TRIBES
and the
AMERICAN CONSTITUTION

Books by

Francis G. Hutchins

A View from the Floor,
The Journal of a U.S. Senate Page Boy
1967
(Frank Madison, pseudonym)

The Illusion of Permanence, British Imperialism in India
1967

India's Revolution, Gandhi and the Quit-India Movement
1973

Mashpee, the Story of Cape Cod's Indian Town
1979

Young Krishna
1980
(translation)

Narayana, *Animal Fables of India*
1985
(translation)

Unicorn Island
1993

Rama and Sita
1996

TRIBES

and the

American Constitution

Francis G. Hutchins

Amarta Press

2000

Amarta Press
31 Cypress Street
Brookline, Massachusetts 02445-6827
e-mail: Amarta@rcn.com
ISBN 0-935100-07-5

Contents

Illustrations

Preface

This book proposes that modern federal law and current historical scholarship reflect serious misunderstanding of the relationship between tribes and the Constitution. Far from being early victims of the American republic, tribes helped shape U.S. prospects and institutions in the republic's first decades. Nineteenth and twentieth century racism spread havoc, but today tribes are once again growing stronger, and the future role of tribes in this country will therefore be quite unlike anything seen in the past century and a half, during which tribes were deemed either too old or too young to participate effectively in the federal system. Although numerous court decisions perpetuate these nineteenth century presumptions, no one today can credibly argue that tribes are archaic relics soon to vanish, or childlike entities "in a state of pupilage" as U.S. Supreme Court Chief Justice John Marshall affirmed in 1831. Fortunately, our eighteenth century Constitution is free of such patronizing attitudes, and an understanding of the mutually adaptive nature of U.S.-tribal relations in the decades before their authoritarian redirection suggests ways to establish twenty-first century tribes on Constitutional foundations, to the benefit of both tribes and the country as a whole.

In the following pages, readers will encounter familiar Euro-American figures such as George Washington, Benjamin Franklin, James Madison, the Marquis de Lafayette, Thomas Jefferson and Andrew Jackson in an unfamiliar setting: tribal treaty sessions. Readers will also encounter Native Americans who are unfortunately not well-known today, among them the highest-ranking Native American to serve in the Revolutionary War on either side, U.S. Colonel Louis Atayataghronghta. Since many early Native American leaders did not read or write, their views must often be reconstructed from accounts left by literate persons who knew them. More dependable sources are speeches made by tribal leaders in their own languages, speeches translated orally by persons who were bilingual but illiterate, then written down by someone literate in French, Spanish or English. Flawed though these translations and transcripts are, the very limitations of translators and transcribers often served the cause of accuracy by making it hard for them to "improve" style or modify meaning, as was done by well-meaning admirers of tribes in later decades. In many instances, these speeches are commentaries on wampum belts which when they survive, if only in the form of a description, serve to supplement what was said. Wampum belts and the transcripts concerning them both document and exemplify how tribal treaty traditions centering around face-to-face discussion of visual symbols came to be constructively combined with the European tradition of writing agreements down, ultimately enabling tribes to modify the course of the American republic by the force of their reasoning as well as by armed resistance.

Support for preliminary research leading to this book was provided by the Institute for Advanced Study, Princeton, New Jersey, the John Simon Guggenheim Memorial Foundation, the National Endowment for the Humanities and the D'Arcy McNickle Center for the History of the American Indian at the Newberry Library, Chicago. Among the many scholars who have shown interest in this project, I wish to express particular gratitude for the encouragement offered more than twenty years ago by Clifford Geertz, Francis Jennings and Judith Shklar.

One

American Revolutionaries and Tribal Tradition

AMERICAN REVOLUTIONARIES RECOGNIZED from the outset that Native Americans imperiled many of their political aspirations. Approximately three million whites, a half-million Africans and a few thousand partially assimilated Native Americans inhabited coastal areas of the thirteen self-proclaimed United States. West of the Appalachians and east of the Mississippi, the tribal population numbered two hundred thousand, organized into more than eighty separate polities which were not only well-armed but familiar with every acre of their homelands.[1] Even their apparent disadvantage in total numbers was deceiving, for in tribal societies all young men were trained to fight. Although less dominant in North America than previously, tribes still controlled vast interior regions by combining their separate strengths into powerful alliances.

White Revolutionary attitudes toward these formidable neighbors ranged all the way from an exterminating hatred to a desire to see them share in the Revolution's promise. George Washington welcomed tribal support for the Revolution. And Benjamin Franklin considered tribes vital to the Revolution's success. Franklin was well-acquainted with the tribes in and around Pennsylvania, and his memory was as long as his foresight was subtle. Between 1736 and 1762, Franklin had printed and distributed the transcripts of thirteen tribal treaty sessions;[2] and in 1754 he supported the Albany Congress to which seven colonies (Maryland, Pennsylvania, New York, Connecticut, Rhode Island, Massachusetts, New Hampshire) sent representatives. Attended by tribal leaders as well, the 1754 Albany Congress significantly strengthened the colonists' capacity to imagine themselves as a collective presence in North America.[3] Urging colonial cooperation in dealings with tribes as well as with the crowned heads of Europe, Franklin pointed out that North American tribes though small successfully coped with European monarchs because confederations transformed tribes into potent forces. Couldn't North American colonists collaboratively regulate their affairs at least as well as the Iroquois? "It would be a very strange thing," mused Franklin, if six Native American tribes

> should be capable of forming a scheme for such an union, and be able to execute it in such a manner, as that it has subsisted ages, and appears indissoluble; and yet that a like union should be impracticable for ten or a dozen English colonies, to whom it is more necessary, and must be more advantageous; and who cannot be supposed to want in equal understanding of their interests.[4]

Great Britain's response to Franklin's consensus-building efforts was to try to set her North American colonies at odds with one another, and to instruct colonists to leave western tribes alone. After 1763, Britain largely succeeded in obstructing interaction between tribes west and colonists east of the Appalachians.

Historians have often dwelt on the irony of the British expectation that the elimination of the French would mean that most of North America would henceforth be safely British-dominated. Although certainly ironic, the reduction of Great Britain's externally unchallenged North American Empire by internal revolt can also be considered just retribution for imperial overconfidence and muscle-flexing. Having bested France for imperial control of North America, King George III's ministers wanted North American colonists to help pay off the resulting war debt; colonial resistance to the Stamp Act and other forms of imperial "taxation without representation" are a well-known chapter in the lore of the American Revolution. Similarly resented were British attempts to refashion and tighten control of colonial governments, described in the Declaration of Independence as involving creation of "a multitude of new offices, and...swarms of officers to harass our people, and eat out their substance"; the Revolutionary response to this imperial initiative is also celebrated in most accounts of the American Revolution. Much less well-remembered today is a third area of British provocation which lent itself less readily to popular dramatization: in addition to heaping new taxes on the colonies and rearranging their infrastructures along authoritarian lines, the King's ministers sought to curb the colonies' ambitions for expansion westward. These efforts, outlined in the Royal Proclamation of October 7, 1763, culminated with the Quebec Act of 1774, which established a royal province whose boundaries extended southward to the Ohio River, westward to the Mississippi River and eastward to the Niagara River, thereby trumping many colonial schemes, large and small, for westward expansion. King George III's plans for the development of the North American interior were of greater concern to illiterate frontiersmen and circumspect land speculators than to the vocal middle class in coastal port cities. But alarm over the future of the North American interior was for more than a few colonists a powerful incentive to overthrow the imperial yoke, as was hinted at in the Declaration of Independence, albeit in a veiled form that disguised its real thrust. Referring to but not identifying the Quebec Act of 1774, the Declaration denounced King George III

> For abolishing the free system of English laws in a neighbouring province, establishing therein an arbitrary government, and enlarging its boundaries, so as to render it at once an example and fit instrument for introducing the same absolute rule into these colonies.

This was not the most incendiary passage of the Declaration, but it meant much to western-oriented Revolutionaries. *Down With Quebec!* was a rallying cry capable of uniting a number of colonies, despite their own incompatible aspirations.

Great Britain's Divide-and-Rule policy was nonetheless moderately successful, and when Franklin in July of 1775 advocated a rebel colonial alliance with tribes and treaty recognition of tribal land rights, he received little support from other colonists, in part because of their British-nurtured ignorance about tribes. Franklin's July, 1775 draft for Articles of Confederation provided that

> No colony shall engage in an offensive war with any nation of Indians, without the consent of the Congress...who are first to consider the justice and necessity of such war.

Furthermore

> A perpetual alliance offensive and defensive is to be entered into as soon as may be with the Six [Iroquois] Nations; their limits to be ascertained and secured to them; their land not to be encroached on, nor any private or colony purchases made of them hereafter to be held good; nor any contract for lands to be made but between the General Council of the Indians at Onondaga and the General Congress. The

> boundaries and lands of all the other Indians shall also be ascertained and secured to them in the same manner.[5]

Unfortunately Franklin's well-reasoned tribal recommendations went unheeded, and warfare between colonies and tribes (which could only benefit Britain) seemed the all-too-likely result.

When royal authority collapsed in the spring of 1775, colonial and tribal governments moved to expand their powers and strengthen their positions vis-a-vis neighboring governments. New collaborative relationships emerged quickly. On April 1, 1775, the Massachusetts Legislature sent this response to an offer of military assistance from the Mahican tribe of Stockbridge:

> Good Brothers: It affords us great pleasure and satisfaction to hear ...that our brothers, the natives of Stockbridge, are ready and willing to take up the hatchet in the cause of liberty and their country....This is a common cause....We are all brothers; and if the Parliament of Great Britain takes from us our property and our lands without our consent, they will do the same by you.[6]

Mixed together in this address were concepts of Native American origin ("the hatchet"), others inspired primarily by European traditions ("liberty," "property") and still others with resonance in both European and Native American traditions: "brothers," "common cause," "lands" and "consent."

Three weeks after receiving this fraternal greeting from Boston, a company of seventeen Stockbridge Mahicans answered a call to help avenge Britain's April 19th attacks on Lexington and Concord. The warriors pitched their wigwams in Cambridge, donned warpaint and fought with bows and arrows as well as muskets against the British in the ensuing siege of Boston. "One thing I ask of you," requested a Stockbridge chief

> that you will let me fight in my own Indian way. I am not used to fight English fashion, therefore you must not expect I can train like your men. Only point out to me where your enemies keep, and that is all I shall want to know.[7]

The Stockbridge Mahicans were prepared to fight against Great Britain alongside rebel colonists, but wouldn't march in step. Tribal warriors rallying to their cause were disconcerting to many white Revolutionaries because, as one colonist observed in 1775, "We make war in an open brave way, a savage by hiding himself surprises."[8] Yet before long, white Revolutionaries were themselves hiding behind trees to "surprise" British redcoats. Indeed the Vermont Revolutionary Ethan Allen and his Green Mountain Boys prided themselves on mastery of such tribal skills. On May 24, 1775, two weeks after seizing control of two British forts on Lake Champlain, Allen informed Canadian tribes,

> I know how to shoot and ambush just like [an] Indian and want your warriors to come and see me and help me fight [British] Regulars. You know they stand all along close together, rank and file, and my men fight so as Indians do, and I want your warriors to join with me and my warriors like brothers and ambush the Regulars.[9]

Colonel Allen's startling raids, purportedly authorized by Connecticut, and the likely spread of such local military initiatives, led to the appointment by the United Colonies of a Continental Commander-in-Chief: Virginia's George Washington, who took command on July 3, 1775. Washington "urged to Congress the necessity of engaging ...[tribes] on our side to prevent their taking an active part against us, which would be a most fatal stroke, under our present circumstances."[10] Washington's logic failed to convince an anxious Congress which on March 8, 1776, ambivalently resolved,

> That Indians be not employed as soldiers in the armies of the United Colonies before the tribes to which they belong shall, in a national council held in the customary manner, have consented thereunto, nor then without express approbation of Congress.[11]

Accepting tribal offers of support continued to provoke debate and thus further delay, until a majority of tribes did as Washington predicted and threw in their lot with the king.

This outcome was made even more probable by the July 4, 1776, Declaration of Independence, which menacingly and inaccurately denounced "the merciless Indian Savages, whose known rule of warfare is an undistinguished destruction of all ages, sexes and conditions." There is no evidence that the Declaration's thirty-three-year-old principal drafter Thomas Jefferson was urged by any member of the Continental Congress—oddly, not even by Franklin—to modify this reckless censure.[12] One can only wish that the Declaration instead had expressed the understanding of tribal motivation evinced by General

Washington who shortly before, on April 19, 1776, wrote that

> human nature is such that it will adhere to the side from whence the best treatment is received. I therefore conjure you, sir, in the strongest terms, to treat all the inhabitants [of Canada] ([French-speaking] Canadians, English, and savages) with tenderness and respect.[13]

Canada occupied much of Washington's attention in his first year as Commander-in-Chief. After the April 19, 1775, battles of Lexington and Concord in Massachusetts, British-rebel conflict quickly spread northward into Canada. This led to General Washington's acquaintance with a Canadian Mohawk named Louis Atayataghronghta, who in 1779 became a Lieutenant Colonel in the U.S. Army. In the spring of 1775, as he later recounted, Atayataghronghta was hunting

> at Lake Saint Francis and there was two Americans came to me, and brought me a letter from General [John] Bailey, to carry to Cagnawagha in Montreal....This letter said, My brothers...don't take up any arms against the Americans, because I want to fight against the British. And I...left all my hunt in the woods...and carried this...letter to Caghnawagha and delivered it to a chief...and he opened the...letter and was likely to be hung for it. And I returned to Lake St. Francis to get my furs and skins. And...General Bailey received me well and he took me to Boston and to Cambridge to see General Washington.[14]

In his meeting with Washington on August 1, 1775, Atayataghronghta related, "the General asked me how would be the best way to keep the Seven Nations from taking up arms against the Americans." Instead of immediately recruiting him for the planned rebel invasion of Canada, Washington requested his assistance in maintaining the neutrality of the French Catholic tribes, known collectively as the Seven Nations of Canada.[15] So Atayataghronghta returned to Caghnawagha, where he was confronted by all three of Britain's top tribal liaisons, Sir Guy Johnson, Colonel Daniel Claus and Colonel John Butler. According to Atayataghronghta, they urged

> me to take up the tomahawk in the Grand Council against the Americans. And they asked me what news. I made them an answer that I did not know but they said I must have known the news by the letter that I carried to Caghnawagha. I then told them that I was for the Americans.

He also reported subsequently holding "a council of war with all the

Seven Nations...and told them all that we must be with the Americans and join them only."[16]

The man eventually known as U.S. Colonel Louis Atayataghronghta was named Lewis Cook when born at Saratoga, New York in 1740. His mother was a Native American of the Maine-Vermont-area Abenaki tribe, and his father African American, though whether slave or free is uncertain. His father was evidently a servant of a British officer stationed at Saratoga and perhaps literally a cook, but seems to have disappeared before or soon after Lewis's birth. In a raid by French troops, Lewis and his mother were captured. Because Lewis looked somewhat African, he was claimed by a French officer who planned to sell him; boys fetched a high price on the slave market. Lewis's mother begged the help of French-allied Mohawk chiefs. They successfully intervened, and Lewis and his mother settled among Mohawks on the Saint Lawrence River at Caghnawagha near Montreal, where he grew up as a French Catholic Mohawk, his Christian name now spelled in French fashion, Louis. He demonstrated prowess in the British-French war between 1756 and 1760, fighting against the British "on Lake Champlain, at Oswego and on the Monongahela"—not too far from where Virginia's Colonel George Washington fought for the British.[17] Following France's surrender and withdrawal from North America in 1763, British promises were made to respect the rights of French-allied Native Americans. But many among the Seven Nations of Canada continued to resent the British, and welcomed Atayataghronghta's 1775 proposal to resume fighting them by aiding the "Bostonian" rebels.

New York's General Philip Schuyler, placed in command of the Continental Army's invasion of Canada, assured General Washington on August 27, 1775, that notwithstanding Congress's desire to insulate tribes from the rapidly spreading rebellion he would personally "not hesitate one moment to employ any Indian that might be willing to join us."[18] In September or October of 1775, Atayataghronghta did command warriors fighting alongside General Schuyler's Continental troops against the British during the siege of Fort Saint Johns on the Richelieu River. "And there I lost two Mohawks, three Caghnawaghas and one chief of the Conasadagas," Atayataghronghta reported. He and other French Catholic tribesmen also carried messages back and forth for all three rebel forces converging on Canada, led respectively by Vermont's self-directed Colonel Ethan Allen, the subsequent traitor General Benedict Arnold, who was marching north through Maine, and General Schuyler, replaced as field commander in September by General Richard Montgomery when Schuyler fell ill and returned to convalesce at his New York headquarters.[19] After initial success, the rebels failed in their climactic attempt to take Quebec City on December 31, 1775, when General Montgomery was slain. A decade later, the painter John Trumbull assigned Atayataghronghta a heroic place by the dying General's side,[20] but at the time this battle occurred Atayataghronghta was already on his way south, back to General Washington's Cambridge headquarters. Atayataghronghta and twelve companions conferred with General Schuyler in Albany on January 5, with Connecticut Governor Jonathan Trumbull (father of the painter) at Lebanon, Connecticut on January 15, finally arriving in Cambridge, Massachusetts a few days later.[21]

After meeting with Atayataghronghta, whose personal merits were by now proven, Washington on January 27, 1776, confided to General Schuyler,

> I am a little embarrassed to know in what manner to conduct myself with respect to the Caghnawagha Indians now here. They have, notwithstanding the treaty of neutrality which I find they entered into with you the other day (agreeably to what appears to be the sense of Congress) signified to me a desire of taking up arms in behalf of the United Colonies. The chief of them, and who I understand is now the first man of the nation, intends, as it is intimated to me, to apply to me for a commission, with assurances of raising four or five hundred men when he returns. My embarrassment does not proceed so much from the impropriety of encouraging these people to depart from their neutrality (accepting their own voluntary offer rather) as from the expense which probably may follow. I am sensible that if they do not desire to be idle, they will be for, or against, us. I am sensible also, that no artifice will be left unassayed to engage them against us; their proffered service therefore ought not to be rejected; but how far, under the little knowledge I have of these people's policy and real intentions, and your want of their aid, I ought to go, is the question that puzzles me. I will endeavor however to please them by yielding in appearance to their demands, reserving at the same time the power in you, to regulate their numbers and movements, of which you shall

Colonel Louis Atayataghronghta. Pencil sketch by John Trumbull, study for *Death of General Montgomery.* Courtesy, Yale University Art Gallery,

> be more fully informed when anything is fixed. At present what they have mentioned is a kind of outdoors talk...before they open themselves fully.[22]

This "outdoors talk" (a tribal-style treaty session) occurred on January 31, 1776, when Washington was told by Atayataghronghta's delegation, "We look upon ourselves to be free, and like our brothers of New England." The Caghnawaghas consequently sought the "liberty to raise men to fight" in defense of freedom alongside their "brothers of New England."[23] The next day, Washington wrote General Schuyler that all "embarrassments" regarding how to respond to the Caghnawaghas had been dispelled by the "talk they honored me with yesterday," in which "they put the matter upon the footing I wished; that is, to join the forces in Canada whenever you shall call for their assistance."[24]

Though by now well aware of Atayataghronghta's prowess, General

Schuyler felt he had his hands full, and advised Washington

> if we can get decently rid of their offer, I would prefer it to employing them. The expense we are at in the Indian department is amazing; it will be more so, when they consider themselves in our service.[25]

Expense or no, General Schuyler before long concluded that he simply couldn't afford *not* to employ Atayataghronghta. On September 19, 1777, with U.S. fortunes at their lowest ebb, Schuyler dispatched Atayataghronghta and the one hundred fifty tribal warriors he then led to help stop General Burgoyne's advance southward along the Hudson River. Surrounded, Burgoyne surrendered at Saratoga on October 17, 1777.[26]

With the British still in control of the Saint Lawrence, Schuyler next sent Atayataghronghta on missions behind enemy lines. On March 15, 1778, Schuyler reported having

> engaged Louis (commonly called Colonel Louis, a friendly Caghnawagha, a man of sense and enterprise, who is going into Canada by the way of Oswegatchie with three or four trusty Oneidas) to learn, if possible, the enemy's vessels on [Lake] Ontario, if not to attempt the destruction of those at Saint Johns, and have promised a thousand dollars in specie as a reward if the one or the other is accomplished. I hope for the approbation of Congress. Louis, who expects to return in less than forty days, is also charged to bring me the most exact account he can procure of the enemy's force in Canada, the posts occupied by them and the numbers at each post, to inform himself if possible what military operations the enemy means to prosecute from Canada in the ensuing campaign and to engage some of our Caghnawagha friends to give the earliest intelligence of the movement of the enemy and what provisions and military stores may be sent to Saint Johns or up the Saint Lawrence.[27]

Obviously such responsibilities could only have been offered to (or accepted by) a person of daring and resourcefulness. What he achieved is unknown.

A year later, in March of 1779, Atayataghronghta again secretly traveled to Canada, to counteract British efforts to enlist Canada's Catholic tribes to fight against the United States.[28] Atayataghronghta's reports may well have contributed to General Washington's decision later in the spring of 1779 to proceed with the long-contemplated invasion of hostile Iroquois homelands, a decision which also led to

Atayataghronghta's long-sought commission as a lieutenant colonel in the U.S. Army.

In his 1778 letter praising Atayataghronghta's "sense and enterprise," General Schuyler had referred to him somewhat slightingly as "Louis (commonly called Colonel Louis...)" because Schuyler evidently disapproved of his desire to be addressed as "Colonel." Washington felt no such disinclination. In a letter to the President of Congress dated January 24, 1776, General Washington reported having been called upon by "thirteen of the Caghnawagha Indians" including "Colonel Louis, who honored us with a visit once before."[29] Atayataghronghta may have styled himself a colonel because of his service in the French army prior to 1763. The British after 1763 would not have been willing to absorb a "savage" French officer into the British Army, and Atayataghronghta may have been hopeful that the Continental Army would restore him to the rank denied him by the British.

Although aware that Atayataghronghta wished to be addressed as "Colonel," General Schuyler preferred as a matter of policy that the U.S. Army go no further than had the British, in awarding "captain's commissions...to some of the chiefs whose fidelity may be depended on."[30] (Captain Joseph Brant, an Anglican Mohawk, is the best-known of Britain's tribal officers.) With the invasion of Iroquois homelands in prospect, Congress accepted Schuyler's recommendation on April 3, 1779, and authorized twelve Native American officers. Four captains and eight lieutenants were then commissioned but Atayataghronghta was not among them, presumably because he refused to accept a captain's commission. Soon thereafter, on June 15, 1779, Congress agreed that one additional commission should be awarded to a tribal chief, and Atayataghronghta at last became a Lieutenant Colonel.

The official reason given by General Schuyler for the request that Congress authorize this additional commission was that, in handing out the twelve previously authorized, he had *forgotten* "to reserve one for the faithful Lewis of the Caghnawagha."[31] This is most unlikely. Schuyler was probably unwilling to admit to Congress that he had failed to persuade Atayataghronghta to accept a captain's commission. The fact that the one additional commission requested was to be at a higher level was nowhere mentioned in the official correspondence, but may have been informally intimated. In any case, Atayataghronghta prevailed, gaining the rank he had long sought, higher than any heretofore awarded by either the British or the United States to a Native American.

Atayataghronghta obtained his precedent-shattering commission because of his ability to lead Native American troops in what seemed likely to be the most significant tribal campaign of the Revolutionary War. On May 31, 1779, Washington ordered New Hampshire's General John Sullivan to invade hostile Iroquois territory and attempt

> the total destruction and devastation of their settlements and the capture of as many prisoners of every age and sex as possible. It will be essential to ruin their crops now in the ground and prevent their planting more.[32]

The success of this campaign through what is now central and western New York State won for Washington his enduring Iroquois name "Town-Destroyer," though Washington only gave the order and the actual destruction was accomplished by General Sullivan, assisted by Colonel Atayataghronghta.

Since most pro-British Iroquois fled long before U.S. troops reached their towns, the U.S. invaders took few captives but did accomplish the other half of their assigned task in dramatic fashion. Sullivan described the Iroquois town of Chemung as "beautifully situated." It

> contained a chapel, with between thirty and forty other houses, many of them very large, and some of them tolerably well finished. There were extensive fields of corn, with great quantities of potatoes, pumpkins, squashes, and, in short, most other things which farms produce. The whole was destroyed.

Proceeding to the Iroquois village of Newtown, Sullivan found it to be

> a large, scattered settlement abounding with extensive fields of the best corn and beans, so extensive and numerous as to keep the whole army this day industriously employed in destroying, and the business is yet unfinished.

Sullivan's 5,000 men also leveled "a number of orchards, one of which had in it 1500 fruit trees."[33]

General Washington decided these measures were necessary after years of increasingly violent raids which had ravaged western settlements in New York State and Pennsylvania, and divided the Iroquois Confederacy into bitterly antagonistic camps. Two tribes—the Oneidas and Tuscaroras—adhered to the Revolutionary cause while the other four Confederacy tribes fought for the British so effectively that Washington in 1779 concluded he must take strong action.

In a letter to the Marquis de Lafayette dated September 30, 1779, General Washington grimly reported

> the entire destruction of the whole country of the Six Nations, excepting so much of it as is inhabited by the Oneidas who have always lived in amity with us; and a few towns belonging to the Cayugas and Onondagas who were disposed to be friendly.

In all, Washington told Lafayette, the invading force had burned

> between fifteen and twenty towns, destroyed their crops and everything that was to be found...with a view to complete the desolation of the whole country, and remove the cruel inhabitants of it to a greater distance, who were...fleeing in the utmost confusion, consternation and distress towards Niagara, distant one hundred miles through an uninhabited wilderness; experiencing a little of that distress, but nothing of those cruelties which they have exercised on our unhappy frontier settlers who (men, women and children) have been deliberately murdered, in a manner shocking to humanity.[34]

Washington was confident that this searing expedition was justified and would make a difference, in demonstrating that the Revolutionaries could and would severely punish hostile tribe, and protect and reward friendly tribes.

Commanding troops who were themselves mostly Iroquois, Colonel Atayataghronghta assisted Sullivan in destroying these pro-British Iroquois towns. Some of Atayataghronghta's men expressed reluctance to obey orders when the campaign's scorched-earth mission became apparent, and were severely rebuked by General Sullivan for their "very surprising" attitude, but he ultimately expressed his satisfaction with their "zealous and very faithful services...in subduing and totally extirpating our common enemy."[35]

As recognition of his efforts during this campaign, Atayataghronghta was invited to lead a delegation of French-speaking Native Americans sent in the summer of 1780 to visit the French army just arrived at Newport, Rhode Island. When received by the French Commander Rochambeau, Colonel Atayataghronghta and his eighteen companions were draped in red woolen blankets. The tribal warriors' faces were also painted red, and all "had one foot unshod as a mark of respect." The French officers at Newport were no less impressed that Colonel Atayataghronghta could speak "French fairly well, and even without an accent." What's more, his French was politic as well as polished, for he affirmed "high regard for Monsieur de Montcalm," the general who died in 1759 defending Quebec from the British. For his part, Rochambeau assured the tribesmen that "The king of France, your father, has not forgotten his children....He hopes that his children whom he loves sincerely, will take part with their father in this war against the English." Like Colonel Atayataghronghta, Comte de Rochambeau saw in the Revolutionary War a welcome opportunity to resume France's contest with Great Britain, so unsatisfactorily halted in 1760, and to involve the French monarchy once again in determining North America's destiny.

At Newport, Colonel Atayataghronghta and his fellow warriors were invited to dine aboard a French vessel, which they thought "wonderful," and also were guests at exercises of the 5,000-strong French army. When "the Hussars galloped past" the tribesmen expressed their approval "by cries which resembled rather the howls of animals"—at least to the ears of their startled hosts. The tribal warriors' way of indicating possibly mocking admiration for the French troops' precision presentation of arms was similarly unexpected: "one after the other walked up to them and bending down their heads, sighted along under the butts of the soldiers' guns." This provoked ill-suppressed mirth among the French soldiers, a reaction Colonel Atayataghronghta may have intended.

Then the Native American delegation served as hosts. Of this event, one officer remarked,

> Never, I think, was there so extraordinary a sight...How can men work themselves into such a state and act so madly? One would think they were wild animals. Frightful cries and howls precede their dances. Some beat time by striking two pieces of wood together, others by hitting a skin stretched over the end of a barrel. This is how they whip up their spirits, while some of them perform dance steps in time and follow the cadence.

Though amazed by such "noisy amusements," this young Parisian was also impressed to find these "savages" so "very civilized." Colonel Atayataghronghta's visit to Newport was a thorough success for the Revolutionary cause, and evidenced General Washington's diplomatic ingenuity as well as his trust in the Colonel's discretion.[36]

The next year, British and Iroquois marauders entered the Mohawk River valley. On September 11, 1781, Atayataghronghta arrived in Philadelphia and informed the President of Congress that he had come "with forty two Indians under my command...to manifest our friendship to America and its cause, and await any orders Congress shall think proper to give."[37] Atayataghronghta's tribal warriors then combined with men under Colonel Marinus Willett to drive the invaders out of the Mohawk valley. A young British officer, Captain Walter Butler, son of Colonel John Butler of Butler's Rangers, was killed with a tomahawk by one of Atayataghronghta's men, who then requested his permission to scalp Captain Butler. Atayataghronghta turned to his fellow officer Colonel Willett and asked "if he should be scalped." Willett answered, "He belongs to your party, Colonel Louis."[38]

Shortly thereafter, on October 19, 1781, British General Cornwallis surrendered his sword to General Benjamin Lincoln at Yorktown. Atayataghronghta then found himself among the commissioned officers "deranged" (i.e., discharged), as of December 31, 1781. Six months later, on July 2, 1782, General Lincoln, now U.S. Secretary at War, sought Atayataghronghta's reinstatement, asserting that the previous fall he had been unaware of the plan to release Atayataghronghta from active service, "or I should have given it as my opinion from the knowledge I have of him and his influence with the Indians that he should have been retained." Indeed, argued Lincoln, "From his interest with the tribes, his sagacity, integrity and firm attachment to the cause of the United States much good has been derived and his further services are necessary."[39] Despite Lincoln's intervention, Atayataghronghta was not returned to active status. When peace came, he directed his attention to re-establishing contacts between pro- and anti-Revolutionary tribes, and to securing their land rights in the post-War United States.

As Colonel Atayataghronghta's career demonstrates, relations between tribal Native Americans and white Revolutionaries were less antagonistic both before and after July 4, 1776 than a reading of the

Declaration of Independence with its unqualified condemnation of "merciless Indian Savages" has led many latter-day analysts to suppose. Despite disparities in culture and interest, white Revolutionaries and Native Americans could sometimes see advantages in emphasizing their complementarity. The colonial patriots who tossed tea into Boston's harbor in 1773 wore feathers and paint to proclaim their conception of themselves as altogether North American, born and bred—and therefore culturally part-Native American. For analogous reasons, colonists in Pennsylvania and New York established a fraternal order called the Sons of St. Tammanend, from which New York City's Tammany Hall descended; Tammanend being a mythical Native American chief whom colonists claimed to reverence, to annoy King George III and mock ultra-loyalist pro-British groups such as the Sons of St. George.[40]

More than mockery was undoubtedly involved. British-descended Revolutionaries needed to distinguish themselves psychologically no less than politically from Great Britain and, by presenting themselves as culturally part-Native American, they strategically denied ancestral bonds to Britain. In 1778 the backwoods patriot George Rogers Clark assured tribes of the Ohio region that Anglo-American Revolutionaries were "very much like the red people" and also didn't

> know well how to make blanket, powder and cloth, etc. They buy from the English (whom they formerly descended from) and live chiefly by making corn, hunting and trade as you and the French your neighbors do.

Since tribes too had been exploited by Britain, Clark reasoned, "Indians had as great a right to fight the English as they [white colonists] did." Only after his economic arguments failed to convince tribes supporting Britain did Clark attack them—with a band of white frontiersmen wielding tomahawks and intoning tribal death chants.[41]

The semi-identification of British-descended Revolutionaries with tribes was perhaps most elaborately expressed by Thomas Jefferson. Though his Declaration of Independence denunciation of "merciless Indian Savages" caused lasting damage, Jefferson's intellectual curiosity about tribes was genuine, and closely allied to his sense of who he was culturally as well as politically. At a Charlottesville treaty session in

1781, Jefferson, then Governor of Virginia, told Kaskaskia chiefs

> I have carefully attended to the figures represented on the skins, and to their explanation, and shall always keep them hanging on the walls in remembrance of you and your nation. I have joined with you sincerely in smoking the pipe of peace; it is a good old custom handed down by your ancestors, and as such I respect and join in it with reverence. I hope we shall long continue to smoke in friendship together.

As for the future, Governor Jefferson assured the chiefs, "We, like you, are Americans, born in the same land, and having the same interests." Native Americans were "brothers" of white Virginians with an equal right to freedom and to "revenge...injury....If the English have injured you...join us in the war."[42] Could not white Revolutionaries and tribes combine to defend common interests against the British, even though differing about how best to organize their societies?

While living in France after the War, Jefferson drew a provocative contrast between the "little societies" formed by North American tribes and the "great societies" of Europe. Native Americans possessed "no law," Jefferson fancifully contended, and were governed only by "their manners" and "moral sense of right and wrong."[43] Even so, Jefferson thought tribes better off than the monarchies of Europe plagued by "too much law," just as "the sheep are happier of themselves than under the care of the wolves." On a scale of political aptitude, the libertarian Jefferson ranked decadent European royalists below valiant Native Americans. He nonetheless believed tribes were *too* free and equal, and sought a happy medium of modest regulation and limited social equality for the post-Revolutionary United States.[44]

Some who had lived on both sides of eastern North America's cultural divide agreed with Jefferson that tribal life was freer, and liked it that way. In 1784, a French visitor to the Oneida tribe encountered a young English-speaking woman who explained

> that she had formerly served at the home of a planter in the State of New York, but that she had tired of the position of a servant and had fled, and that the Indians had welcomed her, and that she lived very happily among them. "The whites," she told me, "treated me harshly. I saw them take rest while they made me work without a break. I ran the risk of being beaten or of dying of hunger, if through fatigue or

> laziness I refused to do what I was told. Here I have no master, I am the equal of all the women of the tribe, I do what I please without anyone's saying anything about it, I work only for myself—I shall marry if I wish and be unmarried again when I wish. Is there a single woman as independent as I in your cities?"[45]

Freedom clearly had distinct meanings, depending on one's social status and values. According to John Heckewelder, tribal chiefs from the Ohio region marveled that

> when the whites meet together, many of them, and sometimes, all, speak at the same time, and they wonder how they can thus hear and understand each other. "Among us," they say, "only one person speaks at a time, and the others listen to him until he has done, after which, and not before, another begins to speak." They also say that the whites speak too much, and that much talk disgraces a man and is fit only for women. On this subject they shrewdly observe, that it is well for the whites that they have the art of writing, and can write down their words and speeches; for had they, like themselves, to transmit them to posterity by means of strings and belts of wampum, they would want for their own use all the wampum that could be made.[46]

Just as the concept of individual freedom differed on opposite sides of the cultural divide, so did the understanding of what sort of North American political structure would be most likely to maximize the freedom of tribes as well as white Revolutionaries. One goal of the Revolution inherent in the Declaration of Independence was to replace Britain as protector of North American tribes. The British monarch had acquired France's tribal responsibilities in 1763, and in 1776 the thirteen colonies-turned-states collectively tried to seize Britain's continental supremacy along with political independence for themselves. But white Revolutionaries found their relationship to tribes more difficult to work out conceptually as well as practically than had the British monarch in replacing the French monarch. One idea was to consolidate pro-Revolutionary tribes into a fourteenth state.[47] This well-meant proposal got nowhere, but many Revolutionaries felt royal pretensions must somehow be answered. In 1771, the British imperial claim to be rightful protector of tribes had been iconographically affirmed by Benjamin West's phenomenally popular painting of Britain's General Wolfe giving his life during the conquest of French Canada. West portrayed Wolfe's sacrifice as having been made not merely to enrich his country or gratify his king but also to benefit tribes, exemplified by a mourning tribal warrior who identified his lot with Britain's cause. In 1786 John Trumbull, the Revolution's leading fabricator of patriotic icons, set out to replace West's *Death of Wolfe* with an image worthy of North America's new future, one which he painted, fittingly, in West's own London studio. Trumbull's *Death of Montgomery*, showing the Revolutionary general dying heroically in the attempted conquest of British Canada, both skillfully followed and deliberately departed from the *Death of Wolfe*, most notably in replacing West's anonymous, passive tribal mourner with an alert, energetic Atayataghronghta seconding the heroics of General Montgomery and exhorting faint-hearted white patriots to renewed courage. Trumbull wished to show that Native Americans supported the Revolution, and that white Revolutionaries joining forces with dynamic tribal leaders such as Atayataghronghta could usher in a North American future beneficial to all. In 1786, the precise relationship of tribes to the United States was still unsettled, but Trumbull felt sure his vision made symbolic sense.[48]

While white Revolutionaries argued about how best to coordinate their interests with those of tribes, tribal leaders were engaged in parallel discussions about possible ways to fit the thirteen United States into the ancient alliance structures used by tribes to manage conflicts among themselves. After 1492, tribes modified these institutions to manage relations with European nations, and after 1775 tribal leaders assumed these institutions could also accommodate the new political situation created by the Revolution.[49] Even before 1492, tribal chiefs were adept at fine-tuning old diplomatic systems which used metaphorical kinship terms to characterize intertribal relationships, including *father, son, uncle, nephew, brother, elder brother, younger brother, male cousin* and *grandfather*. All these fictive statuses except the last were those of able-bodied males because war-making was central to tribal alliance systems; a *grandfather* was thought of primarily as a noncombatant adviser. All participants in such a system, including *son* and *nephew*, were considered to be fully adult. And all statuses were specific to a particular alliance. A tribe could participate simultaneously in more than one alliance, occupying a quite different status in each; the Delawares were for example at one

Death of General Montgomery.
Oil Painting by John Trumbull, 1786. Courtesy, Yale University Art Gallery.

time called *grandfather* by the Iroquois, but *nephew* by the Wyandots. And yet, while a tribe might remain indefinitely the *nephew* or *younger brother* of another tribe, even a longstanding association was not considered binding in the absence of a desire on both sides to preserve it.[50]

Although periodic adjustments in status were obviously called for, no conceptual changes seemed needed after Europeans arrived. Asked by tribal chiefs in 1540 what role Spain coveted in their diplomatic family, the explorer Hernando de Soto chose *uncle*. Prior to giving this answer, de Soto had undoubtedly ascertained that any role a European regime might occupy in the tribes' contractual kinship system entailed obligations as well as rewards; reciprocity was fundamental.

This alliance system derived from the relationships of members of extended families in tribal societies, and tribes consequently assumed that decisions would be reached among members of a diplomatic family consensually, rather as they would be among the adult males of a traditional tribal family. Europeans accustomed to monarchical polities and patriarchal societies were in contrast disposed to think of families in more rigidly hierarchical terms, and tended to view even *uncle-nephew* relationships in authoritarian terms. In due course, European emissaries thus demanded the diplomatic role of *father* for their monarchs, and assumed that tribes would understand the term *father* as Europeans did, despite the fact that many tribes, though male-dominated, were matrilineal and recognized nothing unique and certainly nothing divine in fatherhood. Notwithstanding these differences in perspective, Europeans and Native Americans often did make their hybrid kinship system work to mutual satisfaction, by means of regular face-to-face consultations clarifying misconceptions on either side.

A tribe aligned to a particular European monarch would typically address his or her representatives as *father*, and those of other European monarchs as *brother*. A shift in alliance was reflected by a shift in terminology, as indicated for example in remarks of the Mahican sachem Sacquans on July 18, 1701. In renouncing his tribe's French ties, Sacquans told the British Governor of New York that henceforth "we will not call ourselves *brethren*, but we are your *children* in fact, with our whole hearts not doubting but you will have a *fatherly* eye over us."[51] Sacquans was a diplomat as supple as any schooled in Europe. Tribal chiefs moreover soon themselves acquired first-hand knowledge of Europe; Mahican and Mohawk chiefs were entertained in London in 1710, a Cherokee delegation in 1730 and a Creek delegation in 1734.[52]

By 1775, many tribes were diplomatic veterans adept at juggling the conflicting pressures of French, Spanish and British imperialists, and also at exploiting tensions between Europe's North American colonies and imperial authorities based in Europe. Confident that their flexible system could cope with anything, tribal chiefs believed even Revolution would pose no insurmountable challenge. If they chose, tribes could readily repudiate ties to their British *father* and adopt Revolutionary states as *brothers*. When the Revolutionary War began, tribes east of the Mississippi anticipated fighting on one side or the other as they had in earlier European-initiated conflicts, and then meeting with their foes to bury the hatchet. But since white Revolutionaries had never buried a hatchet before, tribes found themselves obliged to instruct U.S. officials in tribal protocols of peace-making. How tribal chiefs did this would decisively alter the future course of the Revolutionary republic.

Two

A Tribal Peace, 1783-1786

WHEN THE REVOLUTIONARY WAR ENDED, no more fundamental question confronted the United States than establishing relations with independent tribes. Because of their long-established political prowess as well as their strategic location between regions controlled by the United States and Great Britain, tribes were in a position to determine whether the Revolution moved forward to political consolidation or descended into squabbling, opening the way for renewed Crown control. In fact tribes did decisively influence the chain of events that led from the 1783 Treaty of Paris to the 1787 drafting of the Constitution, especially those events concerning the formation of the Northwest Territory. But while historians commonly recognize this arduous political achievement as an indispensable preliminary to the drafting of the Constitution, it has usually been conceptualized as an issue involving "western lands" or even "vacant lands," which ignores the fact that these were lands occupied by tribes that were prepared to fight if not conciliated by appropriate U.S. recognition of their rights.

The Treaty of Paris merely described a perimeter which Great Britain promised to stay beyond. The Treaty thereby acknowledged collective United States ownership of lands extending to the Mississippi River, but said nothing about the rights of any tribes. The Treaty did mandate that there would be "no future confiscations" of property punishing individuals for the side they took in the War, and provided

> that the Congress shall earnestly recommend it to the Legislatures of the respective States to provide for the restitution of all estates, rights and properties which have been confiscated belonging to real British subjects.

The 1783 Treaty also affirmed that

> persons of any other description shall have free liberty to go to any part or parts of any of the thirteen United States and therein to remain twelve months unmolested in their endeavours to obtain the restitution of such of their estates, rights and properties as may have been confiscated.

This provision arguably comprehended tribes, and certainly implied that restoration of land rights to pro-British tribes would be in keeping with the conciliatory spirit of the Treaty.

It was soon apparent however that "real British subjects" would not get their U.S. estates back. Indeed only the most sanguine monarchist could have placed much hope in Congress's "earnest" recommendation of such action to the thirteen sovereign states. For their part, the British pronounced the states' refusal to take such action justification for not evacuating royal troops from lands ceded in Paris. With the United States still unfriendly to monarchists, and Britain now determined to disregard its Treaty obligations, tribes that fought for King George III had little reason to expect generous treatment from U.S. authorities, whether Congress or state.

Unlike Loyalists who had lost private estates, pro-British tribes on U.S.-claimed soil were often still in possession of lands nominally confiscated from them during the War. Even so, reversing such formal confiscation posed problems because some of these lands had already been designated bounty land for Revolutionary soldiers. Seeing no other way to recruit troops, both states and Congress resorted to the dubious expedient of issuing promissory notes payable in land—land to be wrested away from those "merciless Indian Savages" denounced in the Declaration of Independence. As early as September 16, 1776, Congress offered land grants ranging from one hundred to five hundred acres to encourage enlistment, even though it did not yet have a single acre to dispose of.[1] Seven states also designated tracts of tribal land in their claimed western regions for eventual award to veterans.

Some Revolutionary leaders, including notably Benjamin Franklin, contended from the outset that tribal lands must be legally acquired before being awarded to veterans. Many more leaders worried about which authority—state or Congress—would do the acquiring, legal or otherwise, and therefore be in a position to award tribal land to ill-paid soldiers, or sell it to raise capital. But until the formation of the Northwest Territory in 1786, Congress possessed no land whatsoever, either to govern or to dispose of. Many states boasted colonial charters defining their limits, and were in a stronger position than Congress. But obscure charter language and overlapping boundary claims rendered states vulnerable as well.

These territorial disputes gave an opening that tribal chiefs were quick to seize. Adept at playing off European rivals to their advantage, tribes hoped that similar benefit could result from exploiting competition amongst states and between states and the Continental Congress. Negotiations with tribes therefore became arenas in which internal U.S. rivalries were laid bare, and formerly British-allied tribes managed by shrewd diplomacy to regain basic elements of their pre-War status.

The most lastingly important of these tribal negotiations took place in what is now central New York State, but which in 1783 was a region very much up for grabs. This area was disputed even during the War, and almost immediately thereafter quarrels erupted involving four states, the Continental Congress, British imperialists and six Iroquois tribes, all eager to control what once had been undisputed Iroquois territory. The strategies evolved in this pivotal struggle have shaped the relations between states, tribes and the U.S. government ever since.

Colonial New York had once dealt with the Iroquois on the Crown's behalf. But pursuant to the 1763 Royal Proclamation, the Crown had taken the Iroquois and their lands away from New York and placed them under direct Crown control. In 1768, this arrangement was confirmed by the drawing of a "Line of Property" south from the vicinity of Oneida Lake, with the province of New York east of this line and, to the west, Iroquois hunting grounds under direct royal protection. After 1768, whether New York could ever again hope to exercise jurisdiction west of the Mohawk River watershed was uncertain. New York consequently hired Edmund Burke, M.P. to be on the lookout for any threat to New York's future territorial ambitions. Burke soon earned his retainer by averting the inclusion of what is now western New York State in the reconfigured royal Province of Quebec, whose eastern boundary was set in 1774 at the Niagara River, leaving Iroquois territory between the Mohawk and Niagara Rivers sandwiched between two royal provinces, each of which craved to absorb it.[2] Freed by the Revolution from all royal constraint, New York State quickly laid claim to all Iroquois territory—including much land that had been assigned by Parliament to Quebec in 1774—reaffirming New York's old colonial theory of Iroquois "dependence." Revolutionary New York could be quite traditional when this proved advantageous. By describing the six Iroquois tribes as "dependents," New York State could claim all erstwhile Iroquois lands, which by some accounts extended from the Tennessee River north to the Great Lakes and beyond. Moreover, since four of the six Iroquois tribes had fought for King George III, New York State could justify confiscating all the lands of these four Loyalist tribes as War booty. But New York was not the only state with an eye on these lands, to which Virginia, Pennsylvania, Connecticut, Massachusetts and Congress all could make some claim.[3] Nor were the pro-British Iroquois prepared to yield their homelands without a fight.

Congress's claim rested on the theory that Iroquois lands excluded from New York jurisdiction by the Crown in 1763 had become U.S. national property through the defeat of Britain—and/or the conquest of British-allied Iroquois. The anticipated conquest of the Iroquois began provoking anxiety in the spring of 1779, as General Washington concerted plans to invade British-allied Iroquois lands south of Lake Ontario. To neutralize New York State fears that Congress might try to seize these lands, General Washington established a dual command: New Hampshire's General John Sullivan led U.S. troops, which included the tribal force headed by Colonel Atayataghronghta; New York State's militia were under General James Clinton, brother of New York Governor George Clinton. Despite Washington's carefully wrought conception, squabbling commenced between New York State and Congress almost immediately after this joint invasion was completed. On October 23, 1779, New York's Legislature pointedly proclaimed that the State had over many years "expended vast sums of money for the protection and maintenance of the Six [Iroquois] Nations" and therefore considered these tribes to be State "dependents" whose lands even if forfeited because of pro-British actions should properly remain forever within New York jurisdiction. Honorably exempting the pro-Revolutionary Oneidas and Tuscaroras, the Legislature grandly asserted that the other four Iroquois tribes

> namely, the Mohawks, Onondagas, Cayugas and Senecas have, without provocation or complaint, ungratefully and perfidiously committed the most cruel hostilities against this State, destroyed the lives of a great number of its inhabitants, carried others into captivity,

> demolished and burned down many settlements and villages and plundered the property of the inhabitants of the same, to our very great distress and impoverishment.

In view of New York's long record of expenditure on behalf of all six Iroquois tribes, as well as the State's recent suffering at the hands of four of these tribes, the New York Legislature served notice on Congress that their State must be "a principal and contracting party...as an independent State" in any "treaty of pacification hereafter to be set on foot between the said hostile nations of Indians of the one part and the United States of America or this State on the other part." Any such "treaty of pacification" was to "demand... compensation and retribution for the abovementioned hostilities and injuries" in the form of dictated land cessions for State use.[4] Even so, on January 29, 1780, New York's Philip Schuyler confided to the State Legislature his fear that Congress might force the four pro-British Iroquois tribes to cede "a part of their country, and that the territory so to be ceded should be for the benefit of the United States in general and grantable by Congress." Congress intended to argue, Schuyler suspected, that this land "was not the property of the State" and that ownership lay instead "either in the natives or by right of conquest in the United States."[5]

In an attempt to placate Congress, the New York Legislature voted on February 19, 1780 to cede to Congress the State's Iroquois-based claims to lands in the Ohio region, a cession that eventually led to the establishment of the Northwest Territory and New York's modern-day western border. But Congress did not accept New York's proferred cession for more than two and a half years and, even when it was accepted in October of 1782, no assurances were given that New York State would retain jurisdiction over the region east of this cession, and south of Lake Ontario. The possibility that Congress might try to confiscate this region directly from the pro-British Iroquois and then deny some or all of this land to New York State thus continued to haunt New York leaders. Indeed the State's fears intensified in the spring and summer of 1783, as Congress prepared to negotiate with the Iroquois Confederacy a peace settlement potentially disastrous to New York hopes.

At this ominous juncture, General Schuyler once again intervened.

As an alternative to permanent exclusion of the anti-Revolutionary Iroquois as enemies, Schuyler on July 29, 1783, proposed that Congress permit all six Iroquois tribes to return to live peacefully in New York State. After its acceptance as national policy, Schuyler's plan came to be regarded—indeed is still commonly regarded—as the foundation of U.S. government assurances to tribes of protection *from states.* But Schuyler's proposal was actually intended to protect New York State interests *from Congress.* Schuyler advocated conciliating the erstwhile enemy Iroquois because he viewed them as pawns in a State-Congress chess game, and believed their return was the best way to make sure they would become State rather than Congress pawns.

Schuyler reported that he had been contacted in his capacity as one of Congress's Indian Commissioners by pro-British Iroquois tribes who were now eager to return home, and in reply had held out hope of their

> attaining a reconciliation, persuaded...that it cannot comport with the interest of the United States to continue a war with a people who although we may expel from their country will if they please return immediately after the force which has ousted them has retired, nor can even such a temporary expulsion be effected without an expense in my estimation infinitely beyond the value of the object.

By conciliating these former enemies, Schuyler reasoned, the United States could develop mutually advantageous trade relations with them, whereas

> their expulsion will totally deprive us of the fur trade, for it cannot be expected that if ever the British permitted, the Indians would suffer traders to reside amongst them from a community who had deprived them of their country.

Even more important, on U.S. soil they might become militarily neutral rather than fearsome avengers. "If driven to reside in the British territory," Schuyler contended,

> they will add strength to that people in the very quarter where they wish it, and in case of a further rupture, expose the western country to the most dreadful calamities; secure of an asylum, they will harass our frontiers, with nearly as much ease and with much more inveteracy...besides, at enmity with the Indians, our western garrisons must be so numerous as to admit large escorts for convoys.

Schuyler's proposal presupposed that the two pro-U.S. Iroquois tribes, the Oneidas and Tuscaroras, who had been assured of the retention of their entire homelands by the New York Legislature, would "return to their country" from their encampments near U.S. forts. To help these tribes regain self-sufficiency, Schuyler urged furnishing them with "provisions to the month of November" and powder, lead, camp kettles, axes, hatchets and hoes. As for the four pro-British Iroquois tribes, Schuyler recommended they *not* be restored to the possession of all their pre-War territories but rather be assigned delimited reservations in the westernmost section of New York State at a considerable distance from the nearest settlements of U.S. citizens. Full restoration of land rights to these erstwhile foes Schuyler deemed neither just nor any longer feasible, because the New York Legislature had already

> assigned and set apart the Onondaga Country and a part of the Cayuga for the bounty lands promised the Army, hence the [formerly hostile] Indians cannot be restored to the entire country they resided in before the war without clashing with the intentions of the State, nor must I admit observing that it is my opinion that no consideration short of absolute necessity would induce a majority of the Legislature to permit the [formerly hostile] Indians a residence anywhere within the limits of the State.[6]

In this respectful letter to the President of Congress, New Yorker Schuyler shrewdly characterized himself as a moderate seeking a middle course that would be acceptable both to Congress and to the New York Legislature. He thus emphasized the advantages of his plan from the perspective of a war-weary Congress—while politely suggesting that New York State could not reasonably be expected to settle for less.

Averting further warfare was clearly attractive to Congress. Equally tempting to New York State's financially straitened legislators was Schuyler's novel way of defining the land rights to be possessed by the returning Iroquois tribes. Schuyler suggested allowing both the pro-Revolutionary and formerly pro-British Iroquois to reside within the State, but only with greatly diminished rights. Schuyler's plan combined elements from two seemingly incompatible British colonial approaches to tribal land rights. One of these approaches presupposed that tribal Native Americans were nomadic hunters lacking all land ownership or durable land occupancy rights, and who could therefore only claim ownership of any game they killed. Seventeenth and eighteenth century

British colonists had often moved onto land presumed "vacant" or "waste" without asking permission of Native Americans who could, so these colonists imagined, readily find some other place to hunt. The second pre-Revolutionary British approach to tribal land rights drawn on by Schuyler posited in contrast that tribes were organized, sub-sovereign entities occupying definable areas by inheritable, Crown-protected tenancy right; and that tribes were capable of choosing rationally whether or not to sell their land rights, and at what price. (A third colonial theory, the one favored by Rhode Island's Roger Williams and on which Schuyler did *not* draw, maintained that tribes were sovereign rulers as well as unfettered owners of their lands.)

Inventively combining elements of two opposed British colonial approaches, Schuyler suggested that tribes be guaranteed an inheritable tenancy right to defined areas but also could be deemed assemblages of drifting hunters for land valuation purposes. Tribes would be said to possess not full fee title ownership of their ancestral lands, nor even a full occupancy or tenancy right, but only a hunting-ground use right whose sale value was to be determined by reckoning the amount of game remaining. This odd amalgam of concepts equated the land rights of commercially and agriculturally advanced tribes such as the Iroquois with those of small groups who actually were nomadic hunters. As if this were not ingenuity enough, according to Schuyler's concept the tiny amounts tribes could expect for relinquishing their hunting grounds would diminish as white settlements neared, reducing the prevalence of game. The price tribes could ask for their lands thus would decrease at the precise time that the land's value was increasing on the U.S. market. Confined to reservations in the extreme western portion of New York State, well beyond the military bounty lands designated by the Legislature, the formerly hostile Iroquois tribes could

> not prevent the settlement of that extensive uncultivated country which lays between what we now occupy and what they might be permitted to retain. It will be little or no obstacle to our future improving the very country they may retain, whenever we shall want it. For as our settlements approach their country, they must from the scarcity of game, which that approach will induce to, retire farther back, and dispose of their lands unless they dwindle comparatively to nothing, as all savages have done, who gain their sustenance by the

> chase, when compelled to live in the vicinity of civilized people, and thus leave us the country without the expense of a purchase, trifling as that will probably be.[7]

Schuyler seemed to have waved a magic wand, in anticipating that New York State could cheaply buy tribal lands as settlement advanced, indeed might even hope to pay nothing at all.

Schuyler was too well-informed about the Iroquois not to realize that his theory was farfetched. But Schuyler also knew that New York State—belligerent and broke—would not even consider payment for tribal lands at current U.S. market rates. The disordered conditions engendered by Revolutionary War conflict may also have influenced Schuyler's reasoning; the Iroquois were indeed for the moment not prosperous agriculturalists. During the War, both pro-Revolutionary and pro-British Iroquois had been driven from their tilled fields and orchards, and forced to seek refuge and handouts near military forts. Schuyler may well have assumed that the "savage...uncivilized" Iroquois could not recover the degree of advancement in "civilized arts" they had earlier attained, and would henceforth be subsistence hunters.

Schuyler's July 29, 1783 letter to Congress President Thomas Mifflin was referred by him to a committee, which in turn solicited the views of the Commander-in-Chief. Replying to the Congress committee's inquiry on September 7, 1783, General Washington endorsed Schuyler's plan enthusiastically:

> Every advantage that could be expected or even wished for would result from such a mode of procedure. Our settlements would be compact, government well established, and our barrier formidable, not only for ourselves but against our neighbors, and the Indians as has been observed in General Schuyler's letter will ever retreat as our settlements advance upon them and they will be as ready to sell, as we are to buy; that it is the cheapest as well as the least distressing way of dealing with them, none...acquainted with the nature of Indian warfare, and has ever been at the trouble of estimating the expense of one, and comparing it with the cost of purchasing their lands, will hesitate to acknowledge....[P]olicy and economy point very strongly to the expediency of being upon good terms with the Indians, and the propriety of purchasing their lands in preference to attempting to drive them by force of arms out of their country; which as we have already experienced is like driving the wild beasts of the forest which

> will return as soon as the pursuit is at an end and fall perhaps on those that are left there; when the gradual extension of our settlements will as certainly cause the savage as the wolf to retire; both being beasts of prey though they differ in shape. In a word there is nothing to be obtained by an Indian war but the soil they live on and this can be had by purchase at less expense, and without that bloodshed, and those distresses which helpless women and children are made partakers of in all kinds of disputes with them.[8]

Optimistically assuming that Schuyler's method of compensating tribes for their lands would prove workable, Washington suggested

> the Indians should be informed, that...as we consider them as a deluded people; as we persuade ourselves that they are convinced, from experience, of their error in taking up the hatchet against us, and that their true interest and safety must now depend upon *our* friendship. As the country is large enough to contain us all; and as we are disposed to be kind to them and to partake of their trade, we will from these considerations and from motives of compassion, draw a veil over what is past and establish a boundary line between them and us beyond which we will *endeavor* to restrain our people from hunting or settling, and within which they shall not come, but for the purposes of trading, treating, or other business unexceptionable in its nature.
>
> In establishing this line, in the first instance, care should be taken neither to yield nor to grasp at too much. But to endeavor to impress the Indians with an idea of the generosity of our disposition to accommodate them, and with the necessity we are under, of providing for our warriors, our young people who are growing up, and strangers who are coming from other countries to live among us. And if they should make a point of it, or appear dissatisfied at the line we may find it necessary to establish, compensation should be made them for their claims within it.[9]

Before learning of Schuyler's proposal, Washington had been taking a line more consonant with the British colonial tradition presupposing a tribal occupancy or tenancy right purchaseable only at a negotiated, mutually agreed price, even if such agreement was obtained with gun in hand. Only a few weeks earlier, on June 17, 1783, Washington had suggested that enclaves of former Revolutionary soldiers might be located on the frontiers

> to combat the savages, and check their incursions...; the appearance of so formidable a settlement in the vicinity of their towns (to say nothing of the barrier it would form against our other neighbors)

> would be the most likely means to enable us to purchase upon equitable terms of the aborigines their right of preoccupancy; and to induce them to relinquish our territories, and to remove into the illimitable regions of the west.[10]

In 1779, Washington had ordered hostile Iroquois towns destroyed, and his allusion here to "their towns" evidenced his continuing awareness that many tribes were in fact territorially-based political entities active in agriculture and trade, and not mere collections of randomly-roving subsistence hunters. And his reference to purchasing "upon equitable terms...their right of preoccupancy" makes clear his assumption that bargaining would be necessary to keep down the price; in June of 1783 he was not thinking in terms of formulaic, game-based remuneration. Washington's admiration for the political ingenuity of Schuyler's concept may have induced him to alter his views. Or Washington like Schuyler may have reasoned that the war-ravaged Iroquois might not be able to regain their previous level of agricultural advancement, and thus become more like "wolves" than town-dwellers.

Between writing his June and September letters, Washington had toured upstate New York. Accompanied by New York's Governor Clinton, Washington first went north to Lakes George and Champlain, returning by way of Saratoga Springs which Clinton and Washington tried in vain to buy. They next went west up the Mohawk River, then to Oneida Lake where they conferred with members of the Oneida tribe before returning by way of Lake Otsego, the future site of Cooperstown.[11] While on the Mohawk River, Clinton and Washington inspected (and subsequently did buy) 6,000 acres near modern-day Utica. Washington liked the land but didn't have the cash, so Clinton lent him 2,500 pounds at seven percent interest to cover his share; Washington was finally able to discharge this debt in 1787, and in time realized a handsome return.[12] When he wrote his September 7th letter, Washington in other words was newly indebted to New York's two principal leaders, both financially and conceptually.

Washington nonetheless added important dimensions to Schuyler's proposal. Schuyler focused narrowly on his own State, viewing the formerly pro-British Mohawks, Onondagas, Cayugas and Senecas as pawns in a high-stakes contest between New York and Congress for control of Iroquois lands. Washington expressed no objection to the specific implications of Schuyler's plan for New York State, that the State be permitted to proceed with its plan to grant Onondaga and Cayuga lands to soldiers, and that all formerly hostile Iroquois tribes be assigned land in the extreme western part of the State, allowing for a buffer zone between these tribes and settlements of New York citizens. But Washington's thinking comprehended all thirteen states, and envisioned all tribes adjoining U.S. settlements as useful inhibitors of unregulated westward movement by U.S. citizens. The manipulative Schuyler was concerned primarily about a loss of tribal land by New York State; Washington pondered national social stability, and predicted that tribes occupying vast tracts for some time to come could help the federal government "people the country progressively" with "compact" rather than dispersed settlements. Washington believed this would promote respect among frontier tribes for the orderliness of U.S. society and government. Conversely, if formerly pro-British tribes were forced to flee U.S. soil and returned as predators, they could foment social disorder.[13]

Tribal conciliation seemed prudent, and Schuyler made it appear virtually cost-free. Apart from casual expressions of solicitude, and the belief that tribes should be left minimally able to support themselves, neither General Schuyler nor General Washington considered the tribes' own perspective or interest. Even more problematic, neither Schuyler nor Washington seems to have considered legally relevant to questions affecting Native American land rights the many differences among Native Americans in culture, religion and political orientation. Both Generals were personally well acquainted with U.S. Colonel Louis Atayataghronghta, and each in his crucial letter (Schuyler's of July 29, 1783 and Washington's of September 7, 1783) made reference to having recently met with the pro-Revolutionary Oneidas. In addition, on July 2, 1783, Washington had conferred with U.S. Captain Hendrick Aupaumut of the Stockbridge Mahicans about their plan to move from lands guaranteed them by the Commonwealth of Massachusetts to lands they would hold only by tribal grant in New York State. In a letter of recommendation, Washington praised the Stockbridge Mahicans as "our friends and brothers...and subjects to the United States of

America" who had "during the whole of the late War...remained firmly attached to us and...fought and bled by our side."[14] Though not citizens, the Mahicans were thus respected allies and trustworthy "subjects." Yet while citizen-soldiers were awarded grants of fee-title land from which hostile tribes had been evicted, Washington assumed that "occupancy rights" with minimal monetary value would suffice for tribes, even those who had "fought and bled by our side." Pro-Revolutionary tribes were not to have their ancestral lands confiscated, but neither were they to be awarded fee title to these lands or to receive full market value for any portion they might wish to sell. Believing that "the country is large enough to contain us all," Washington felt tribes should be left to fend for themselves in the way of life they had freely chosen.

After receiving General Washington's endorsement, Schuyler's New York State-oriented tribal conciliation plan was formally considered by a Continental Congress committee consisting of New York's James Duane, chairman, Richard Peters of Pennsylvania, Daniel Carroll of Maryland, Arthur Lee of Virginia and Benjamin Hawkins of North Carolina. This committee drafted a report designed to apply to all sections of the frontier with the exception of the south, and which included (albeit with qualms) all the particular provisions desired by New York State. The committee echoed Washington in concluding "that the hostile tribes of Indians...are not in a temper to relinquish their territorial claims, without further struggles" and warned that

> if an Indian war should be rekindled, repeated victories might produce the retreat of the Indians, but could not prevent them from regaining possession of some part of the distant and extensive territories which appertain to the United States; that while such temporary expulsions could only be effected at a great charge, they could not be improved to the smallest advantage but by maintaining numerous garrisons and an expensive peace establishment.

The committee consequently suggested, and Congress agreed, to waive

> the right of conquest...[nonetheless insisting on] the obligation they [hostile tribes] are under to make atonement for the enormities which they have perpetrated, and a reasonable compensation for the expenses which the United States have incurred by their wanton barbarity; and they possess no other means to do this act of justice than by a compliance with the proposed boundaries.

Treaty Commissioners representing Congress were to meet with hostile tribes and insist that they surrender ownership claims to sufficient land to "be speedily improved into a fund towards the security and payment of the national debt." If tribes yielded what was desired, they would be allowed to reside peacefully on, and be deemed rightful occupants of, the remainder of their lands.[15] With respect to New York State, the committee recommended that

> whereas the Legislature of the State of New York have granted lands at Onondaga and Cayuga to certain officers and privates in the service of the United States, not only as bounties for recruiting and enlisting, but to appease the discontents which prevailed for want of their pay, and as a reward for their meritorious services, the said Commissioners are therefore further instructed to take care as far as will be consistent with the public peace that in the establishment of the proposed lines the said military grants be not prejudiced or impeached; but if it shall appear that the persisting in such grants and appropriations may so far irritate the Indians as to expose these United States to the dangers and calamities of an Indian war; that then it will be proper for the Commissioners to report the difficulties which shall so occur in their negotiation to the Legislature of the State of New York, and in such case it is earnestly recommended to the Legislature of the State of New York to revise the laws by which such appropriations have been made, so as to prevent the calamities of a new rupture with the Indians.

Evidently the committee was uncomfortable with Schuyler's insistence that the formerly hostile Iroquois tribes must only be assigned lands in the far western portion of New York State, and came up with a temporizing formula that included a procedure for resolving possible future differences. The full Congress was even more uncomfortable than their committee, and eliminated this already-qualified language from the final version approved on October 15, 1783.[16]

Months in the making, the tribal policy that Schuyler set in motion was admittedly problematic but also flexible enough to supply guidelines within which mutual agreement might have been attained. Sadly, the implementation of this policy lurched from controversy to disaster. After his Iroquois-oriented plan had been strongly applauded by General Washington and adopted by Congress, Schuyler assumed that Congress would invite him to negotiate with the Iroquois. Indeed, since

Congress had declined to commit itself formally to New York State's Iroquois agenda, who was to negotiate for Congress became a matter of intense concern to Schuyler and other New York leaders. Other statesmen might appropriately be appointed to negotiate with other tribes, but surely no one other than Schuyler could be trusted to handle the explosive issue of offering erstwhile anti-Revolutionary tribes territorial rights within New York's claimed bounds. Who else could hope to work out a compromise acceptable to both the Iroquois and the New York Legislature?

So little did Schuyler imagine the possibility of his being bypassed by Congress that on January 11, 1784, Schuyler held a preliminary meeting in Schenectady with a number of formerly hostile Iroquois to prepare the way for the upcoming Continental Congress treaty session over which he expected to preside. The Iroquois who had fought against the Revolution were at this moment landless refugees, having been driven from their homes by General Washington in 1779 and then expropriated by New York State and not yet provided for by their British allies. Pro-British Iroquois tribes were negotiating for land in Canada, with two sites under discussion, one at the Bay of Quinte north of Lake Ontario, another on the Grand River north of Lake Erie. Land at both these places was ultimately granted, but in January of 1784 nothing was certain. Having been ignored by the British in the 1783 Treaty of Paris was moreover an inducement even to the staunchly pro-British Mohawk Captain Joseph Brant at least to explore possibilities on the U.S. side of the border.

In their opening remarks at Schenectady, the formerly pro-British Iroquois chiefs lamented that the sun had seemingly "fallen from his place, and...a thick darkness had overspread the earth." Indeed "the path of peace was so overgrown with brush" that they had only with difficulty reached the treaty ground .[17]

"It is true that the sun has long been [so] obscured to you that the path of peace has been obstructed and rendered impassable," Schuyler retorted. "But the Americans have not in the least been the occasion of this, they wished to maintain a friendly intercourse with the Indians" and still were subjected to "barbarous and atrocious conduct...and none of the Six Nations except those trusty men who sit there, the Oneidas and Tuscaroras, fulfilled their engagements." After issuing this reprimand, Schuyler grandly "plucked the hatchet out of our heads with which the Indians had struck us, buried it, collected our bones, covered them, as also the ruins of our buildings, burnt by the Indians lest our resentment should rekindle at the sight." With "a magnanimity and generosity peculiar to a free people," Schuyler informed the Iroquois, the Continental Congress was disposed to re-establish friendly relations with their former enemies, on terms not yet announced but which Schuyler felt confident transgressor tribes "ought thankfully to accept."

Schuyler further noted that the 1783 Treaty of Paris did not "contain a single stipulation for the Indians, they are not so much as mentioned in the Treaty, they are therefore left to settle matters with Congress." If "the Indians should continue the war" instead of agreeing to the just concessions they would be expected to make, they would "thereby render themselves so obnoxious as to oblige us to extirpate them." As for Captain Brant's contention that all territory west of the Mohawk River watershed was still "our lands, acknowledged to be ours at the Treaty held at Fort Stanwix in the year 1768," Schuyler conceded that "a line of property was settled in 1768" but refused to speculate regarding "whether this agreement and every other heretofore made is become void or not, by the unprovoked war which the Indians have waged against the Americans, after they had in the most solemn manner pledged their faith to observe a strict neutrality." Only at the upcoming Congress treaty session would boundaries "be established between property to be appropriated to the use of the Indians, and...that for the use of the Americans." Schuyler concluded by urging that Captain Brant's followers "come to the General Meeting with truly pacific dispositions reflecting on the past, the present and the future, and ...regulate their conduct with regard to the Americans in such manner as not to afford fresh cause of complaint."

At Schenectady in January of 1784, Schuyler made clear what sort of treaty he intended to conduct on behalf of the Continental Congress. He would be polite but firm. He would set forth negotiation guidelines and announce terms which were to be accepted without demur. These terms would begin from the premise that the Mohawks, Onondagas, Cayugas and Senecas had by their conduct during the Revolutionary

War forfeited all their pre-War land rights and currently possessed no land rights anywhere within the United States. Schuyler however was prepared to help them if they would conduct themselves contritely and peaceably, by endeavoring to secure for them modest land rights within New York State's bounds. Schuyler felt confident he could serve successfully as an intermediary between the New York State Legislature and the Continental Congress on the one hand and the four formerly pro-British Iroquois tribes on the other. If instructed to function in this role by Congress, he would do his utmost to fashion an amicable multi-party post-War peace settlement guaranteeing the four Iroquois tribes presently encamped in British-controlled territory the right to occupy demarcated reservations in western New York State. In the process, New York State would secure a large amount of Iroquois land for award to veterans, as well as an implicit acknowledgment of the State's claimed western boundary from Congress.

Momentously, Schuyler was bypassed when Congress appointed Treaty Commissioners in March of 1784; in fact no New Yorker was selected. Schuyler discerned in this turn of events the work of New York's enemies, and advocated an assertive State response.[18] The most disquieting explanation of why Schuyler might have been passed over implicated Massachusetts, which had decided in the fall of 1783 to assert ownership (based on its ancient colonial charter) of territory already claimed by the Iroquois and New York State. In response to the Massachusetts intervention, Congress resolved on June 3, 1784, "That the first Monday in December next, be assigned for the appearance of the...States of Massachusetts and New York, by their lawful agents" to argue this boundary dispute. The following day Charles De Witt, a New York delegate to Congress, wrote New York Governor Clinton,

> I hope the [New York] Legislature have taken every precaution respecting the W[estern] Territory. I believe, Sir, a plan is formed and perhaps wrought into system to take that country from us. Massachusetts Delegates have put in a petition yesterday from the Legislature of that State setting forth that New York is possessed of a part of their land...The whole world seems to look on that W[estern] country with a wishful eye.[19]

This was scarcely an exaggeration. In addition to Massachusetts, Connecticut and Pennsylvania hoped to acquire a piece of what De

Witt called the western country: that area *east* of what was to be the Northwest Territory. Agreement was being painstakingly secured from state after state that the proposed Northwest Territory would belong to the nation, but rampant state rivalries flourished regarding the Iroquois homelands just to the east. Pennsylvania desired a Great Lakes port, finally acquired in 1792 when the federal government awarded Pennsylvania the Erie Triangle. Connecticut and Massachusetts maintained that their ancient colonial charters gave them title to lands stretching westward right through what is now New York State. In 1763 the British Crown had sought to end such overlapping colonial claims to western lands by taking direct control of all territory west of the Appalachians. But in 1776 these old claims were revived, and none had been settled by 1784. Since the three Congress Commissioners appointed to negotiate with the Iroquois were from Pennsylvania, Connecticut and Virginia, New York officials had good reason to fear that a Congress treaty with the Iroquois could frustrate their State's hopes and abet the aspirations of Pennsylvania, Connecticut and Massachusetts. Ironically, General Schuyler's plan to make the Iroquois pawns of New York State had induced three other states to test whether the Iroquois might not be turned instead into pawns of these states. Worse yet, they had evidently succeeded in persuading Congress to become their collective agent.

Mulling over these developments, James Duane decided to join Schuyler in opposing the Commissioners appointed by Congress to negotiate with the Iroquois, and thus ostensibly to implement the tribal policy he had helped draft as chairman of the Congress committee that recommended favorable action on Schuyler's proposal. Like Schuyler, Duane was a New York aristocrat with strong confederal tendencies, and it was of great symbolic as well as practical significance that Duane and Schuyler now turned their backs on Congress and urged New York's populist Governor Clinton to devise a tribal policy to counter the threat to New York State's boundaries posed by Congress's plan to negotiate with the Iroquois without Schuyler. Duane and Schuyler had long been political rivals of Clinton; indeed in 1777 when the office of governor under the new State constitution was first contested, Schuyler expected to be chosen but instead was beaten by Clinton running as the poor man's candidate.

As a prominent member of Congress, Duane understood both the political and legal risks of what New York now contemplated. "Great difficulty arises," he warned Clinton, "from the interference of the proposed treaty with the authority and the views of Congress." Duane cautioned that some in Congress would argue that the Iroquois tribes were "*independent nations*, detached from the State, and absolutely unconnected with it." For New York State to negotiate with enemy nations living beyond its borders would be an undeniable violation of the Articles of Confederation. "There is then an indispensable necessity," reasoned Duane, "that these tribes should be treated as *ancient dependents on this State*....On this ground the tribes in question may fall under the character of *members of the State* with the management of whom Congress have no concern." Duane suggested that Governor Clinton confer with the formerly hostile Iroquois as if this were not a "treaty" at all but merely a meeting with a group of former New York residents who desired to return to live within the State. After all, New York State had already confiscated their lands and thus did not need to ask anything of *them.* Rather, *they* would be asking the State to restore some of the lands they had forfeited by their conduct during the Revolutionary War. Duane recommended that Clinton assert New York State's rightful, already perfected jurisdiction over the ancestral homelands of these dispossessed refugees, and greet them as petitioners with no current rights. Duane advised against using or allowing the Iroquois to use

> the word "Nation," or "Six Nations" or "Confederates," or "Council Fire at Onondaga," or any other form which would revive or seem to confirm their former ideas of independence....I would say nothing of making peace or burying the hatchet, for that would be offensive to Congress, perhaps very justly. But I would study to carry on the intercourse (for I object even against the term *treaty*, which seems too much to imply equality) with as much plainness and simplicity as possible, and as if I was actually transacting business with the citizens.

Duane proposed that the State express willingness that the formerly pro-British Iroquois "should be restored once more in their native land" and offer to "establish a line between the settlements of the white people and the lands to be reserved for the use of the Indians within our State, in such a manner as would be for the advantage and comfort of both parties" but only on the condition and with the understanding that "the Indians on their part would be reasonable in their claims, equitable in their concessions and inoffensive in their future deportment." Duane lamented that

> They are used to be called, *Brethren, Sachems and Warriors of the Six Nations*. I hope it will never be repeated. It would be not less absurd than mischievous. They should rather be taught [that] by separating from the Oneidas and entering into a wicked War, they had become wretched and destroyed themselves, and that the public opinion of their importance had long since ceased.[20]

Duane here urged a new way of thinking about the Iroquois as "dependents." He realized that if the Iroquois were merely deemed "dependent" in a feudal sense they would still have to be considered autonomous polities with which Congress under the Articles should perhaps negotiate. So Duane suggested that Governor Clinton deal with the Iroquois not as *dependent nations* but rather as stateless refugees *dependent* on the charity of New York State.[21] As it turned out, though Clinton may have preferred Duane's approach, when face-to-face with the Iroquois he felt obliged to employ many of the flattering formulas Duane deplored. Despite the risk of offending Congress, Clinton could not proceed as Duane desired, because the Iroquois were not hapless, and realized they had options.

In the summer of 1784, all six Iroquois tribes were confusingly invited to attend separate, competing treaty sessions to be hosted respectively by the United States and by New York State. Before setting out, Congress's Treaty Commissioners asked Governor Clinton to supply them with a military escort. Clinton replied that raising troops was beyond his power when the New York Legislature was not in session, adding defiantly,

> The Indians of the Six Nations, whom I have requested to convene at Fort Schuyler, have advised me that they will be accompanied by deputies from other nations possessing...territory within the jurisdiction of the United States; I shall have no objection to your improving this incident to the advantage of the United States, excepting however and positively stipulating that no agreement be entered into with the Indians, residing within the jurisdiction of this State (and with whom

> only I mean to treat) prejudicial to its rights. Those engagements being made on your part, you may rely on every exertion in my power and that of my colleagues to promote the interest of the United States; which I flatter myself no State in the federal Union has at any time more cheerfully and efficiently supported than this.[22]

Undaunted, Congress's Commissioners decided to enter New York State with a guard of New Jersey troops; and on August 19, 1784 reaffirmed their intention to "conclude a peace in the name of the United States with such of those nations as have been hostile." Clinton was invited to attend Congress's treaty session—but only if he would agree to avoid the subject of war and peace and limit himself to matters of proper concern to New York State. Congress's Commissioners blandly pointed out that "such conduct on the part of the State of Pennsylvania has been generally approved for its wisdom and confederal policy." After consulting with General Schuyler, Clinton decided not even to reply to this, since "an answer, such as their letter merits, might occasion altercation."[23]

Pennsylvania wished on this occasion to acquire only a tract of Iroquois-claimed land within that State's acknowledged bounds, and Pennsylvania's representatives dutifully waited until after the Congress Treaty had been signed, at which time they were "introduced" to the Iroquois with whom they concluded a separate Treaty one day after the Congress Treaty. Pennsylvania's conduct remained throughout "entirely satisfactory to the Continental Commissioners."[24]

The entirely uncooperative Governor Clinton tried to head off Congress's Commissioners by convening a preemptive State-Iroquois treaty session amidst the devastated remains of the old British Fort Stanwix. Called Fort Schuyler by New York State in honor of General Schuyler, both the Iroquois and Congress's Commissioners preferred for distinct reasons of their own to call this monument to the imperial past by its old British name.[25] Governor Clinton initially proposed that the Iroquois confer with him at the German Flats (modern Herkimer), clearly within New York State's jurisdiction. Congress's Commissioners on the other hand proposed convening "the Great Council Fire of Congress" at Fort Niagara, then still in British possession and outside of New York State's current control. But the Iroquois insisted that the treaty take place at Fort Stanwix, to underscore their demand for restitution of all their pre-War lands as confirmed to them there by the British in 1768. New York State agreed, and Congress's Commissioners decided they had no choice but to head for Fort Stanwix themselves.

With future President James Monroe, who happened to be traveling in the area, looking on, Clinton opened New York State's Iroquois conference on September 5, 1784, announcing as his objective

> settling those differences and animosities which have arisen between us, by reason of your conduct during the late War; to establish boundary lines between you and us, on such just and equitable terms as will be satisfactory and prevent all future animosities.[26]

Since the assembled Iroquois chiefs were all aware that Congress's Commissioners were due to arrive in two weeks, Governor Clinton unflinchingly addressed his State's quarrel with Congress. *"Brethren!"* he proclaimed,

> The right and power of managing all affairs with the Indians, not members of any of the states, is vested in Congress, who have, as we are informed, appointed Commissioners for the purpose. We are appointed by a Law of the Legislature of this State, to superintend Indian Affairs within the same, by virtue of which we are authorized and required to enter into compacts and agreements with any Indians residing within this State. It is in consequence of this Law and these powers that we appear now to treat with you our *Brethren,* with whom, when our present differences are adjusted, we are inclined to live as heretofore, on terms of the most sincere friendship: in testimony whereof we give you this belt.

By presenting the Iroquois with wampum belts and employing other ceremonial elements of traditional tribal treaty-making, Clinton did his best to conciliate the State's arch-enemies, whose delegation at Fort Stanwix was led by the widely detested Captain Joseph Brant.

On September 7, Brant replied to Governor Clinton's opening remarks, subtly apologizing for the "difficulty in our minds, that there should be two separate bodies to manage these affairs, for this does not agree with our ancient customs." The chiefs, Brant confessed, were disposed to think "we should first meet Commissioners of the whole thirteen States and after that if any matters should remain between us and any particular State, that we should then attend to them."

Clinton saw no choice but to accept this Iroquois decision rebuffing his defense of New York State's priority. Believing nothing further could be accomplished, Clinton left Fort Schuyler/Stanwix on September 11, 1784. Reaching Albany by September 14, Clinton immediately reported all that had transpired to General Schuyler.[27]

Events were unfolding precisely as predicted by one exasperated Congress Commissioner who warned,

> while the Indians are induced to believe...that there are distinct, independent and perhaps jealous powers to treat with them, they will certainly avail themselves of it.[28]

Just how "jealous" Clinton felt toward Congress's Commissioners was evidenced by his decision to depart before they arrived, leaving behind a State representative with instructions to attend the Congress treaty session and "frustrate" measures inimical to New York interests.

On October 3, 1784—this time with a second future president from Virginia, James Madison, and the Marquis de Lafayette in attendance—Congress's Commissioners convened their Iroquois treaty session. In opening remarks lavishly embellished with Native American metaphors, they proposed

> to kindle a Council fire at this place, where we may smoke the calumet together undisturbed by evil thoughts, and renew the friendship, and brighten the chain of alliance with *you our faithful brothers* [the pro-Revolutionary Oneidas and Tuscaroras], and give peace and good counsel *to those* who have been unfortunately led astray by evil advisers.

In case the chiefs might still be thinking of keeping their New York State options open, Congress's Commissioners assured them

> We know from experience that ill winds blow from every quarter, and birds fly about with evil chirpings....We...have full authority to transact all business between the United States, and you, and...without the authority of Congress no business can be valid that may be attempted by particular people or states.[29]

The Congress Commissioners then introduced Lafayette, whom they described as "one of the head warriors of the great Onondio," the Iroquois name for the French monarch. Lafayette urged the assembled chiefs to "Be wiser than the white men—keep peace among you." He also expressed hope that trade with France would once again flourish.

"The products of France are known to you," Lafayette reminded the Iroquois, "and you are clever enough to prefer them." These themes were tame enough; not so, his decision to claim for France's King Louis XVI the title of tribal *father.* General Washington had suggested to the young Marquis that his presence at Fort Stanwix might usefully impress Iroquois such as Colonel Louis Atayataghronghta who had pro-French leanings, and encourage them to support the United States. Instead the flamboyant Marquis, employing what he imagined was platitudinous rhetoric, induced the chiefs to suppose that France actually intended to resume France's pre-1763 role as *father*—i.e., patron and protector—of tribes. The chiefs responded with such eagerness to his speech that the following day Lafayette wrote his wife he was "very weary of the role of father of the family which has been forced on me here." All he wished to accomplish, he assured her, was to facilitate "a treaty that will give us a small commercial outlet and will ensure the tranquillity of the Americans." Already embarrassed by New York State's tribal negotiations, the Congress Commissioners now had to cope with the impression that France sought a key role in post-Revolutionary tribal politics. Greatly alarmed, they insisted that the Marquis must leave because, as he confided to his wife, "the savages had been too occupied with me to pay attention to the Commissioners." He left Fort Stanwix two days later, escorted by Madison.[30]

Congress's Commissioners then had only Iroquois chiefs to contend with—and Governor Clinton's representative Major Peter Schuyler, a nephew of General Schuyler. When on October 9 the Commissioners asked Major Schuyler for a copy of his instructions, he handed them over. The next day, belatedly realizing their antagonistic wording would give offense, Schuyler rashly grabbed them back and tore them up. The Congress Commissioners retaliated on October 12, barring him and his Iroquois-speaking interpreter Peter Ryckman from attending further treaty sessions.[31]

Congress's Commissioners also became enmeshed in controversy with another sector of New York officialdom. Discovering a violation of their prohibition against "selling or giving spirituous liquor to the Indians during the negotiation," the Commissioners

Resolved, that all strong liquors in the hands of persons at, or near

> Fort Stanwix, other than such as shall be detained by the special approbation of the Commissioners, be immediately seized and...stored in the Commissioners' store.[32]

But when New Jersey Lieutenant John Mercer attempted to carry out this order, he was arrested by Montgomery County Sheriff James Yale, and ordered to appear before the justices of the County's inferior court. The Commissioners forbade Mercer's appearance and portentously demanded of the justices an

> exemplary animadversion against all who have been concerned in it, for such an indignity and injuries offered to the authority of the United States, to the Commissioners vested with the powers, and to the officer acting by their orders, if encouraged by passing unpunished must necessarily involve this country, and this State in the most serious consequences.[33]

Apparently their ploy worked, and the next day Lieutenant Mercer was again ordered to seize liquor supplies and told, "It is our intention that Mr. Peter Schuyler and Mr. S. Rightman [an apparent reference to Peter Ryckman] should not be excepted from this order."[34] Montgomery County and New York State had been successfully faced down.

While Congress's Commissioners sought the cooperation (or at least the neutrality) of the representatives of France, Pennsylvania and New York State, tribal leaders at Fort Stanwix were attempting to mend their own fractured alliance. For the Iroquois, the Revolutionary War had become a civil war, and skillful use of the tribes' ages-old techniques of reconciliation was needed to restore harmony. As Iroquois delegates began arriving, a fight broke out between two Oneida brothers, one of whom "had served in the British army, and the other had joined the Americans." The brothers'

> conversation grew more and more animated, and one of them struck the other violently with his club. The one who had been struck began to cry and seemed to want to return the blows he had received, but an old man took him in his arms and held him down on the ground until some women who had come led the other out of the hut. The old man was the father of the two young people, and his son, though strong, made no attempt to escape from his arms. He even consented to smoke the peace pipe with his brother. We saw him smoke half a pipe and give it to the aggressor, who finished it, and peace was made.[35]

The person who recorded this incident was Francois Marbois, at Fort Stanwix with the Marquis de Lafayette. Marbois also

> witnessed the reconciliation of the Oneidas with their Indian enemies.... The [Oneida] Great Grasshopper, wearing the cloak M. le Chevalier de La Luzerne had given him and followed by five other savages dressed with the same care, went to the huts of the Senecas. They walked with dignity and stopped from time to time. The chief of the Senecas came out and received them at some distance. They sat down on the grass, the two chiefs exchanged greetings, they smoked the peace pipe, and they parted. The next day the visit was returned, the Senecas going to the Oneidas with the same ceremony and the same formalities.[36]

Congress's Commissioners imagined they were as attentive to tribal rituals as the French, but also presumed to make improvements, giving wampum belts to the Iroquois while refusing their requests for written copies of accompanying remarks, stating disingenuously

> we did not choose you to be deceived, and our meaning to be misrepresented by the few persons among you who understood English, and might have explained our speech if we had gave a copy of it, as they pleased....We did not wish to put you into the power of such persons, but to clear your eyes and your understandings. We explained at your desire over and over again our speech to you, and the [wampum] strings and belts which accompanied every part of it.[37]

In tribal understanding, a properly handled treaty session would have begun with ceremonies intended to induce a mood of harmony. Discussion would then be introduced by an exchange of wampum belts ornamented with symbols specific to the occasion. By 1784, tribes nonetheless expected written supplements and understood what the Commissioners' evasions implied. Despite their ostentatious use of Native American metaphors, Congress's Commissioners at Fort Stanwix displayed contempt for the deeper conventions of tribal diplomacy. To employ elements of traditional Native American diplomacy without attempting to enter into the ceremonial ambience of the tribal meeting ground was an insult, one not lost on the Iroquois.

The increasingly exasperated Commissioners also read from the 1783 Treaty of Paris and contended peremptorily,

> in this treaty, no mention is made by the King of Great Britain of any Indian nation or tribe whatever...he has left those tribes to seek for

> peace with the United States, upon such terms as the United States shall think just and reasonable.

Undeterred, Mohawk Aaron Hill replied,

> Certainly the Great King did not look up to that Great Spirit, which he had called as a witness to that treaty, otherwise common justice would not have suffered him to be so inattentive, as to neglect those who had been so just, and faithful to him; and we think that our brothers the United States did not think of the Great Spirit, otherwise they would have mentioned to the Great King those persons who had been so faithful to him, when they found that he had entirely neglected them.

Hill prefaced his pointed rebuke with this crucial assertion:

> We are free, and independent, and at present under no influence. We have hitherto been bound by the Great King, but he having broke the chain, and left us to ourselves, we are again free and independent.

The Commissioners retorted contemptuously, telling Hill

> you are mistaken in supposing that having been excluded from the United States and the King of Great Britain, you are become a free and independent nation, and may make what terms you please. It is not so. You are a subdued people; you have been overcome in a war which you entered into with us, not only without provocation, but in violation of most sacred obligations. The Great Spirit who is at the same time the judge and avenger of perfidy, has given us victory over all our enemies. We are at peace with all but *you; you* now stand out *alone* against our *whole force.*

Although Congress's Commissioners dismissed his claim, Aaron Hill was justified in describing the four formerly pro-British Iroquois tribes as independent. Britain's failure in the Treaty of Paris to secure the rights of allied tribes infuriated the pro-British Iroquois, who responded by proclaiming themselves unbound by any agreement to which they were not parties. Embarrassed British officials in Canada were the first to hear this declaration. Congress's Commissioners heard next, and in refusing it credence imprudently forced the newly-neutral Iroquois back toward alliance with Britain.

Neither the Commissioners' tone nor their policy of demanding abject surrender accorded with the fundamentally conciliatory views of Generals Schuyler and Washington, or of Congress. But Congress's Commissioners were by now quite angry. Realizing they were nowhere near agreement, Congress's Commissioners broke off negotiations, demanded hostages (including Aaron Hill) and imposed a Treaty specifying a boundary line that appeared to take land from both the Iroquois and New York State, while simultaneously confirming (in disregard of the desires of many in Congress) some land to the Iroquois that New York State had already designated for award to veterans.

By the dictated Treaty completed on October 22, 1784, the "Six Nations" purportedly renounced all claims to territory west of a line four miles east of the Niagara River, and were then "secured in the peaceful possession of the lands they inhabit east and north of the same [line], reserving only six miles square round the fort of Oswego to the United States for the support of the same." Some of the western land to which the Iroquois renounced claims was destined for the proposed Northwest Territory but nothing was said about this in the Treaty, which was only one in a series of necessary preliminaries and not an affirmative establishment of the Northwest Territory. What land if any the "Six Nations" actually would "inhabit" east of the line was not identified, although this was of great consequence since none of the four formerly pro-British Iroquois tribes currently inhabited any land east of the line; most still were encamped under British military protection near Fort Niagara, and thus on land to which they ostensibly renounced their claims by the 1784 Treaty. Were the lands "secured" —wherever they were—possessed collectively by the "Six Nations" or was each tribe to have its own allotment? By what tenure would these lands be held, and under which U.S. jurisdiction? Could Congress by fiat guarantee tribal land rights in regions claimed by states, or would state confirmation be required?

On October 15, 1783, Congress had adopted a measured policy of conciliation for anti-Revolutionary tribes. These tribes were to be told that they had forfeited all their land rights by their wartime conduct, but that they would now be granted new land rights by a magnanimous government. These land rights were to be less than tribes previously held, but still considerable and—perhaps most important—clearly demarcated and strongly guaranteed. Disastrously disregarding this pragmatic policy, the Treaty Commissioners at Fort Stanwix decreed incoherent terms they couldn't enforce, leaving both the Iroquois and

New York authorities furious.

Congress's Fort Stanwix Treaty was soon repudiated by the then-sovereign Iroquois Confederacy. Since some Iroquois had signed the Treaty under duress, an Iroquois council session was convened at Buffalo Creek (modern-day Buffalo) which formally denounced the Treaty. Finally in 1794, by approving the replacement Treaty of Canandaigua, the U.S. federal government also repudiated the Treaty. Iroquois chiefs justifiably recalled in 1794 how at Fort Stanwix, "the Commissioners would always do the business as they pleased: they behaved terribly." In any treaty expressing the spirit of the tribal meeting ground, explained these chiefs, "it is pleasing to have both parties advance and meet; each having a voice in the agreement."[38] Instead of ushering in peace with the four formerly pro-British Iroquois tribes, the 1784 Treaty of Fort Stanwix drove many of these Iroquois to seek refuge in Canada, from which "asylum" they continued for decades to fight against the United States, just as Generals Schuyler and Washington had predicted.

Unlike tribes near the Atlantic coast which lost their autonomy in the seventeenth century and accepted ordinary colonial jurisdiction, or midwestern tribes that remained independent well into the nineteenth century, the once-mighty Iroquois Confederacy gradually declined in power during the eighteenth century, and was badly splintered by the Revolution. Complete dissolution of the Confederacy seemed all too likely, but the post-War years reopened possibilities, some of which the Iroquois successfully grasped. Iroquois attempts to regain leverage prospered because of rivalries between the British and the United States, as well as rivalries within the United States among several states and between these states and the central U.S. government. Two hundred years later, the Iroquois still derive benefit from the standing they secured in the Revolutionary era from rival U.S. governments, each of which sought to use the autonomous Iroquois as pawns but whose competition instead empowered these intended pawns.

New York State also had to work hard to undo damage done by the 1784 Congress Treaty. One dilemma for the State was what to say to soldiers who had been granted land in the region now "secured" by Congress to Iroquois tribes that had fought against the Revolution. To assist veterans granted land in what was now a contested region, the New York Legislature on May 5, 1786, declared that

> *whereas* by virtue of acts heretofore passed, for granting bounty lands, sundry locations have been made on lands belonging to the Onondaga, Cayuga and Seneca nations of Indians, *and whereas* an attempt to settle such lands...may involve this State in a disagreeable controversy with the said Indians

veterans might choose land elsewhere.[39] The same law established a second Military Tract to replace that laid out in 1782 just west of the lands of the Oneidas and Tuscaroras. The State's second Military Tract was located in erstwhile Mohawk territory far to the north and east, where the State's jurisdiction would hopefully not be contested. The reason given was "sundry circumstances" which had rendered "the lands so intended to be granted...of little use."

Another dilemma for New York State was what could establish in the eyes of the other twelve states New York's rightful jurisdiction west of the Mohawk River watershed. To resolve their incompatible claims, New York and Massachusetts in 1784 prepared for legal proceedings to be orchestrated by Congress. But after numerous delays, the two states decided in 1786 to meet on their own, using substantially the same people who would have represented their states before a Congress tribunal. Bilateral discussions began in Hartford, Connecticut in late November, and were successfully concluded on December 16, 1786.[40] Massachusetts was accorded the right to acquire and resell tribal occupancy rights in portions of western New York State, in return for acknowledging New York State's jurisdiction there.

The Hartford Compact was approved by the Legislatures of New York and Massachusetts early in 1787. These two States then attempted to have their Compact "filed in the secretary's office" of Congress but on October 8, 1787, this motion was defeated. After Massachusetts and New York settled their differences, the result was presented to the Continental Congress—*and not approved.*[41] The independent route taken by Massachusetts and New York, skirting around the procedure outlined in the Articles of Confederation for the settlement of such disputes, may have been seen by some members of Congress as a bad precedent. Others no doubt perceived that the Hartford Compact could not be reconciled with the 1784 Treaty of Fort Stanwix. Even critics of the Treaty may have felt that it should not be simply ignored. Whatever the reasons, New York State had once again failed to gain Congress recognition of its western boundary claims. The legal status of Iroquois land and the related question of the location of New York State's western boundary remained unresolved when the Constitution was drafted.

After their diplomatic "triumph" at Fort Stanwix in October of 1784, two of Congress's three Commissioners proceeded on to negotiate the January 21, 1785, Treaty of Fort McIntosh with Ohio-region tribes, reiterating the refrain that "we claim the country by conquest; and are to give not to receive." This contention made no better sense in the midwest than it had in New York State. Affirmed one final time in a treaty with the Ohio-region Shawnees dated January 31, 1786, the Commissioners' conquest premise was finally repudiated by Congress in the face of the tribes' logical retort: How can we be said to have been conquered if we haven't surrendered and are prepared to continue fighting?[42]

An opportunity to ascertain whether a more conciliatory approach might achieve better results was presented in the fall of 1785 when Congress attempted to negotiate with southern tribes. This effort was led by North Carolina's Benjamin Hawkins, one of the five members of Congress who drafted the measured post-War tribal policy approved on October 15, 1783. Despite methodical efforts, Hawkins and his fellow Congress Commissioners failed to conclude a treaty with the Creek Confederacy. But amicable treaties were completed with the Cherokees, Chickasaws, Choctaws, treaties that were models of the best that could be achieved within the cumbersome framework provided by the Articles of Confederation.

In marked contrast to the angry showdown with New York State at Fort Stanwix, for the Congress treaty sessions at Hopewell, South Carolina, the States of North Carolina and Georgia were politely invited to send delegates, who participated courteously even when expressing forthright disagreement. Congress's Commissioners also made efforts to establish good relations with southern tribal chiefs, working to create an atmosphere in which negotiations might proceed toward mutually advantageous solutions to common problems. The Chickasaws for example were told

> We sincerely wish you to live as happily as we do ourselves, and to promote that happiness as far as [is] in our power, regardless of any distinction of color, or of any differences in our customs or manners, or particular situations; and as a proof of the sincerity of our declarations, we propose to enter into articles of a treaty, as equal as may be.

The Cherokees were similarly assured that Congress was "your father and friend...who will see justice done you." Many chiefs responded positively, one addressing the Commissioners as "our eldest and first brothers" while others aptly praised the "unexpected justice" of the proceedings.[43]

Congress's Commissioners conceded that numerous outrages had been committed during the past decade by Revolutionaries as well as pro-British tribes. But when the Cherokee chief Tassel demanded a return to the boundaries guaranteed them by British authorities before the War in what is now eastern Kentucky and eastern Tennessee, the Commissioners replied candidly, "you must not expect from us any promise which we know cannot be done but with great inconveniency to our citizens." Tassel retorted, "Are Congress, who conquered the King of Great Britain, unable to remove those people?"[44]

The Cherokee line ultimately drawn by the Commissioners pleased no one altogether, and was defensible primarily because it seemed injurious to the fewest people "regardless of any distinction of color." Some white squatters were to be removed, and North Carolina and Georgia would be asked to find alternatives to some land grants already made so that the Cherokees could recover some land, although not as much as they had previously been guaranteed by British authorities. Tassel accepted this conditionally, declaring himself

> satisfied with the promises of the Commissioners to remove all the people from within our lines, except those within the fork of Holston and French Broad; and I will agree to be content that the particular situation of the people settled there and our claims to the lands, should be referred to Congress, as the commissioners may think just, and I will abide by their decision.

The Commissioners agreed to refer these remaining Cherokee

grievances to Congress, and also to recommend compensation should the Cherokee claim be denied.[45] But the representatives of North Carolina and Georgia refused to go along with this compromise. Hours before the Cherokee Treaty was to be completed, North Carolina's agent William Blount submitted a written protest, stating

> Should you, by treaty...[alter existing] boundaries...within the limits of...North Carolina, between the...Cherokee Indians and her citizens, that State will consider such a treaty a violation and infringement upon her legislative rights.

The Congress Commissioners replied at once, telling Blount

> The local policy of some States is certainly much opposed to federal measures, which can only, in our opinion, make us respectable abroad and happy at home.[46]

Hawkins and his fellow Commissioners went forward despite Blount's protest, hoping that the North Carolina Legislature would ultimately acquiesce. In North Carolina, Hawkins possessed almost as much influence as Blount, and planned to do what he could to defeat Blount's faction and gain State approval. But Hawkins realized the three Congress Treaties with southern tribes could not be enforced if either North Carolina or Georgia remained opposed. Days after completing the Cherokee Treaty, the Commissioners advised the President of Congress that

> We have required the aid of the agent of North Carolina, and the commissioners of Georgia, in the execution of the treaty, and we foresee that difficulties will frequently arise, and indeed, render it ineffectual, if these two States should refuse their cooperation.[47]

North Carolina's Legislature ultimately sided with Blount against Hawkins, resolving in November of 1788

> that all treaties made with any tribe or nation of Indians whereby lands allotted to them for hunting grounds within the chartered limits of this State other than those allotted by the law of the State heretofore made are a violation of the Constitution and not warranted by the Confederation of the United States... [and] all and every person holding land under grants legally obtained from this State shall be protected in the possession of the same, any Treaty made by the Commissioners appointed by the United States with any tribe or nation of Indians to the contrary notwithstanding.[48]

Georgia's Legislature similarly proclaimed the Congress Treaty with the Cherokees "a pretended treaty" which was

> a manifest and direct attempt to violate the retained sovereignty and legislative right of this State, and repugnant to the principles and harmony of the Federal Union; inasmuch as the aforesaid commissioners did attempt to exercise powers that are not delegated by the respective States to the United States, in Congress assembled.[49]

Southern courtesy had fared little better than northern rudeness. Even though Congress negotiations with the southern tribes were handled much more consensually than those in the north, the ultimate result was not significantly different.. As Hawkins lamented to Thomas Jefferson on June 14, 1786, "The interposition of Congress without the cooperation of the southern states is ineffectual, and Georgia and North Carolina have refused by protesting against their authority."[50]

On August 7, 1786, Congress approved "An Ordinance for the Regulation of Indian Affairs." This created an "Indian Department" within the War Department, consisting of northern and southern districts. The southern district was to "comprehend within its limits all the nations in the territory of the United States, who reside southward of the river Ohio." The northern district was to "comprehend all the other Indian nations within the said territory, and westward of Hudson river." This excluded New England, while explicitly including most of the claimed territory of New York State—without expressing an opinion about state boundaries "westward of Hudson river." Under the Ordinance, tribes within state boundaries would be clearly a Congress responsibility. But before the Ordinance was approved by Congress, an amendment backed by Georgia's William Few was added, providing

> in all cases where transactions with any nation or tribe of Indians shall become necessary to the purposes of this Ordinance, which cannot be done without interfering with the legislative rights of a state, the Superintendent...shall act in conjunction with the authority of such state.[51]

The states' power to obstruct intrastate tribal initiatives by Congress continued.

Creation of the Northwest Territory through cession to Congress of all state claims there eliminated this obstacle in the Northwest. But elsewhere even well-conceived attempts by Congress to function in tribal relations as a national government served principally to embitter tribes and gratify the nation's foes. After the fracas he witnessed at Fort Stanwix, James Monroe expressed concern to James Madison that nothing could "remove the impressions which this variance has made with the Indians and in the Court of Great Britain respecting us."[52] Fortunately Madison, Monroe and others with similar worries turned their attention to remedying the defects in the Articles of Confederation that tribal negotiations had so painfully exposed. The next phase in the history of North America consequently produced not the collapse of the United States, so eagerly anticipated by royalists, but rather the framing of the Constitution.

Three

Writing Tribes into the Constitution

CONVENTIONAL WISDOM AMONG SCHOLARS of U.S. tribal policy posits that centralized protection for tribes was one of the good aspects of British imperialism; that the American Revolution brashly rejected this along with other good ideas emanating from London; but that the 1789 Constitution sensibly re-instituted a royal-style monopoly of tribal relations, mandating "exclusive" federal authority. This perspective was first outlined in the 1830s by U.S. Supreme Court Chief Justice John Marshall, and after more than a century and a half of elaboration stands virtually unchallenged. It relies however on an understanding of the transition from British imperial to Revolutionary and then Constitutional tribal policy that is so misleading that it now forms a substantial barrier to progress in resolving today's tribal issues.

Because each of Great Britain's North American colonies originated in separate circumstances extending over more than a century, the colonies varied considerably in their governmental structures, and therefore in how frontier tribes as well as colonially governed groups of Native Americans were dealt with. When the British Crown in the 1750s began articulating the framework of a more centralized North American regime, Native Americans were part of the plan, as was exploitation of the trans-Appalachian interior. The Royal Proclamation of October 7, 1763 sought to make the Appalachian watershed a barrier between white colonists and western lands, which were designated tribal hunting grounds "for the present" though intended ultimately for development controlled from London rather than by coastal colonies. While tribal land sales and future colonial settlement west of the mountains were arrogated to royal control, coastal colonies continued to supervise the daily life of many Native American groups east of the Appalachian watershed, and to trade with politically autonomous trans-Appalachian tribes. Thus even at the height of imperial centralization, Native American policy was not so unitary as later supposed, when a mythologized notion of a benign British rule gripped the imaginations of federal officials frustrated by state resistance. Nor did the Crown's plan to separate western tribal lands from coastal colonial jurisdiction imply a royal intent to protect these lands indefinitely for tribal use.

In 1776, Britain's still-sketchy policy for Native Americans was torn apart, and all thirteen colonies-turned-states began pursuing their own Native American policies. Most states revived practices followed prior to the 1750s, giving them new sanction as the acts of "sovereign" polities. Simultaneously, Congress sought to replace the Crown as a continental "sovereign" equivalent in stature to the Crown itself. Patriotic feeling ran high at the outset of the Revolution, and many in Congress talked and acted as if the United States were governed by an entity which, though collective and representative, was almost as unitary as the Crown. Half a century later Chief Justice Marshall endorsed this view that a unitary entity had in fact emerged, writing in 1832 that the Revolution

> was a great popular movement, not perfectly organized; nor were the respective powers of those who were intrusted with the management of affairs accurately defined. The necessities of our situation produced a general conviction that those measures which concerned all, must be transacted by a body in which the representatives of all were assembled, and which could command the confidence of all: Congress, therefore, was considered as invested with all the powers of war and peace, and Congress dissolved our connection with the mother country, and declared these United Colonies to be independent States. Without any written definition of powers, they employed diplomatic agents to represent the United States at the several courts of Europe; offered to negotiate treaties with them, and did actually negotiate treaties with France. From the same necessity, and on the same principles, Congress assumed the management of Indian affairs, first in the name of these United Colonies, and afterwards in the name of the United States. Early attempts were made at negotiation, and to regulate trade with them. These not proving successful, war was carried on under the direction, and with the forces of the United States, and the efforts to make peace by treaty were earnest and incessant.[1]

Spontaneous, sovereign national government continued, Marshall argued, until acceptance of the Articles of Confederation provided a written basis for U.S. government, spelling out a formal division of authority between the Continental Congress and the thirteen state governments that for the first time articulated limits on the power of

Congress as the national government of the United States. Although not implemented until 1781, the Articles were put in final form for submission to the states in 1777, and Marshall's image of legitimacy flowing more or less directly from the people of the United States to the Continental Congress presumably has greatest application to the years 1775-1777.

The tribal policy stance articulated during this period of imagined near-unanimity assumed that Congress possessed authority over tribes extending well beyond that claimed by George III. Benjamin Franklin's draft for Articles of Confederation, considered by Congress in July of 1775, stipulated for example that the "boundaries and lands of all the...Indians shall be ascertained and secured to them" by Congress. "And all purchases from them shall be by the General Congress for the general advantage and benefit of the United Colonies."[2] Had Franklin's plan been adopted, it would have placed all tribal lands beyond the jurisdiction of individual colonies, and authorized Congress to do as it wished with any tribal land acquired.

After the Revolutionary War began, advocates of this approach further asserted that Congress could claim as national war booty the lands of tribes that fought against the Revolution. The Supreme Court later considered an argument based on theories first evolved in this era, that the 1763 Royal Proclamation had, as Chief Justice Marshall put it in 1810, legally severed trans-Appalachian lands

> from the colonies within whose bounds they would otherwise have been, and that...[a]ll acquisitions during the war...were made by the joint arms, for the joint benefit of the United States, and not for the benefit of any particular state.[3]

But the draft of the Articles of Confederation ultimately submitted to the several states in 1777 contained nothing comparable to Franklin's forthright plan for central regulation of tribal lands. Nor was there a bold declaration that conquered tribal lands must become national property. Instead the Articles contained numerous phrases susceptible of varying interpretations. The key provision, destined to become notorious for ambiguity, was

> The United States in Congress assembled shall also have the sole and exclusive right and power of...regulating the trade and managing all

affairs with the Indians, not members of any of the states, provided that the legislative right of any state within its own limits be not infringed or violated.[4]

The contested meanings of "members...of states" and "legislative right" greatly perturbed James Monroe and James Madison as they exchanged letters trying to make sense of the 1784 Fort Stanwix fiasco, of which each had witnessed a different phase. Monroe, at Fort Stanwix during New York State's attempt to negotiate with the Iroquois, told Madison he doubted

> 1. Whether these [Iroquois] Indians are to be considered as members of the State of New York, or whether the living simply within the bounds of a state ...while they acknowledge no obedience to its laws...nor enjoy...any of the rights of citizenship within it, is a situation which will even in the most qualified sense admit their being held as members of a state? 2. Whether on the other hand this is not a description of those whose management is committed by the confederation to the U.S. in Congress assembled?

Madison responded to Monroe's questions by noting that the Articles

> give Congress the exclusive right of *managing all affairs* with the Indians *not members* of any state, under a proviso that the *legislative authority* of the state within its own limits be not violated. By Indians not members of a state must be meant those, I conceive, who do not live within the body of the society, or whose persons or property form no objects of its laws. In the case of Indians of this description the only restraint on Congress is imposed by the *legislative authority* of the state.
>
> If this proviso be taken in its full latitude, it must destroy the authority of Congress altogether, since no act of Congress within the limits of a state can be conceived which will not in some way or other encroach upon the authority [of the] state. In order then to give some meaning to both parts of the sentence as a known rule of interpretation requires, we must restrain this proviso to some particular view of the parties. What was this view? My answer is that it was to save to the states their right of preemption of lands from the Indians. My reasons are 1. That this was the principal right formerly exerted by the colonies with regard to the Indians. 2. That it was a right asserted by the laws as well as the proceedings of all of them, and therefore being most familiar, would be most likely to be in contemplation of the parties. 3. That being of most consequence to the states individually, and least inconsistent with the general powers of Congress, it was most likely to be made a ground of compromise. 4. It has been always said that the proviso came from the

> Virginia delegates, who would naturally be most vigilant over the territorial rights of their constituents.[5]

Madison valiantly sought to ascribe specific meanings to the Articles, suggesting that "members...of states" probably referred only to those Native Americans to whom lands had been assigned by legislatures, and whose day-to-day affairs—schooling, apprenticing, indebtedness and the like—had long been supervised by colonial and then by state commissioners possessing legal authority to approve contracts on behalf of Native American wards. "Legislative right" on the other hand Madison supposed might refer simply to the pre-emptive right of states to tribal lands which might some day be no longer used by tribes. Such future rights could accord states no current authority whatsoever over the political activities of tribes. A believer in the value of written contracts and an advocate of central authority, Madison was reluctant to accept New York State's expansive vision of the still-martial Iroquois as "members" or New York State's interpretation of its "legislative right" to include authority to negotiate treaties with autonomous tribes. But Madison's alternative interpretation was really only wishful thinking, as he himself was to admit (in *Federalist 42*) once a replacement for the Articles of Confederation had been drafted. After earnestly endeavoring to construe the Articles in a manner that would leave Congress with some basis for exercising authority over tribes within a state's claimed limits, Madison conceded that New York State undoubtedly held the stronger position at Fort Stanwix because New York's land claims were at issue and the Articles of Confederation were explicitly protective of state land claims. There was nothing ambiguous about Article Nine, Clause Two of the Articles, which declared that "no State shall be deprived of territory for the benefit of the United States." Thus, even if New York State had acted discourteously at Fort Stanwix, Congress had been altogether out of bounds. Madison informed Monroe that in his opinion

> as far as New York may claim a right of treating with the Indians for the purchase of lands within her limits, she has the confederation on her side; as far as she may have exerted that right in contravention of the general Treaty, or even unconfidentially with the Commissioners of Congress, she has violated both duty and decorum.... But whatever may be the true boundary between the authority of Congress and that of

> New York or however indiscreet the latter may have been I join entirely with you in thinking that temperance on the part of the former will be the wisest policy.

Monroe was even stronger in his censure of Congress's Commissioners for presuming to resolve in concert with the Iroquois, and over the express objections of New York State, land right questions within the claimed bounds of that State. Observed Monroe,

> the land held by these Indians having never been ceded either by New York or Massachusetts belongs not to the United States; the only point then in which New York can be reprehensible is, for preceding, by a particular [treaty], the general Treaty. This must be attributed to a suspicion that there exists in Congress a design to injure her. The transaction will necessarily come before us, but will it not be most expedient in the present state of our affairs to form no decision thereon? I know no advantages to be derived from one....If the right of Congress hath been contravened shall we not derive greater injury by urging it to the reprehension of New York who holds herself aggrieved in other respects than by suffering our sense of that delinquency to lay dormant? Our purchases must be made without her bounds and those Indians whose alliance we seek inhabit a country to which she hath no claim.

In August of 1787, a still more elaborate effort to read a coherent meaning into the Articles was made by a committee of Congress headed by Nathan Dane of Massachusetts. The Dane committee's report began by arguing that management of tribal affairs was so inherently "indivisible ...that the parties to the confederation must have intended to give them entire to the Union, or to... the State." The committee then proposed that the phrase "legislative right" might be understood to authorize limited state jurisdiction within tribal territory over "debtors, criminals, and other proper objects" of state laws. Under "this distinction" which "may perhaps serve to explain" the Confederation's language, the central U.S. government could still possess all the "powers necessary" to "make stipulations with any such tribe, secure it in the enjoyment of all or part of its lands, without infringing upon the legislative right" of the state within which such tribal lands were located.

Forty-five years later, Chief Justice Marshall expressed admiration for this reading of the Articles, which expanded the concept of a state's "legislative right" beyond what Madison would have allowed but preserved unrestricted U.S. authority to enter into land negotiations with independent tribes even within claimed state bounds. But Marshall stopped short of affirming that this was the "true construction" of the Articles, noting that whether the Dane Committee had indeed discerned "the correct exposition" of the Articles "is rendered unnecessary by the adoption of our existing Constitution."[6]

Like Marshall in 1832, and Madison and Monroe in 1784, the Dane Committee in 1787 worked hard to interpret the 1777 Articles in ways that might salvage the spirit of the early war years 1775-77 when Congress successfully dealt with tribes and states from a position of superior authority. But since Georgia and North Carolina as well as New York read the Articles differently—following New York State's lead, Georgia's 1785 Creek Treaty for example described the self-governing Creeks as "members" of Georgia[7]—and since coercion of a state was clearly not an option under the Articles, the Dane committee wanly concluded their proposed reading of the Articles by acknowledging that the "most eligible" way of dealing with Georgia and North Carolina was to solicit voluntary land cessions from these two states. In the committee's words,

> whatever may be the true construction of the recited clause, the committee are persuaded that it must be impracticable [for Congress] to manage affairs with the Indians within the limits of the two States, so long as they adhere to the opinions and measures they seem to have adopted. The difficulties in fact exist; the States think it is their duty to counteract the powers of Congress, when carried, in conducting affairs with those Indians, beyond those narrow limits which the said States prescribe....The committee discern but two ways practicable; the one is for the two states to make liberal cessions of territory to the United States, the other is for those States to accede to Congress's managing, exclusively, all affairs with the Cherokees, Creeks, and other independent tribes within the limits of the said States, so that Congress in either case may have the acknowledged power of regulating trade, and making treaties with those tribes, and of preventing on their lands, the intrusions of white people. That of making liberal cessions of territory, all things considered, appears to be the most eligible and likely to meet the approbation of the two States.

Voluntary state cession of western land claims in effect revived in a consensual, post-Revolutionary form the dual system proclaimed by King George III in 1763, of direct royal control of tribes in the west combined with continuing colonial control east of the Appalachians. Neither the old British nor the new Confederation policy offered a complete solution because some tribes, such as the Iroquois in New York State, remained within the post-cession bounds of states, just as some tribes had in fact remained subject to colonial jurisdiction under Britain's pre-Revolutionary system.

Dissatisfaction with Britain's dual system of tribal control had contributed to the outbreak of Revolution. Similarly, dissatisfaction with the way tribes were dealt with by the Articles of Confederation added impetus to the calling of the 1787 Constitutional Convention. It is therefore tempting to follow Chief Justice Marshall's lead, and to conclude that the Constitutional Convention achieved the desired goal of unambiguously affirming exclusive federal authority over tribes. Indeed most scholars today assume that the Constitution's minimal reference to tribes and the scant record of discussion of the issue at the Constitutional Convention are evidence of a consensus to this effect. Quite the contrary, it was continuing disagreement about this issue among delegates at the Constitutional Convention—combined with their desire to accentuate areas where they did agree—that curtailed what was said about tribes in the Constitution. The few scraps of contemporary commentary that do survive about the drafting of the Constitution support this interpretation, as do concurrent deliberations in the Continental Congress involving key members who were also delegates at the Constitutional Convention.

In its final form, the Constitution contains only two direct references to Native Americans. One provision (Article One, Section Three) excludes "Indians not taxed" from enumeration as citizens of a state. The other (Article One, Section Eight) specifies, "The Congress shall have power...to regulate commerce with foreign Nations, and among the several States, and with the Indian Tribes." How state populations (citizen as well as non-citizen) should be calculated for purposes of apportioning representation needed to be settled at once —i.e., before the 1790 census—so in addition to the obviously bartered, morally indefensible plan to count African American slaves as three-fifths of a person, the Constitution excluded from census enumeration "Indians not taxed." This alluded principally to non-citizen groups of "Indians" resident on the numerous state-administered, tax-exempt "Indian reservations" but also acknowledged the possible presence within state boundaries (then and in the future) of "Indians" of varying statuses, since logically there could also be some "Indians" who were taxed. With equal caution, the second provision authorized federal regulation of *commercial* relations with tribes. This language emerged only after several drafts, and entirely pleased no one.

The Constitutional Convention met in Philadelphia from May 25 to September 17, 1787. In the first several weeks, deadlock appeared unavoidable. As Georgia delegate William Few recalled years later,

> The different interests and diversity of opinions seemed for some time to present obstacles that could not be surmounted. After about three weeks' deliberation and debating, the Convention had serious thoughts of adjourning without doing anything. All human efforts seemed to fail. Doctor Franklin proposed to appoint a chaplain and implore Divine assistance, but his motion did not prevail. It was an awful and critical moment. If the Convention had then adjourned the dissolution of the Union of the States seemed inevitable. This consideration no doubt had its weight in reconciling clashing opinions and interests. It was believed to be of the utmost importance to concede to different opinions so far as to endeavor to meet opposition on middle ground, and to form a Constitution that might preserve the Union of the States. On that principle of accommodations, the business progressed, and after about three months' arduous labor, a plan of Constitution was formed on principles which did not altogether please anybody, but it was agreed to be the most expedient that could be devised and agreed to.[8]

As Few suggests, several distinct "accommodations" resulted. Large, populous states were balanced against small states, slave states were balanced against those opposed to slavery—and states with claims to jurisdiction over tribally-occupied lands were balanced against states that preferred central U.S. government jurisdiction. One public signal of the compromises emerging behind the Convention's closed doors in Philadelphia was the passage on July 13 of the Northwest Ordinance by the Continental Congress, which was then meeting in New York City and which included individuals who were simultaneously members of the Philadelphia Convention. The significance of the Ordinance for the handling of slavery in the Constitution has been much discussed by scholars, but the equally momentous implications of the Ordinance for Constitutional regulation of tribes has not been noted.[9]

The Northwest Ordinance provided that slavery would not be permitted in the federal Northwest Territory, but that fugitive slaves could be pursued there and returned to their legal owners. Since slave states still claimed all lands south of the Northwest Territory's Ohio River boundary, the Ordinance implicitly accepted at least a temporary slave future for lands that many hoped would be ceded by slave states to the control of the U.S. government, but which had not yet been ceded. Paralleling the distinction between the future of slavery north and south of the Ohio, the Ordinance implicitly endorsed a division of authority in tribal relations between the federal Northwest Territory and the region south of the Ohio, where the authority of Virginia, North Carolina and Georgia would continue for at least a few years to come. In the Northwest, the Ordinance proclaimed full and direct central U.S. control over tribes:

> The utmost good faith shall always be observed towards the Indians; their lands and property shall never be taken from them without their consent; and in their property, rights, and liberty they never shall be invaded or disturbed, unless in just and lawful wars authorized by Congress; but laws founded in justice and humanity shall, from time to time, be made, for preventing wrongs being done to them, and for preserving peace and friendship with them.

This might almost be called a Bill of Rights for tribes in the Northwest Territory. No similar affirmation concerning the rights of tribes within state boundaries could have been agreed on by the Continental Congress—or by the Constitutional Convention.

On August 3, three weeks after passage of the Ordinance, a motion was made in Congress by Georgia's William Few and seconded by William Blount of North Carolina, which would have required the U.S. Superintendent of Indian Affairs for the Southern Department to "explain and confirm" to the Creek Confederacy "all former treaties" made with the Creeks by Georgia.[10] Vigorous opposition to this bold initiative was voiced by the Dane committee in the context of its pro-Congress reading of the Articles. Surely, the Dane committee argued scornfully, "the delegates of Georgia do not mean that Congress is bound to send their forces to punish such nations as the State shall name...such an idea cannot be consistent with the dignity of the Union, and the principles of the federal compact."[11] The Few-Blount motion failed, but so also did the Dane committee's counter-proposals for voluntary state land cessions.

Serving simultaneously as members of Congress and delegates to the Constitutional Convention, Few and Blount missed many sessions of both. But the two men were in New York City when Congress discussed western land issues, and in Philadelphia to sign the final draft of the Constitution. Between August 7 and September 17, Blount participated actively in the crucial latter stages of the Constitutional Convention. His not altogether admiring biographer William Masterson concluded that North Carolinian Blount's behind-the-scenes influence on the Constitution may well have been extensive, but that this "work, as he ever sought to make it, was completely hidden."[12] Though commonly described as among the silent non-participants at the Constitutional Convention, in Congress Blount and Few were aggressively opinionated regarding state control of tribal land, and their willingness to recommend the finished Constitution for ratification to their respective states undoubtedly reflected their sense that in Congress and the Constitutional Convention they had helped fend off all attempts to affirm that the central U.S. government had unrestricted authority to regulate tribal affairs within state bounds.

Considering the recent fate of the Dane committee's efforts in the Continental Congress, Madison could scarcely have been optimistic of success when on August 18 he proposed to the Constitutional Convention that Congress be assigned the power "To regulate affairs with the Indians as well within as without the limits of the U[nited] States."[13] Four days later the Committee of Detail, to which Madison's suggestion was referred, recommended specifying only that Congress could regulate *commerce* "with Indians within the limits of any State, not subject to the laws thereof."[14] A limited definition of tribal *commerce* had been earlier advanced by Georgia, which contended that "a right of regulatory trade" had nothing to do with "the fixing of any boundary between the Indians and citizens."[15] The Committee of Detail's restriction of federal authority to "commerce" could be interpreted as sanctioning state power over any and all matters relating to "Indians" within state bounds other than the narrow federal power here acknowledged. Moreover, a state could logically claim the power to determine for itself which "Indians" were not subject to its laws, and when state laws might be extended over them. Under this provision, states might have claimed unrestricted authority over all Native American groups within state bounds deemed to be not tribes, and even authority to supervise the non-commercial "affairs" of tribes within state bounds, which might arguably include land transactions. Instead of quietly establishing federal power, as Madison had hoped, the Committee of Detail's version explicitly confirmed continuing state power. Madison must have wondered whether it had been wise even to raise the issue of tribes, since it had once again stirred up state vigilance. One of the five members of the Committee of Detail was Nathaniel Gorham, who subsequently purchased from Massachusetts the pre-emption rights to Iroquois lands in New York State and, just prior to the ratification of the Constitution, negotiated under Massachusetts supervision a state treaty acquiring some of these rights from the Iroquois.

No formal action was taken on the Committee of Detail's proposal. Unrecorded efforts, presumably spearheaded by Madison, resulted in the emergence of the compromise language that was ultimately adopted. This final formula accepted the Committee of Detail's basic approach, but spoke of "Tribes" rather than "Indians" and made no mention of state laws. "Tribes" were polities, and were thus—wherever located—worthy of federal attention, unlike individual "Indians" who might be supposed appropriately subject to control by the state within which they resided.

Although the Committee of Detail's explicit pro-state language was pared away, the Constitution as adopted did not, as is generally assumed today, establish "exclusive and plenary" federal jurisdiction over tribes within states. Ironically, this modern interpretation relies in large part on a misreading of Madison's own later words. Advocating ratification of the Constitution in his *Federalist 42*, dated January 22, 1788, Madison derided the troublesome elusiveness of terms in the Articles such as "legislative right"—terms which he had himself once earnestly sought to construe. By contrast in the proposed Constitution, he maintained,

> The regulation of commerce with the Indian tribes is very properly unfettered from two limitations in the Articles of Confederation, which render the provision obscure and contradictory. The power is there restrained to Indians, not members of any of the States, and is not to violate or infringe the legislative rights of any State within its own limits. What description of Indians are to be deemed members of a State, is not yet settled, and has been a question of frequent perplexity and contention in the federal councils. And how the trade with Indians, though not members of a State, yet residing within its legislative jurisdiction, can be regulated by an external authority, without so far intruding on the internal rights of legislation, is absolutely incomprehensible. This is not the only case in which the Articles of Confederation have inconsiderately endeavored to accomplish impossibilities; to reconcile a partial sovereignty in the Union, with complete sovereignty in the States; to subvert a mathematical axiom, by taking away a part, and letting the whole remain.

In *Federalist 42,* Madison was trying to argue that the Constitution's final language had at least some of the merits of his original proposal. Since he was defending the Constitution as drafted, he spoke of tribal *commerce*, and simply finessed the question of whether or not this was identical with *affairs*, the term he had proposed. Madison similarly implied that contentious issues "not yet settled" were a consequence of the Articles and not necessarily a constraint on the Constitution. Deftly, Madison scorned the ambivalent posturing of the Confederation's Article Nine, Clause Four while bypassing the opposite problem posed by the Constitution's elegant conciseness. In Madison's astute words, the Constitution was *unfettered from* specific linguistic formulas which had proved unproductive. Madison was expressing relief that the Constitution was not fettered by either the pro-state language of the Articles or the pro-state language that came so close to acceptance at the Constitutional Convention. Madison was *not* suggesting, as is frequently imagined, that the federal government could expect to be entirely *unfettered* in exercising authority over all tribal concerns, whether within or without states, and whether or not directly related to "commerce." Indeed, as the complete text of *Federalist 42* reveals, Madison recognized that "not yet settled" jurisdictional struggles were certain to continue, as well-established states, ancient tribes and an unproven new central U.S. government maneuvered to define enigmatic phrases.[16]

The unfettering of Madison's word "unfettered" was abetted by Chief Justice Marshall's 1832 version of Constitutional history. To counter President Andrew Jackson's support for Georgia's defiance of federal authority to regulate intrastate tribes, Marshall declared on behalf of a unanimous Supreme Court that those "ambiguous phrases" in the Articles of Confederation—"legislative right" and "members of States"—designed to qualify central U.S. power

> were construed by the States of North Carolina and Georgia as to annul the power itself....The correct exposition of this Article is rendered unnecessary by the adoption of our existing Constitution. That instrument confers on Congress the powers of war and peace; of making treaties, and of regulating commerce with foreign nations, and among the several states, and with Indian tribes. These powers comprehend all that is required for the regulation of our intercourse with the Indians. They are not limited by any restrictions on their free actions. The shackles imposed on this power, in the Confederation, are discarded.[17]

Marshall's word "shackles" echoed Madison's word "unfettered" and indeed the words can be linked, through an 1831 Dissent by Justice Thompson in *Cherokee Nation vs. Georgia,* on which Marshall in 1832 clearly drew, and which referred directly to *Federalist 42.*[18]

Madison in 1788 had tried to put the best face possible on a consciously compromised situation. Marshall in 1832 was trying to avert a complete triumph—with full federal government backing—for state regulation of tribes. Confronted with strong opposition, both Madison and Marshall asserted as unqualifiedly as they felt they could that federal authority over tribes transcended state rights. Ironically, their efforts have proved so successful with later generations that the actual compromises between federal and state authority, of which Madison and Marshall were all too aware, have been forgotten. Selective summaries of the contentions made by Madison and Marshall have encouraged federal courts to leap from the valid assertion that the Constitution established federal *primacy* in one area of tribal relations to the assumption that the Constitution established an exclusive federal monopoly of tribal relations, a step neither Madison nor Marshall took.

The Constitution is deservedly esteemed as a document devised by persons of great foresight, public commitment and political acumen.

Less well-recognized is the fact that these qualities were manifested as much in what was left out of the Constitution as in what was put in. Pressured by circumstances beyond their complete control, Madison and his collaborators prepared a deliberately elliptical document with few fixed parameters. The experienced politicians who pieced together the Constitution had come to realize that compromise and silence are integral parts of statecraft, and were therefore willing to outline a spare national agenda and to postpone other issues for subsequent resolution. Because the future of slavery was unresolved, the Constitution provided only for abolition after twenty years of the importation of more slaves, a clear sign that the more fundamental questions posed by slavery were left to be addressed later. The future of tribes was also unclear, and to many questions concerning them the Constitution answered in effect, "Wait and see." The Constitution was not pro-slavery or anti-slavery, pro-tribe or anti-tribe, it was a compromise accepted by advocates of all these views. Neutral about issues, it was nonetheless affirmative about process, and thus also about future change. The Constitution was both a compromise and pro-compromise, both an accomplishment in itself, a triumph of discourse and bargaining, and a model of how yet further accomplishments might be reached.

Many modern-day commentators imagine that the Constitution's drafters anticipated every later contingency. In fact, as Georgia's William Few observed, the Constitution was a chastened, minimal document, a product of failed experiments as well as of forward-looking statecraft. Drafted for an unfinished nation, the Constitution was a set of terse rules for an on-going political process embracing thirteen states, a central government—and about eighty tribes which didn't participate officially in the rule-writing but had a major impact on what rules could be adopted, and how far they would be carried. What the political status of tribes would, could or should be was finessed in the Constitution because long-standing battles affecting tribal rights were still underway. The fact that tribes had fought on both sides in the Revolutionary War complicated resolution of these dilemmas, as did the great disparities in perspective of state, Congressional and tribal authorities regarding control of tribally-occupied lands. Not entirely satisfactory to any of the recognized participants in the political process of the United States, the Constitution was a framework within which competing goals could be peaceably pursued. By the Constitution, tribes were conceded a right to exist within the bounds of the United States, and other tribal rights were also implicitly acknowledged to exist. For tribes, the Constitution was thus a landmark—no more, but also no less—in their ongoing struggle for defined rights, a struggle that began before the Constitution was drafted and would continue long after it was ratified. While the Constitution gave the federal government more power to regulate tribes than Congress possessed under the 1777 Articles of Confederation, this was still not power to act in disregard of state authority, and definitely not as much power as Congress would have had under the 1775 draft of the Articles proposed by Benjamin Franklin. Franklin knew that nothing short of full acknowledgment of tribal land rights could satisfy tribes, and recommended that "The boundaries and lands of all the...Indians...be ascertained and secured to them."[19] The Constitutional Convention of 1787 was neither the first nor the last time that central control of tribal affairs was advocated—and failed to obtain the necessary political support. Long after the inception of the Constitution, tribes were still working to acquire by their own efforts the rights that Franklin failed to secure for tribes from his fellow Revolutionaries in 1775, and which remained unimaginable to most U.S. citizens in 1787.

Why the Constitution needed to be open-ended is apparent from even a quick glance at a contemporary map of the country. Produced in Philadelphia shortly before the Constitutional Convention convened there, Francis Bailey's "Map of the United States of North America" for example leaves the limits of all states undefined. The italicized names of many tribes are sandwiched in, but these also lack fixed bounds. Potential states with fanciful names such as Polypotamia and Pelisipia are sketched in, but much of the map is dominated by blank spaces. No Constitution for this nation-in-flux could have been agreed on that had no comparable blanks waiting to be filled in.

After the thirteen British colonies declared themselves independent states in 1776, perhaps the most likely outcome was war among these new states, opening the way for a reimposition of imperial control. Much less likely was what resulted: the fashioning of a unique, made-in-

A Map of the United States.
From *Francis Bailey's Pocket Almanac for 1787* (Philadelphia, 1786
Courtesy, American Antiquarian Society.

...graved by H. D. Pursell for F. Bailey's Pocket Almanac

America government excluding European imperialism—and including tribes. By charging the British monarch in the Declaration of Independence with fomenting slave insurrections and inciting "merciless Indian Savages" to attack coastal colonial settlements, the thirteen states in 1776 indicted a belief that even in going beyond a "quarrel" with their "mother country" into Revolution, Britain's North American colonies were political communities composed primarily of persons of European descent and were thus not yet committed to forming a polity within which African American slaves and Native Americans would participate. The Constitution in contrast is a North American document, which moved decisively away from Jefferson's Anglo-Saxon-sounding Declaration of Independence as well as from the British Parliament-influenced Articles of Confederation, and moved toward formal recognition of the need for a government specific to North America, for a country with a culturally diverse populace, which would have to work systematically to achieve unanimity. The Declaration of Independence had been an act of defiance, focused on the past; the Constitution was a forward-looking document aimed at establishing orderly process in a complex and polyglot polity. In the Declaration of Independence, American Revolutionaries presented themselves as disaffected British colonists, rebelling to establish a new and better (albeit vaguely defined) political order. Near-chaos prevailed for more than a decade, in part because of international warfare but also because of internal conflicts over definition of that future polity. In these momentous struggles, tribes participated with important success. As a result, the Constitution to which all U.S. citizens are heirs comprehended tribes as compatible entities.

Drafted in 1787, ratified in 1788, the Constitution was a landmark achievement, yet one that might not have survived for long had it not been implemented creatively. Fortunate in its brand-new Constitution, the United States was no less fortunate that the first President elected under the Constitution was to prove equal to the task of launching an untested government of uncertain powers.

Four

President Washington's Tribal Policies

WHEN GEORGE WASHINGTON ASSUMED OFFICE as President in 1789, he recognized that the Constitution left much to be resolved. Having presided over the 1787 Constitutional Convention, Washington knew well how many issues, including control of tribal relations, were finessed then which now must be confronted. As Commander-in-Chief, Washington had mediated in countless central-state disputes involving tribes, and he understood that the Constitution had not ended such disputes but simply provided a new mode of dealing with them, in which he himself had greatly enhanced responsibility, both formally and personally. Notwithstanding the ambiguity of the Commerce Clause, Washington devised effective ways to interpose federal authority between states and tribes that drew on the Constitution's outline of the President's powers as Commander-in-Chief and on the Treaty Clause, neither of which referred directly to tribes. The more constructive spirit that characterized the conduct of U.S. tribal relations under the Constitution derived in other words not from its lone reference to "Tribes" but from the innovative institution of the Presidency, as well as from the character and imagination of the person who first held that office.

During the Revolution's first phase, King George III loomed large in the thinking of all Americans, and anything resembling monarchical authority was suspect. By 1787, the United States had learned from experience what confusion could result from the absence of administrative continuity. A non-monarchical mode of centralized decision-making was moreover now visible. By his conduct as Commander-in-Chief between 1775 and 1783, General Washington in effect invented U.S. executive authority. Nominally only a military officer, Washington offered balanced advice on all sorts of public questions, including tribal affairs. Thus when post-War U.S. tribal policy was being formulated in 1783, Congress sought the Commander-in-Chief's recommendations, which were national in scope, well-reasoned—and quickly adopted by Congress. Then on December 23, 1783, Washington resigned as Commander-in-Chief to return to private life as a Virginia planter and land speculator. Almost immediately, U.S. tribal policy unraveled. Numerous other national problems became comparably aggravated.[1] Bringing Washington back was an irresistible solution, and the office of President was tacitly constructed to institutionalize the position he had quietly defined for himself, in tribal affairs as in so many other policy areas.

Tribal relations under the Constitution logically became a responsibility of the President as Commander-in-Chief. In *Federalist 24* for example, Alexander Hamilton defended the need for a standing federal army by pointing to the "constant necessity for keeping small garrisons on our western frontier" to guard against "the ravages and depredations of the Indians." North American territories were still held by Great Britain and Spain, Hamilton warned, and "The savage tribes on our western frontier ought to be regarded as our natural enemies, their natural allies; because they have most to fear from us and most to hope from them."

Potentially even more important than the President's power as Commander-in-Chief of an army whose most likely foes were tribes was the fact that, insofar as the Presidency was conceptualized as a republican, elective monarchy, inherent within it was the unstated prospect of reviving aspects of King George III's role as peacetime protector of tribes; in tribal terminology, their *father*. What might come of this was entrusted to the President's discretion. King George III had attempted to develop his role as tribal protector into a means to circumscribe coastal colonies. Comparably, President Washington saw in the federal government's public duty to protect tribes a tool to counterbalance the strong position assured states by the Constitution, especially once supplemented by the Bill of Rights. But Washington was still a Revolutionary at heart, and had no desire to revive King George III's Divide-and-Rule strategy. Washington hoped rather to bring tribes and states closer together, by demonstrating how a strong federal government through mediation could remove some of the grievances that aggravated state-tribal relations and might even provoke hostilities that could endanger the nation's survival. Boldly yet deliberately, Washington insisted that the federal government must play a role in tribal affairs both within and without state boundaries. Approaching the Constitution as simply a "more perfect" form of U.S. government rather than a repudiation of the Articles of Confederation, Washington as President sought do a better job of conciliating tribes than had the Continental Congress, and a better job of pressuring New York, Georgia and North Carolina into allowing the federal government to take charge of relations with the militant tribes within the claimed limits of these states. Though prepared to use force against both states and tribes, Washington never supposed that the Constitution had in fact established exclusive federal control of tribes, and never forgot that his ultimate goal was to promote willing cooperation among states, tribes and the federal government.

As President, Washington inherited the various treaties negotiated with tribes by Continental Congress Commissioners, which remained in force under the Constitution. He thus had to decide at an early date which of these treaties might prove ultimately beneficial to tribes, even if opposed by states, and which were so unsatisfactory either to tribes or to states that they should be quickly renegotiated. The Treaties negotiated in 1785-86 with the Cherokees, Chickasaws and Choctaws though disliked by Georgia and North Carolina, seemed to him well-conceived, in contrast to the abusive Treaties negotiated with the Iroquois and tribes in the Northwest Territory, which from the outset were strongly resisted by these tribes. The post-Revolutionary War tribal policy adopted by Congress in 1783 (after consulting General Washington) had been flexible and attentive to reasonable tribal desires. Its basic purpose was to work out an amicable compromise enabling both U.S. citizens and tribes to share the vast territory guaranteed to the United States by the 1783 Treaty of Paris. Tragically, implementation of this policy was then recklessly pursued by Congress-appointed negotiators who provoked bitterness by disregarding tribal customs as well as tribal aspirations. Being long-established polities, tribes expected proper acknowledgment of their past accomplishments and present prowess, and insisted on protection of their land rights by any government that desired to establish treaty relations with them. Tribes moreover refused to consider having fought against the Revolution a punishable crime. For centuries, tribes had waged war and then buried the hatchet with their erstwhile foes. Post-war relationships and their attendant rights might well be different, depending on the outcome of war, but merely having fought was not considered reason for ill treatment such as the Iroquois were subjected to at Fort Stanwix in 1784.

Washington was a private citizen when these abuses occurred, and restoring the spirit originally intended for post-Revolutionary War tribal relations was consequently high on his agenda during his first months as President. In this effort, Washington had the earnest support of Henry Knox, Secretary at War during the last two years of the Continental Congress government and then President Washington's first Secretary of War, as well as the encouragement of Benjamin Hawkins, one of North Carolina's first two U.S. Senators. After negotiating Continental Congress Treaties in 1785-86 with the Cherokees, Chickasaw and Choctaws, only to see his handiwork denounced by North Carolina and Georgia, Hawkins returned to Congress, where his conciliatory views found expression in the tribal provisions of the Northwest Ordinance, as well as in a committee report, submitted on August 9, 1787, suggesting that Congress's Treaty Commissioners had offended tribes in the Northwest Territory not only by failing to follow tribal protocol but also by acquiring land rights from the wrong tribes. Many tribes, observed Hawkins and his fellow committee members, "now complain that these lands were not purchased of the Indian nations, the proper proprietors of them." Indeed it was hopeless, in the committee's view, to ascertain legalistically "what tribes can justly set up claims...but to quiet them in some form or other appears...highly expedient, and necessary." The most eligible way to do this, the committee urged, was to hold "a general treaty with the tribes which make claims to those lands, and adjusting all disputes about them." Hawkins had adopted this consensual approach with southern tribes in 1785-86, and the committee on which Hawkins sat recommended that a similar course be followed northwest of the Ohio. Candid discussion with tribal chiefs and pragmatic attempts to work out a consensual agreement with them made sense, since "The Indians appear to act a natural part for men in their situation, they express a concern about their lands and their desire of peace with the United States, in whose power and limits they are." The committee therefore recommended "collecting the chiefs of many tribes to the same treaty, where all interests relative to the same subject may be adjusted." Without directly criticizing the conduct of the Congress Commissioners who had so deeply offended tribes north of the Ohio, the committee politely asked,

> May it not be politic and just to treat with the Indians more on a footing of equality, convince them of the justice and humanity as well as power of the United States and of their disposition to promote the happiness of the Indians?[2]

On May 2, 1788, Secretary at War Knox followed up on these suggestions by recommending to Congress

> that the United States may conform to the modes and customs of the Indians in the disposal of their lands, without the least injury to the national dignity. Were an opposition to the custom of the Indians in this respect to be a material part of national character, it would not be highly estimated in the opinion of the world. But your Secretary conceives that the Commissioners may negotiate an extinguishment of the Indian claims, to the territory described by former treaties ...without calling in question the validity of the said treaties. In case of a new purchase, or the modification of the former boundaries, a sum of money may be given according to the Indian custom, on the chiefs signing the deeds in the usual form.[3]

This 1788 Knox letter is commonly called the source of the U.S. policy of purchasing tribal lands. But Washington in 1783, commenting on General Schuyler's proposals, had urged that if tribes should "appear dissatisfied at the line we may find it necessary to establish, compensation should be made them for their claims within it."[4] And both Washington and Knox identified tribal pressure as the policy's real source.

Though he missed its deeper causes, Knox recognized the problem that had been created in the Northwest by the conduct of Congress's Treaty Commissioners. Simplistically characterizing tribal dissatisfaction almost as a business dispute, Knox advised Washington on May 23, 1789, that

> the Indians are greatly tenacious of their lands, and generally do not relinquish their right, excepting on the principle of a specific consideration expressly given for the purchase of the same. That the practice

> of the late English colonies and government in purchasing the Indian claims has firmly established the habit in this respect, so that it cannot be violated but with difficulty and an expense greatly exceeding the value of the object. That the Treaties of Fort Stanwix and Fort McIntosh do not state that the limits therein defined are by virtue of a purchase from the Indians. That the said Treaties have been opposed and complained of.[5]

In non-recriminatory fashion, Knox declined to fault those who had negotiated the Treaties of Fort Stanwix and Fort McIntosh, or to distinguish between the pragmatic policy adopted by Congress on October 15, 1783, and its rash implementation in New York State and the Northwest Territory by Congress's Treaty Commissioners. Many modern-day commentators have in consequence described the policy Knox urged in 1788-89 as a *reversal* of former U.S. policy, whereas in fact Knox proposed a revision of treaties negotiated by foolhardy Treaty Commissioners, and a *return* to the conciliatory spirit of General Schuyler's July 29, 1783 letter and General Washington's September 7, 1783 endorsement of it, which informed the policy recommended to Congress by Hawkins and his fellow committee members, adopted by Congress on October 15, 1783.

The approach backed by Washington in 1783, and which he was finally in a position to implement in 1789, entailed respect for the tribes' insistence that their land rights must never be extinguished except after full discussion and in the most consensual and elaborately ceremonial manner. To tribes, this meant properly negotiated treaties, whether or not they involved payment. Reconciling this with the Constitution suggested using the Constitution's most formal procedure, that involving Senate advice and consent and Presidential proclamation. Washington and the Senate therefore accepted Knox's recommendation that in construing the Constitution's Treaty Clause, "The independent nations and tribes of Indians ought to be considered as foreign nations."[6] Washington articulated his own thoughts in a letter dated September 17, 1789.

> Gentlemen of the Senate:
>
> It is doubtless important that all treaties and compacts formed by the United States with other nations, whether civilized or not, should be made with caution, and executed with fidelity.

> It is said to be the general understanding and practice of nations, as a check on the mistakes and indiscretions of Ministers or Commissioners, not to consider any treaty negotiated and signed by such officers, as final and conclusive, until ratified by the sovereign or government from whom they derive their powers. This practice has been adopted by the United States respecting their treaties with European nations, and I am inclined to think it would be advisable to observe it in the conduct of our treaties with the Indians; for though such treaties being, on their part, made by their chiefs or rulers, need not be ratified by them, yet, being formed on our part by the agency of subordinate officers, it seems to be both prudent and reasonable that their acts should not be binding on the nation until approved and ratified by the government. It strikes me that this point should be well considered and settled, so that our national proceedings, in this respect, may become uniform, and be directed by fixed and stable principles.[7]

The Constitution specified use of the full treaty procedure in dealings with what Washington called "civilized" nations, and Washington "was inclined to think it would be advisable" to use the same procedure in tribal negotiations as well. Washington did not allude to the tribes' own expectations in this letter to the Senate, but from personal experience was well aware of this factor as well. The result of this decision was the emergence of a unique process through which the written U.S. Constitution was combined with the tribes' oral tradition of establishing familial-style relations among tribes and nations.

Washington was so determined to establish honorable guidelines for the conduct of tribal relations that on August 22, 1789, "The President of the United States came into the Senate Chamber, attended by General Knox" for an advance discussion of the possible terms of treaties with the Creeks, Cherokees, Choctaws and Chickasaws. These were the first treaties of any sort to be initiated under the Constitution by the federal government, and proved to be both the first and last time that Washington (or any subsequent President) entered the Senate to be advised in advance about a prospective treaty's terms. Washington did not enjoy listening to two days of inconclusive speech-making, and as he departed reportedly remarked that he would "be damned" if he ever again came to the Senate to ask them to "advise and consent" to a treaty's proposed terms prior to its negotiation.[8] Yet another precedent was thus established by Washington with care—and decisiveness.

In the north, the Revolutionary War had splintered the Iroquois Confederacy, which would never again regain its former military might. South of the Ohio River, on the other hand, the four long-dominant tribal federations, although weakened and divided during the Revolutionary War, were by 1789 once again influential, having regained much of their former strength through individual leadership, *brotherly* tribal cooperation—and a fair amount of European backing. The Creek chief Alexander McGillivray had proved particularly resourceful, and so became an urgent priority for U.S. treaty diplomacy under the federal Constitution. The monarchically-inclined McGillivray had openly scorned the quarrel-plagued Continental Congress, but federal officials were hopeful that McGillivray might be better-disposed toward a U.S. republic headed by President Washington, and on April 20, 1789, six weeks after the Constitution went into effect and ten days before Washington actually took the oath of office, a federal emissary joyously (if not quite accurately) informed the McGillivray-led Creeks,

> We are now governed by a President who is like the old King over the great water; he commands all the warriors of the thirteen great fires. He will have regard to the welfare of all the Indians; and when peace shall be established he will be your father and you will be his children so that none shall dare to do you harm.[9]

Alexander McGillivray's genetic father Lachlan McGillivray had come from Scotland to Creek country as a trader, married a Creek woman and settled down. Alexander, born in 1750, was raised as a Creek until he was about fourteen but then sent to live with relatives in Charleston, South Carolina.[10] There young Alexander studied Greek and Latin as well as English history and literature. His Latin tutor William Henderson became a literary figure in London and no doubt helped shape McGillivray's grand rhetorical style. McGillivray's father arranged a position for him in a "counting house" in Savannah run by Samuel Elbert, subsequently Governor of Georgia. Young McGillivray however proved "so fond of study, that he devoted much more of his time to reading of history, than to the acquisition of mercantile knowledge." Frustrated, his father brought him back to Creek country, where he could employ to the full all his diverse abilities.

Equally at home in an Alabama forest clearing, the British drawing-rooms of Charleston or the Anglo-Spanish salons of Pensacola, the mature Alexander McGillivray thrived by ingeniously combining the traits of several cultures. His principal residence, at the Upper Creek town of Little Tallassee on the Coosa River in what is now central Alabama, was a "log house" with a stone chimney and "embellished with dormer windows." After being sumptuously entertained at this "rural humble palace," the traveler and diarist John Pope exulted that "his table smokes with good substantial diet, and his sideboard displays a variety of wines and ardent spirits." Pope spoke admiringly of his "atticism of diction aided by a liberal education" and his "great fund of wit and humor, melioriated by perfect good nature and politeness." Pope considered McGillivray's Creek wife at Little Tallassee a "model of prudence and discretion."[11] As was not without precedent in his tribe, McGillivray also had a second Creek wife in another Upper Creek town.

This talented man was quick to grasp the opportunities afforded by the American Revolution. Shortly after War broke out, McGillivray entered British service as a special agent charged with shoring up Creek support for King George III. When the Creeks' royal *father* failed them in 1783, McGillivray next devoted his energies to strengthening the institutions of Creek government, while deliberating future options.[12] East of the Creeks loomed the sovereign and Revolutionary State of Georgia. To the south, the Spanish as successors to the British presided imperially over East and West Florida, and thus over the Seminoles, sometimes called "wild Creeks" because they occasionally functioned as part of the Creek Confederacy. The Cherokee, Choctaw and Chickasaw tribal *brothers* of the Creeks resided to the north and west. A European presence was also discernible in these tribally-ruled regions, as persons representing British, Spanish and French interests all sought footholds. Freebooters abounded as well, many of these being stateless persons of mixed national origin. The Creeks managed to function successfully in this chaotic context because they possessed a leader known to Europeans by the name Alexander McGillivray and simultaneously to his Creek compatriots as *Isti Atcagagi Thlucco*, Great Beloved Person.[13]

McGillivray's first major post-War initiative was to write the newly-appointed Spanish Governor at Pensacola, observing in carefully phrased language that the British government had been "compelled to withdraw its protection from us" but since the Creeks were "allies and not subjects" in a treaty relationship of limited loyalty to their *father* the king, the British monarch had "no right to transfer us with their former possessions to any power whatever contrary to our inclination and interest." Like the Iroquois to their north, McGillivray's Creeks in 1784 considered themselves wholly independent. Therefore, McGillivray concluded grandly,

> We certainly as a free nation have a right to choose our protector and on our search what power is so fitting as the Master of the Floridas. I shall offer some reasons to show that it would be good policy in the Crown of Spain to grant us our desires.

McGillivray's diplomatic overture was sympathetically received, and led to the signing on June 1, 1784, of the Treaty of Pensacola, by which the Spanish monarch took the Creeks under his *fatherly* protection. McGillivray was given a salary in return for his promise to facilitate Spanish trading interests.[14]

Though an atypical Creek, McGillivray did identify with his tribe as they collectively assessed where they stood in the wake of British withdrawal from their region. McGillivray's success also reflected the fact that his own personal ambitions accorded well with the inclinations of a majority of the Upper Creeks, who lived farther from the Atlantic coast, and had grown increasingly concerned about Lower Creek ties to Georgia. The Creek Confederacy was quite unlike the Iroquois Confederacy of five (later six) large, well-organized tribes. The Creeks were divided into two loosely grouped assemblages, called the Upper and Lower Towns, each having several score towns and villages of widely varying size, which meant that political coherence was dependent on whether there was a strong individual leader in one of the larger towns, capable of controlling one assemblage and then gaining a following in the other. Only Lower Creek towns had ratified the pre-Revolutionary treaties of 1733, 1763 and 1773 with colonial Georgia. The post-Revolutionary Creek treaties ceding land to the State of Georgia, completed in 1783, 1785 and 1786, were not considered valid even by many Lower Creeks, and McGillivray steadily gained backing here as well for his determination to repudiate the Georgia State treaties as deceitful and therefore not legally binding on the Creek Confederacy.[15]

Because of the ineffectiveness of Congress, maintaining Creek independence in these years involved playing off the Georgians against the Spaniards in Florida. Both claimed Creek territory, since Spain considered the Tennessee River to be the northern limit of its Florida domain and Georgia claimed the Mississippi River as its western limit. The political viability of Spanish Florida was however highly uncertain. Culturally, Florida combined Native American elements with various European national influences and those of both enslaved and escaped Africans. The principal trading house in Spanish Florida was an old British firm: Panton, Leslie. And the most adroit agent of Spanish power was a footloose Irishman named Carlos Howard.

The Spaniards in Florida desired Creek trade but preferred to avoid trouble with the United States. One Spanish Governor "displayed the portrait" of Spain's King Charles IV to a Creek delegation, while offering little tangible assistance. McGillivray was obliged to exert continual pressure on the Spaniards to assist him in his efforts to force back Georgians, and once protested he was "miserably disappointed" with the guns supplied him by Spain. Creek warriors, he pointed out archly, were "accustomed to the best English guns."[16]

Despite such frustrations, McGillivray reasoned in 1784 that the "protection of a great monarch [i.e., Spain] is to be preferred to that of a distracted republic."[17] This was a credible enough description of the thirteen semi-united States linked by the Articles of Confederation. The pretensions of Congress notwithstanding, the Creeks' choice of alliance prior to 1789 had been in effect between Revolutionary Georgia and imperial Spain, with Spain looking like the better bet. Once Washington became President of the new federal republic, the Creeks reconsidered their options and expressed willingness to meet U.S. representatives at the Oconee River, in modern-day eastern Georgia.

To negotiate with McGillivray and other Creek chiefs, Washington chose prestigious Treaty Commissioners, the most prominent of whom was former Secretary at War Benjamin Lincoln. Also appointed was Washington's longtime personal aide, Colonel David Humphreys, formerly a diplomat in Paris and London. On his way to the Creek treaty ground, Humphreys wrote Washington a series of chatty letters recounting the exotic hardships of a type of diplomacy new to him. His carriage wheels became mired in "deep sands" and his spirits drooped during a "fatiguing journey...through a dreary wilderness, in which there was not a single house" for a span of thirty miles.

Commissioner Lincoln and Georgia's Senator William Few, who planned to attend the treaty session as an observer, sailed from New York City in two sloops laden with "goods and presents necessary for the Indians." They reached Savannah after a "boisterous and dangerous passage" and reached their camp on the eastern bank of the Oconee River on September 20, 1789.[18] From his base in Creek territory on the river's western bank, McGillivray sent greetings delivered by his principal Creek rival, who was known in Georgia as the Tame Chief but to Creeks as Hoboiethle Mico or more simply as the mico or chief of the Upper Creek town of Tallassee. Assisted by two other chiefs and an interpreter, the Tallassee Mico introduced the U.S. Commissioners to ceremonies quite different from those Humphreys had participated in at the court of Louis XVI. The "pipe of friendship" was smoked and the welcoming chiefs touched the Commissioners' faces with an elegant fan of feathers signifying that past differences were brushed aside by the "white wing of reconciliation." The Commissioners reciprocated as best they could; Colonel Humphreys wrote Washington that McGillivray's emissaries "dined with us, and seemed well satisfied."[19]

The next day the U.S. Commissioners crossed the Oconee and met informally with McGillivray, and finally he visited them in their camp. Throughout these negotiations, the celebrated chief dressed "altogether in the Indian fashion," Humphreys later reported to Washington, "and is rather slovenly than otherwise." McGillivray's demeanor also drew mixed comments: "His countenance has nothing liberal and open in it. It has, however, sufficient marks of understanding." On balance, he looked like a person they could do business with. "McGillivray dined with us," Humphreys confided,

> and although he got very much intoxicated, he seemed to retain his recollection, and reason, beyond what I had ever seen in a person, when in the same condition. At this time I became intimate to a

> certain degree with him and endeavored to extract his real sentiments and feelings, in a conversation alone confidentially.[20]

For his part, McGillivray was not overly impressed by the person he later described as "that puppy Humphreys."

After two days of exploratory visits, the U.S. Commissioners spent September 23 preparing a draft treaty for presentation to the Creeks in the U.S. camp. In the evening, the Commissioners were informed that McGillivray desired they meet "on the west side of the Oconee." The Commissioners agreed, and at eleven in the morning of September 24 at the Creeks' own meeting ground, "we were received," Humphreys later conceded, "with more etiquette than ever I had before witnessed." Nine hundred Creek warriors greatly outnumbered the U.S. guard of four hundred, and also wholly outshone them in splendor. The Creek national standard surmounted by eagle tail-feathers was carried by honor guards, followed by separate town contingents. The warriors of each town walked in single file behind their chief, every warrior stepping carefully in the tracks of the one in front. Their heads were shaved to create a wedge of hair narrow near the crown of the head, broad at the nape of the neck, then gathered in several braids twined with ribbons. The chiefs wore turbans, some of these being strips of colored cloth wound into intricate shapes while others were fez-like caps adorned with the plumage of flamingoes, trumpeter swans, whooping cranes or egrets. Breechcloths, fringed white leggings and moccasins of deerskin and a cloth shawl or long shirt completed the chiefs' dress. At each warrior's side swung deerskin pouches containing gunpowder and tobacco, embellished with representations of animals and birds in red, blue and black, outlined with porcupine quills or shell beads. In the fabric of turbans and shawls, yellow, red and green tartan plaids contrasted notably with the solid colors and stylized ornamentation of traditional Creek taste. Like Spanish guns, Scottish plaids hinted at the substantial strength Creeks drew from trade with Europe.[21]

Even more striking than a Creek warrior's apparel and equipage were the embellishments of his body. Tattooed decorations recorded his past martial accomplishments, while freshly painted designs of red, white or black bespoke his present inclination toward war or peace. The message conveyed by the body paint of McGillivray's entourage was a methodical mixture of the white color of peace with the red and black of war. Traditionally, when two tribes met to end a war, no outward display would hint of hostile thoughts. McGillivray had not come to the Oconee in this spirit, he had come to bargain, with no expectation of attaining perfect harmony with the Revolutionary United States. Nonetheless both sides hoped for a truce based on limited mutual advantage; McGillivray wanted a free port for Creek trade with Europe, Washington's Commissioners hoped to pry the Creeks away from alliance with Spain.

Opening ceremonies culminated with what Humphreys called "the great ceremony of *Black Drink*." Creeks called it White Drink because for Creeks white was the color of peace and purity, and the ritual consumption of this black-colored, caffeine-rich beverage brewed from the leaves of the yaupon or Gulf holly roused good feelings and calmed jealous thoughts.

> [A]fter all participants were properly seated according to rank, some young men bearing gourds of the brew would appear and open the ceremony with the shout of *Choh!* The shouters then advanced to the principal chiefs and offered them the gourds. In each instance the server would step back and aspirate the prolonged cry or wail called the black drink note. This utterance was then repeated on a finer key, with the chief drinking away all the time, as long as the crier's wind could hold out.[22]

The U.S. Commissioners then attempted to rise to the occasion, declaring in opening remarks,

> Brothers of the Creek Nation, Attend! We trust that the great Master of Breath who formed us all brothers, whether white men or red men, has created this day to be the time for preventing our people and your people from taking away that breath which none but he can give, or should take away....Although, brothers, we cannot entirely forget the calamities we suffered in the late war with Great Britain, yet we have buried all resentments for the part which the allies of Britain acted in that bloody scene. That war left many of our cities, villages, and towns, in a ruinous condition; but we obtained liberty and independence. Our country has recovered from desolation. We are at peace with all the nations of the world. We are increasing every day in numbers....Our lands are so extensive that they enjoy all seasons, and yield all productions. Our great ships are made to go in every part of

> the world, where goods and merchandise can be obtained. Our Union, which was a child, is grown up to manhood; so that it can speak with a louder voice, and strike with a stronger arm, than ever it has done before; for you must know, that a happy change has taken place in our national government. One Great Council is established, with full powers to promote the public good. General Washington, who led our armies to conquest wherever he turned his face, is now the headman of all our councils, and chief of all our warriors. You know him, and he never speaks the thing which is not.[23]

The Commissioners then presented their draft treaty and waited for McGillivray's response. This came the next day when after conferring most of the night with his fellow chiefs McGillivray simply pulled up stakes and marched away. Washington's high-level Treaty Commissioners discovered on the morning of September 25 that they had no one to talk to. Senator Few set out in pursuit and finally caught up with McGillivray at his encampment for the night more than thirty miles distant. Arriving about midnight, Few was "admitted into his tent" but McGillivray "would not give us any reason why he fled from us, nor would he return. Thus," Few summed up, "by the obstinacy or wickedness of one perfidious savage, the benevolent intentions of the President and Commissioners were defeated."[24] The first negotiation of Washington's administration ended in humiliating failure.

The real reason talks had broken down concerned Creek autonomy. Before the Revolution, the Creeks had called the British monarch their *father*. After 1776, the Creeks deemed the unproven United States "truly their younger brother."[25] In 1789, McGillivray was prepared to accord the new federal government the position of *elder brother* or even that of *co-father* (along with Spain), but only if persuaded that the United States understood how to behave as a *father* should in dealing with an adult *son*. Instead, McGillivray complained, he had been pressured to relinquish seemingly unlimited quantities of Creek land, including even the game-rich Okefennoke swamp. The Commissioners did offer access to a Georgia port, but only under federal supervision and only if the Creeks terminated ties with Spain. As the Commissioners reported back to President Washington, McGillivray "would not renounce the close connection which he had formed with the Spanish Government... without obtaining a full equivalent for the sacrifice...a free and exclusive port...upon the Altamaha, or the river Saint Mary."[26]

Unknown to the Commissioners was a letter McGillivray received a day before he left for the Oconee, containing what he described as a

> favorable report of the benign condescension of our great protector King Charles IV, conceding us our trade on terms as advantageous as the Americans could or would wish to do....These reports made me (to use the Indian expression) stout in my heart and strong in my mouth.

In a subsequent letter congratulating McGillivray on his firmness, the Spanish Governor announced a further gift of 785 guns, adding "I have no doubt that you will be satisfied, for they assure me that they are of superior quality."[27]

Washington's prestigious Commissioners returned to New York City much annoyed, filing a report accusing McGillivray of "deception" and urging that the Creek Confederacy be brought to heel by force. The Commissioners estimated Creek armed strength at 4,500 and suggested that a federal army of 4,250 be raised to carry "the arms of the Union into the very heart of the Creek country" in order that the Creeks might "be taught to feel the weight and superiority of the United States." Ever dutiful, Secretary Knox began drawing up plans, noting however in a letter to President Washington dated January 4, 1790, that

> The present military arrangement of the United States consists of one battalion of artillery, of two hundred and forty non-commissioned and privates; and one regiment of infantry, of five hundred and sixty non-commissioned and privates. This force, for the following objects, is utterly inadequate.

The standing federal army totaling less than a thousand men obviously could not supply the proposed force of 4,250. And since he did not share the Commissioners' confidence that nineteen U.S. soldiers were the equal of twenty Creek warriors, Knox recommended recruiting for a year 5,000 men—twenty two and a half men for every twenty Creek warriors—at a cost of $1,152,836.[28]

At this ominous juncture, Senator Benjamin Hawkins offered to write McGillivray. The Senate's leading expert on southern tribal affairs was hopeful McGillivray would attend to his initiative, and Washington deferred to "that ingenious gentleman, Mr. Hawkins." The North Carolinian's letter was delivered to McGillivray at Little Tallassee in

May. "Come forward yourself," Senator Hawkins wrote earnestly, "with a few of the principal chiefs of the Upper and Lower Creeks to the President of the United States, lay before him a real state of the case, and I will answer with my honor and my life that you will be received and treated with."[29]

McGillivray may have been already prepared to renew negotiations because within weeks of receiving Hawkins' letter he was headed north in a grand caravan accompanied by twenty-three other Creek chiefs, including his unpredictable rival the Tallassee Mico. Throughout the ensuing negotiations, the Tallassee Mico supported McGillivray, maintaining for example when questioned by Knox that he had signed treaties with Georgia only under duress, and that he had never been authorized to sign away Creek land. "I and the others never did consent to that," he insisted of the 1785 Georgia Treaty, adding "I tried...to destroy the paper while the man was writing it but was prevented....I told them...I had no right, that the lands belonged to the whole body of the nation."[30]

The arrival of McGillivray's splendidly plumed party created a sensation in New York City, then the nation's capital. The Creek chiefs too must have been impressed to be greeted by white men in full Native American regalia, calling themselves the Sons of St. Tammanend. These self-styled aboriginal warriors of what became Tammany Hall escorted the Creek chiefs

> up Wall Street to Federal Hall where Congress was in session, then to the President's house, and finally to the City Tavern, where Governor Clinton and Secretary of War Knox were hosts at dinner.[31]

McGillivray was a guest in the home of Secretary Knox; the other Creek chiefs lodged in a nearby inn. The following days were crammed with social events of all descriptions. Vice President Adams' wife Abigail informed her sister that the

> Creek savages...visit us daily....They are very fond of visiting us as we entertain them kindly, and they behave with much civility....They are very fine looking men, placid countenances and fine shapes. Mr. Trumbull says, they are many of them perfect models. McGillivray dresses in our fashion, speaks English like a native, and I should never suspect him to be of that nation, as he is not very dark. He is grave and solid, intelligent and much of a gentleman, but in very bad health.[32]

This renewed attempt at negotiation succeeded, and the U.S.-Creek

Treaty of New York was concluded on August 7, 1790. Following formal signing, Washington presented a wampum belt

> as a token of perpetual peace, and a paper of tobacco to smoke in remembrance of it. Mr. McGillivray rose, made a short reply to the President, and received the tokens. This was succeeded by the shake of peace, every one of the Creeks passing this friendly salute with the President.[33]

One article of the Treaty declared dramatically

> If any citizen of the United States, or other person not being an Indian, shall attempt to settle on any of the Creeks' lands such person shall forfeit the protection of the United States, and the Creeks may punish him or not as they please.

An article approved by the Senate but kept secret added,

> In order to effect a consolidation of interests between the United States and the Creek nation, it is hereby stipulated that Alexander McGillivray the beloved chief of the said nation shall also be constituted the Agent of the United States in the said nation with the rank of Brigadier General and the pay of one thousand two hundred dollars per annum, on his taking the usual oaths required by law.[34]

McGillivray's commission as Brigadier General made him the highest ranking Native American U.S. officer ever (Colonel Louis Atayataghronghta having formerly held this distinction), and qualified him for appointment as U.S. Agent to his own nation. Even more important, the Treaty of New York acknowledged the Creeks' right to deal directly with other nations. McGillivray gained an alliance with the United States without surrendering his nation's freedom to maintain foreign relations. Washington was certainly aware what this concession meant because while McGillivray and his party were making their slow way overland, word of the negotiations reached Spanish Florida and the Irish Spaniard Carlos Howard was quickly dispatched to New York by sea. His ship arriving before McGillivray, Howard journeyed down to Philadelphia to intercept him and kept in close touch throughout the negotiations, even appearing by his side at a reception at the home of President Washington. The 1790 Treaty was, as matters turned out, not unacceptable to Spain.[35]

Chief McGillivray did swear allegiance to the United States, and

Alexander McGillivray? Pencil sketch by John Trumbull, 1790. Trumbull sketched members of McGillivray's party when he visited New York City in 1790, and this drawing is related in date and format. His commissioning while in New York City could explain the U.S. officer's uniform. Courtesy, Yale University Art Gallery.

acknowledged U.S. sovereignty over Creek lands located within the territorial boundaries claimed by the United States. But federal officials assumed this meant the bounds ceded by Great Britain to the United States by the 1783 Treaty of Paris, which encompassed virtually the entire Creek nation. McGillivray knew this border had not yet been agreed to by Spain, and since the New York Treaty specified that "American sovereignty is to extend no farther than to such parts of the Creek nation as shall fall within the limits" of the United States, and, "Resting in full confidence that the King...[of Spain will defend] his claim and rights from the Americans," McGillivray assured the Spanish Governor that in all likelihood "no part of our country will fall within the United States." In McGillivray's eyes, the New York Treaty was contingent: the Creeks had agreed to consider their territory within U.S. bounds if (and only if) Spain should relinquish its own claims to suzerainty over Creek lands. After his trip to New York, McGillivray politely informed visitors from the United States that he considered Washington "my political and adopted Father" but made no reference to the fact that Washington shared this role with Spain's King Charles IV. So far as McGillivray was concerned, two *fathers* were better than one.[36]

McGillivray did his best to preserve friendly relations with both of his "political and adopted" *fathers* despite the resistance of both Spain and the United States to this arrangement. When forced to choose, McGillivray sided with Spain. Though willing to test the intentions of the new federal government, he seems to have finally concluded that collaboration with the United States was not possible, in large part because Georgians refused to accept the 1790 Treaty, and Washington's administration could not compel them to do so. In July of 1792, McGillivray traveled to New Orleans to sign a new Treaty with Spain which reaffirmed the 1784 Treaty of Pensacola and pledged Spanish support to the Creeks in expelling intruders. McGillivray's retainer was increased from 2,000 to 3,500 pesos annually. In return, McGillivray promised to give up his U.S. salary and titles. "It is far from my heart," he asserted, "to wish to have the least dependence on a people whom I know to be the natural and determined enemy of all the Indian nations and whom it is incumbent on us to resist." That fall, McGillivray "gave out in general orders" that the cattle of Georgia squatters "should be all seized on and the huts burnt."[37]

Six months later, McGillivray was dead. He died on February 17, 1793, "of complicated disorders—of inflamed lungs and the gout on his stomach," his Pensacola trading associate William Panton informed old Lachlan McGillivray, now back in Scotland. "Taken ill on the path coming from his cow-pen on Little River, where one of his wives, Joseph Cornells' daughter, resided," McGillivray died eight days later.[38] The sudden passing of this extraordinary leader left uncertain the future direction of Creek politics—and of Constitutional *fathership*.

The Treaty of New York did secure to the Creeks in the name of the federal government some land claimed by Georgia. Significantly however, before yielding to McGillivray, Secretary Knox *attempted* to win his approval of the cessions earlier made by a few Creeks to Georgia. The federal starting point in negotiating with McGillivray was Georgia's claim, as President Washington explained to the Senate in urging ratification of the Creek Treaty. Even though it had not been possible to obtain Creek cession of all lands claimed by Georgia on the basis of its pre-1789 State treaties, Washington expressed the cautious hope that the 1790 federal Treaty would nevertheless

> afford solid grounds of satisfaction to the State of Georgia, as it contains a regular, full and definitive relinquishment, on the part of the Creek Nation, of the Oconee Land, in the utmost extent in which it has been claimed by that State and thus extinguishes the principal cause of those hostilities from which it has more than once experienced such severe calamities.[39]

Knox and Washington would have preferred an agreement by which Georgia's pre-1789 Treaties were confirmed by the federal government. Failing to achieve Creek acquiescence, the federal government went forward and reached an agreement with the Creeks that was a compromise between what the Creeks demanded and what Georgia demanded. As a result, the 1790 federal Treaty of New York was pronounced "unconstitutional" by Georgia, just as had been the 1785 Continental Congress Treaty of Hopewell with the Cherokees.[40] (Prior to the adoption of the U.S. Constitution and the establishment of the Supreme Court practice of construing what was and was not Constitutional, the term "unconstitutional" was in widespread use by politicians in both Great Britain and the United States, who freely applied it to any action they deemed disruptive of fundamental political order.)

President Washington and Secretary Knox thought of themselves as honest brokers trying their best to work out a general settlement acceptable to both Georgia and the Creeks. The post-1789 federal government wasn't sure how to compel Georgia to accept a bilateral settlement between the U.S. government and a tribe any more than had been the Continental Congress. The 1790 U.S.-Creek Treaty did become a federal commitment, urgently commended to Georgia. But if Georgia resisted, President Washington was prepared only to make a renewed effort to seek a compromise agreeable to both the Creeks and Georgia. As Commander-in-Chief, President Washington and his successors did remove individual Georgians from land guaranteed by the federal government to the Creeks. But Georgia's contention that its pre-Constitutional treaties were proper exercises of the State's "sovereign, territorial and legislative rights"[41] was never formally contested by the federal government, which in fact accepted Georgia's position in the State-federal settlement of 1802 by which Georgia ceded its remoter western claims to the federal government.

Both before and after 1789, state cessions of western land offered the best chance of mitigating state-central disputes over boundaries and tribally occupied lands. But state cessions could never be a complete solution because each cession that was made came with strings, and no state was willing to cede all its tribally-claimed lands. Thus even after a state cession questions persisted, both in the territory ceded and in relations with tribes within the state's now-reduced bounds. With these tribes, federal treaties became a vital tool after the Constitution put treaties beyond state reach. To establish a presence, federal officials negotiated treaties with tribes within state bounds about lands occupied by tribes and claimed by states. Hopefully, once the federal government had been accepted as arbiter by both states and tribes, peaceful negotiations could bring states and tribes ever closer to agreement. The federal government presumed that tribal territories would shrink eventually, and in the meantime tribal use of ancestral hunting grounds might beneficially discourage the disorderly dispersal of U.S. citizens.

Georgia refused to take even the first step toward agreement until 1802, when the State finally ceded the territory that became the States of Alabama and Mississippi. But President Washington did oversee western land cessions by North Carolina in 1790 and Virginia in 1792. The process by which Virginia ceded its remaining western claims to the federal government and Kentucky was simultaneously admitted to the federal Union as its fifteenth state involved minimal tribal repercussions because Virginia had dispensed with tribal land claims in Kentucky long before 1789. The process by which North Carolina gave up its western claims and Tennessee in 1796 became the sixteenth state was not so smooth.

North Carolina wasn't even a member of the federal Union when Washington took the oath of office. But at a second State convention on November 21, 1789, North Carolina did decide to join the Union, the twelfth state to do so (Rhode Island being the thirteenth). A month after ratifying the Constitution, North Carolina also offered to cede what became the State of Tennessee to the federal government, and on April 2, 1790, President Washington signed into law "An Act to Accept a Cession of the Claims of the State of North Carolina to a Certain District of Western Territory." This federal Act accepted without alteration North Carolina's Deed of Cession, which included stiff terms.[42] These terms sought to minimize North Carolina's share of Revolutionary War debt, and to insure the continuance of slavery in the region ceded, even after it came under federal control. The bulk of North Carolina's Deed of Cession however had to do with North Carolina's insistence that any and all land grants made by the State must be honored by the federal government, even if these grants conflicted with commitments made to tribes in U.S. treaties. Acceptance of North Carolina's Deed of Cession placed the federal government in a compromised position, as President Washington candidly acknowledged. Although the 1785 Continental Congress Treaty of Hopewell remained on paper a federal commitment to the Cherokees, there now existed an agreement between the federal government and the State of North Carolina that was partially incompatible with it.

What should be done? In August of 1790, Washington informed the Senate that

> I shall conceive myself bound to exert the power entrusted to me by the Constitution in order to carry into faithful execution the Treaty of Hopewell, unless it shall be thought proper to attempt to arrange a new boundary with the Cherokees, embracing the settlements, and compensating the Cherokees for the cessions they shall make on the occasion.[43]

The Senate consented to Washington's initiative but the Cherokees refused to go along with federal attempts to persuade them to relinquish the boundaries secured them by the 1785 Treaty of Hopewell, and accept instead tribal boundaries that would coincide with what North Carolina and the federal government had together agreed on. By the July 2, 1791 Treaty of Holston, the Cherokees agreed only to a partial reduction of their territory, and not to the full cession desired by the federal government. Ironically, the federal negotiator who in 1791 accepted the Cherokees' refusal to acquiesce in North Carolina's position was none other than William Blount, who in 1785 had called the Congress Treaty of Hopewell unconstitutional for doing precisely the same thing.

The problems resulting from the Cherokees' unwillingness to extract the federal government from a quandary of its own making were assessed in a report submitted to President Washington on November 8, 1791, by Secretary of State Thomas Jefferson. After outlining the boundaries of the territory ceded by North Carolina's Deed of Cession, Jefferson noted that "The Indians, having claims within the said tract of country, are the Cherokees and Chickasaws, whose boundaries are settled by the Treaties of Hopewell, concluded with the Cherokees on the 28th day of November, 1785, and with the Chickasaws on the 10th day of January, 1786, and by the Treaty of Holston, concluded with the Cherokees July 2nd, 1791." Jefferson then acknowledged that the two Continental Congress treaties were not compatible with the terms of the North Carolina Deed of Cession accepted by the federal government on April 2, 1790. Jefferson estimated that "perhaps a fourth or a fifth" of the "bounties in land given by the said State of North Carolina" and still considered valid by North Carolina lay "in a country wherein the Indian title is acknowledged and guaranteed by the United States." Well aware that much sorting out needed to be done, Jefferson candidly informed Washington that "I have not presumed to decide on the merits of the several claims."[44]

Undeniably, the tribal catastrophes of the 1820s and 1830s, when the federal government coercively removed southeastern tribes from their homelands, trace back to these pre-1789 state-tribe controversies, which the Continental Congress had been helpless to end, and which Washington's administration also sought in vain to resolve through peaceful persuasion.

Not surprisingly, the clearest expression of President Washington's strategy toward tribes came in dealings with tribes of the Northwest Territory, where no state claims to land or tribal jurisdiction remained.

After years of alternating negotiation and warfare, federal *fathership* was accepted by more than a dozen formerly hostile tribes in an elaborate, indeed paradigmatic U.S.-tribal mutual adoption process at Greenville in what is now Indiana. In the summer of 1795, General "Mad Anthony" Wayne met to bury the hatchet with tribes he had bested the previous fall.[45] Advisers from tribes allied with the United States guided Wayne's conduct with great astuteness.

The chiefs were greeted graciously by their conqueror. "The heavens are bright, the roads are open," General Wayne assured the assembled tribes; "we will rest in peace and love, we will have a little drink to wash the dust out of our throats."

Throughout the first weeks of deliberation, not much seemed to be happening. A Shawnee chief addressed the Wyandots as *uncles*; a Wyandot chief rejoined by calling the Shawnees *younger brothers*. Both Shawnees and Wyandots referred to the Delawares as *grandfather*. General Wayne was addressed as an *elder brother*, while he referred to all the chiefs as *younger brothers* and to the British and French as "your *fathers*." Finally after more than a month, the Chippewa chief Masass expressed the hope that "Perhaps, at a future day, your *younger brothers* may be made happy, by becoming your *children*, should you extend to us your *parental* protection."

"*Brother* Indians," declared the Wyandot chief Tarke in a general gathering called to announce final agreement, "we do now, and will henceforth, acknowledge the fifteen United States of America to be our *father*...you must call them *brothers* no more." Turning to General Wayne, Tarke said, "You see, we all acknowledge you to be our *father*. I take you by the hand, which I offer as a pledge of our sincerity, and of our happiness in becoming your *children*." Wayne then addressed the assembly:

> Listen! all you nations, to what your *uncle*, the Wyandot, has said....I have hitherto addressed you as *brothers*. I now adopt you all, in the name of the President and fifteen great fires of America, as their *children*, and you are so accordingly....The United States of America gives peace to you and all your nations, and receives you and them under the protecting wings of her eagle.[46]

Federal officials seemed at last to have got it right, with substance and spirit combined in the ritually informed manner tribes expected. Even wampum was used appropriately, as a basis for oral explication during the treaty session and a memory aid afterwards. By their nature, wampum belts could be made sense of only through group discussion, and thus represented perfectly the tribes' understanding that any treaty was meaningless unless entered into with due ceremony and regularly re-examined in reflective interchanges. Tribes never thought of treaties as simple sign-and-record transactions. Although they tolerated writings as supplements to their traditional wampum belts, tribal leaders did not consider parchment agreements substitutes for on-going communication. Tribal treaty sessions today are often imagined to have involved nothing more than land sales, set down on pieces of paper borne away by officials to be filed and enforced in court. Treaties were never regarded by tribes in this way, and since independent tribes were prepared to negotiate only on their own terms, U.S. officials advised by friendly chiefs began at any early date designing and presenting wampum belts at treaty sessions. But wampum used ineptly—as at Fort Stanwix in 1784—made no sense. At Greenville in 1795 all the elements coalesced. Indeed fourteen years later, President Jefferson accepted a credibly expounded wampum belt given by General Wayne to the Wyandots at Greenville as enforceable evidence of a U.S. treaty obligation. Yielding to Wyandot persuasion in 1809, Jefferson told them

> Of this, besides other evidence, you now produce the belt of wampum reserved by you, in memory of it, the counter-belt given us having probably been destroyed in the fire which consumed our War Office in the year 1800. Such evidence, therefore, being now produced as induces a belief of the agreement, it shall be committed to writing...and you shall have a copy of these writings which shall be firm and good to you forever.[47]

At Greenville, tribes were diplomatically transformed from adult *younger brothers* into adult *sons*. This change was negotiated in a traditional tribal manner, and accepted as appropriate by those present, under the altered circumstances created by Wayne's military victory. Few if any tribes had a fundamental objection to calling the United States *father* rather than *brother*. The concept of a non-tribal nation serving as tribal *father*, understood in 1789 to be part of tribal tradition, in the seventeenth century had been an innovation in the tribal system, worked out in consultations between tribal chiefs and Europeans. Pressures from European *fathers* over time changed tribes, and pressures from their new federal *father* were expected to bring further changes. Tribes were not inflexibly opposed to U.S.-promoted alterations in their way of life. But tribes insisted that in any familial political arrangement reciprocity and consultation were indispensable, and if unsatisfactory the relationship would be broken off. Alexander McGillivray's Creeks had terminated federal *fathership* in 1792 after a two-year trial.[48] At Greenville in 1795, tribes similarly looked forward to testing federal reliability through periodic consultations on matters of mutual concern.

Tribal treaties negotiated under the Constitution thus inaugurated not only federal *fathership* of tribes but also an effort to define its nature and limits. In tribal reckoning, a *father* nation could expect deference; in return, a tribe maturely choosing to be adopted insisted on paternal protection of its vital interests. Being a contractual relationship, such an international *father-son* alliance was implicitly conditional, to be sustained only so as long as it served the perceived needs of both parties. As the Seneca chief Cornplanter remarked to Washington in 1791, "We called you *father* because you promised to secure us in the possession of our lands." Eleven years later, Creek Chief Efau Hadjo observed with equal pointedness to a federal Treaty Commissioner, "When a *man* has a *child*, he considers him, and is not willing to distress him and make him poor."[49]

President Washington proved to be a different kind of tribal *father* than George III had been, more constrained by states and personally more motivated to advance western settlement and encourage tribes to abandon hunting. Dissatisfied chiefs consequently berated Washington by contrasting him unfavorably to the kings of Great Britain, Spain or France. But notwithstanding his failings as a tribal *father*, Washington did set a pattern of federal practice destined to survive for several decades, in which the Constitution's international treaty procedure was often impressively combined with the ancient Native American concept of contractual *fathership*. Washington worked flexibly to negotiate mutually satisfactory settlements. He thought about fairness, he conferred, he shifted course, he was a gracious host, he personally partook in traditional tribal treaty rituals, he acceded to some tribal demands, and overruled advisers who pressed for war. Though not an advocate for tribes, he was for their conciliation, and to this end attempted to ascertain and respond to reasoned tribal preferences. Washington did not favor according tribes more rights, land or money than they themselves insisted on, but he did favor peace, and knew how to listen and experiment constructively, bearing in mind the aspirations of the entire republic he led. Throughout his Presidency, Washington sought peaceful relations with tribes, and worked creatively to establish a place for tribes within the Constitution's framework. Properly negotiated subordinate tribal alliances, he believed, would safeguard long-range U.S. strategic interests, while guaranteeing tribal leaders sufficient time and space in which to implement modifications in their "savage" societies. If tribes preferred to follow their own ancient customs in adopting the United States into familially defined alliances, while the federal government put faith in forms that were meaningful to the United States, Washington was more than willing to extend tribes this *civil* courtesy.

Why then do people today find it difficult to think of Washington as in any sense a friend of tribes? Critics for example delight in recalling that the Iroquois dubbed Washington "Town-Destroyer" because of his 1779 order to raze hostile Iroquois settlements. Certainly General Washington's Revolutionary War decisions differed from his peacetime policy recommendations. But even in wartime, Washington held fellow soldiers such as Colonel Atayataghronghta in high personal esteem, and received them with *civility* even though he thought of them as "savages." In Washington's eighteenth century lexicon, adult "savages" were rational human beings who usually lacked personal *civility* but who might be expected to display *civil* manners if treated *civilly*, and whose societies could be made *more civil* by a process of institutional reform called *civil*-ization, making a society *more civil* by progressive introduction of orderly governmental institutions and settled agricultural practices, which would gradually encourage desire for private property and thus for laws protecting it. Only in the nineteenth century did the redefined word *civilization* (connoting an entire society's cultural level rather than a reform process thought of as beneficial to any society) come into conventional use as a defining attribute of "higher" races, along with the term *savage state* as an indicator of racial incapacity.[50] Washington viewed *savage* tribal leaders as rational champions of a flawed way of life, and thus best opposed with measures demonstrating why his preferred mode of life was worth their emulation. Washington favored letting tribes decide their future course, while obstructing their continuance in their ancient mode of living. To Washington, tribes remained alien groups even when they were not allied to enemies of the United States. His plan of *civil*-ization, recommended for the mature consideration of *savage* tribes, was thus joined to a warning that they would have to deal with the U.S. Army if they defied U.S. jurisdiction over any of the territories King George III had ceded by the 1783 Treaty of Paris. Washington in effect said, "Let's see if tribes can survive. Meanwhile, we should render our own government respectable in their eyes, and avoid unnecessarily antagonizing them."

As *father* of tribes and Father of his country, Washington combined two quite distinct concepts. Washington was hailed as Father of his country because by leading the nation to victory in the Revolutionary War and inaugurating the Constitutional system as President he had more than any other one person brought his country into existence. As *father* of tribes, Washington was filling a ritualized role in a pre-Revolutionary tribal system, a role that was institutional, not personal. The government of the United States collectively (e.g., the "fifteen fires" spoken of at Greenville) and not any individual was understood by tribes to be their *father*. None of Washington's successors was referred to as Father of his country, but all subsequent presidents were routinely referred to as *father* of tribes.

A cruel consequence of the racism that transformed later tribal relations was the belief that it was senseless to expect reasoned discourse from tribal chiefs, who therefore were imagined to be calling the President *father* because they desired discipline rather than an ally to fill a role carefully delimited by the tribes themselves. Accepting this inverted understanding, the twentieth century scholar Francis Prucha candidly explained why he entitled one of his books *The Great Father*:

> In the nineteenth century, it was common for Indians to refer to the president (head and symbol of the United States government) as the Great Father, and the term was adopted by government officials as

> well. It was an appropriate usage for the paternalistic attitude of the federal government toward the Indians as dependent children.[51]

By the time "Great Father" in this corrupted sense had become an accurate characterization of federal thinking, tribal usage had been rejected by U.S. officials, and a non-tribal notion of autocratic fatherhood substituted.

In the wake of nineteenth century efforts to undo the tribes' achievement, many have faulted President Washington (who died in 1799) for not anticipating that his successors would abuse tribes and render them desperate. These critics are scornful of Washington's presumption that tribes were worthy antagonists fully capable of defending themselves and discerning their own best interests. But thinking of eighteenth century tribes only as prospective victims obscures accomplishments that tribes can now build on. Washington's measured challenge energized numerous tribes, which one-by-one established themselves by treaty within the U.S. federal system so successfully that no subsequent shock ever entirely dislodged them.

Five

The Constitution and "Indian Lands"

THE CONSTITUTION'S TRIBAL AMBIGUITY did not deter President Washington or the first federal Congress from moving rapidly to forestall states, land speculators and squatters from attempting to seize the lands of independent tribes. This objective was affirmed by passage on July 22, 1790—days before negotiation of the Treaty of New York with the Creek Confederacy—of "An Act to Regulate Trade and Intercourse with the Indian Tribes," providing

> That no sale of lands made by any Indians, or any nation or tribe of Indians within the United States, shall be valid to any person or persons, or to any state, whether having the right of preemption to such lands or not, unless the same shall be made and duly executed at some public treaty, held under the authority of the United States.

"Indian lands" could henceforth be legally transferred only at a federal treaty. But what was meant by "Indian lands"? The federal government wanted to assure Creek chiefs visiting the nation's capital that Georgia's independent efforts to acquire Creek lands were now prohibited. Just as clearly, a federal treaty was not contemplated each time a U.S. citizen of Native American descent wished to dispose of a tract of privately owned "land." How to define those "Indian lands" properly subject to federal treaty supervision certainly entered into discussion of the 1790 Act because the Senate committee that handled it consisted of tribal affairs veterans William Few of Georgia, Benjamin Hawkins of North Carolina and Philip Schuyler of New York. These three senators representing states with claims to juris-diction over tribal lands agreed that the federal government must regulate, by formal treaty, sales of "Indian lands" even if such lands lay within state boundaries. In agreeing to this, Senators Few, Hawkins and Schuyler undoubtedly made a distinction between "Indian land" transactions now subject to federal law and other "Indian" land sales over which states would continue to exercise jurisdiction.

As used in the first Trade and Intercourse Act, "Indian lands" evidently referred only to lands where tribes possessed "Indian title." "Indian title" was the monetarily "nearly worthless" hunting ground use right which Congress in 1783, adopting Philip Schuyler's suggestion, had concluded was all that tribes could be said to possess aboriginally and inherently, in the absence of a specific grant of more substantial land rights. "Indian title" was understood to be most often temporary, and thus compatible with a right of preemption that could be sold to private parties anticipating an early end to tribal hunting in a particular area. The category of "Indian lands" seems to have excluded not only lands owned individually by "Indians" but even numerous tracts of land held in common by tribes. Many tribes in coastal regions had for a century or more occupied colonial reservations where they held much more valuable land rights than the presumptively temporary hunting ground use right with negligible sale value to which the federal government extended protection in 1790.

Federally-protected "Indian lands" were typically located in "Indian Country," a zone encompassing much federal territory but extending as well into regions claimed by several states. In "Indian Country," tribes continued to hunt and pursue their ancient ways of life, regulating their affairs as autonomous polities. In "Indian Country," tribes could govern themselves and pursue whatever customs they wished, so long as they did not challenge fundamental U.S. jurisdiction or disturb the peace of U.S. citizens. On the other hand, tribes in "Indian Country" were barred from privileges and protections available to U.S. citizens, as well as from privileges and protections available to tribes residing on state-granted reservations under "ordinary" state jurisdiction. Federally-protected "Indian Country" possessed features that many tribes found attractive. But as they made the transition advocated by federal policy to a more settled agriculture life, some of these tribes were expected to embrace yeoman agriculture, along with more secure and valuable forms of land tenure. As this happened, "Indian Country" would recede gradually, since tribes still intent on pursuing game would presumably emigrate to regions where game was more plentiful. Since preemption rights to tribally-occupied lands in "Indian Country" were often held by private land speculators with a financial interest in inducing tribes to leave, and since states holding such preemption rights were similarly tempted to pressure tribes into leaving, the federal government decided to insure that tribes left voluntarily and at a time of their own choosing, by requiring a federal treaty for removal of a region from aboriginal hunting ground status. Transfer of lands from independent tribal use and control, and their inclusion within "the limits of our society" was in other words declared by Congress to be so consequential, and so inherently susceptible of abuse by preemption right holders, that its regulation in every instance by a cumbersome and costly federal treaty was imperative.

This objective for the land sale provisions of the 1790 Trade and Intercourse Act is implicit in the letter that proposed it. On July 7, 1789, Secretary of War Henry Knox urged passage of a

> declarative law...that the Indian tribes possess the right of soil [i.e., federally secured land tenure] of all lands within their limits, respectively, and that they are not to be divested thereof but in consequence of fair and bona fide purchases made under the authority or with the express approbation of the United States....No individual state could, with propriety, complain of invasion of its territorial rights. The independent nations and tribes of Indians ought to be considered as foreign nations, not as the subjects of any particular state. Each individual state, indeed, will retain the right of preemption of all lands within its limits, which will not be abridged; but the general sovereignty must possess the right of making all treaties, on the execution or violation of which depend peace or war.[1]

In this letter, Knox deplored the posture of states such as Georgia, which considered tribal lands beyond the frontier "vacant" and tribes mere tenants-at-will. The 1790 Act passed in response to Knox's urging seems to have been designed to protect tribes that had not been accorded any durable land rights either by a state or the central U.S. government. Independent tribes living on U.S. soil but not subject in any manner to U.S. jurisdiction were declared by Congress to possess legal rights to use the lands they occupied, rights to be spelled out formally when tribes signed federal treaties replacing a tribe's inherent aboriginal right with positive guarantees.

The dynamics of this process were discussed early in 1793, when a threat of tribal war northwest of the Ohio River prompted President

Washington to ponder whether it would be desirable or even legal to retrocede "Indian lands" that had been earlier ceded by tribes at a U.S. treaty. To Secretary of State Thomas Jefferson, Secretary of War Henry Knox, Treasury Secretary Alexander Hamilton and Attorney General Edmund Randolph, the President posed this question: "Have the Executive, or the Executive and Senate together authority to relinquish to the Indians the right of soil of any part of the lands north of the Ohio, which has been validly obtained by former treaties?" Knox, Hamilton and Randolph advised Washington they thought it possible, where state or private interests were not affected, to return federal territory to the status of "Indian lands." Jefferson disagreed and explained his reasoning as follows:

> I considered our right of preemption of the Indian lands, not as amounting to any dominion, or jurisdiction, or paramountship whatever, but merely in the nature of a remainder after the extinguishment of a present right, which gave us no present right whatever but of preventing other nations from taking possession and so defeating our expectancy: that the Indians had the full, undivided and independent sovereignty as long as they chose to keep it and that this might be forever: that as fast as we extended our rights by purchase from them, so fast we extended the limits of our society, and as soon as a new portion became encircled within our line, it became a fixed limit of our society: that the Executive with either or both branches of the legislature could not alien any part of our territory: that by the law of nations it was settled that the unity and indivisibility of the society was so fundamental that it could not be dismembered by the Constitutional authorities except 1. where *all power* was delegated to them (as in the case of despotic governments) or 2. where it was expressly delegated. That neither of these delegations had been made to our general government, and therefore that it had no right to dismember or alienate any portion of territory once ultimately consolidated with us: and that we could no more cede to the Indians than to the English or Spaniards, as it might according to acknowledged principles remain as irrevocably and eternally with the one as the other. But I thought that as we had a right to sell and settle lands once comprehended within our lines, so we might forbear to exercise that right, retaining the property, till circumstances should be more favorable to the settlement, and this I agreed to do in the present instance if necessary for peace.[2]

Washington and his other senior Cabinet officers seem to have agreed with Jefferson about what usually occurred when tribal lands were acquired by treaty, and to have disagreed only as to whether this process might in special circumstances be reversed.

The complex process Jefferson described was underway in both federal territory and states, and many state/federal implications remained unexplored. In 1790 for example, the term "Indian reservation" referred to state-regulated tracts, many of which had been originally established by colonial legislatures in the seventeenth century. Federally protected tribal hunting grounds in "Indian Country" and state-protected "Indian reservations" were separate legal categories. But what if at a federal treaty to extinguish tribal use rights to a tract in "Indian Country" a portion was reserved for the tribe? And what if this portion of "Indian land" came in time to be isolated from other portions of "Indian Country" and surrounded by areas under ordinary state jurisdiction? Was this isolated tract still in federally regulated "Indian Country" or now a state "Indian reservation" comparable to those established in earlier years by colonies and states, or possibly a hitherto unknown category, a "federal Indian reservation"? If so, would a federal relationship with that tribe and federal regulation of that separated tract continue indefinitely? Because of his commitment to state sovereignty, Jefferson resisted this prospect, whereas Federalists saw it as a way to expand intrastate federal authority. Disagreement about the extent of federal jurisdiction over tribes within state boundaries is not usually perceived today as a reason for the emergence in the mid-1790s of the Republican and Federalist parties, because of the mistaken assumption that in tribal matters the federal government's authority, having been categorically affirmed by the Constitution, was unchallenged even by Jeffersonians. Historians have tended to view controversies regarding tribal lands within claimed state boundaries as motivated by greed rather than by credibly divergent interpretations of the Constitution, and thus have missed the importance of tribal policy controversies in polarizing political party alignments. The most pivotal confrontation occurred in 1794-95 over whether New York State or the federal government should supervise Iroquois land transactions. This showdown had immediate consequences for the Republican-Federalist party split, and a delayed but profound impact on modern U.S. tribal policy.

During the Confederation era, New York had maintained that the Iroquois tribes were "dependent members" under State jurisdiction primarily because the State's boundary claims relied so heavily on the Iroquois. After the drafting of the Constitution, the State's boundary anxiety persisted, and with it determination to hold onto jurisdiction over tribes to the greatest extent legally allowable. Aware that the Constitution would introduce new uncertainties about tribal jurisdiction, New York's Jeffersonian Governor George Clinton sought to preclude at least some future federal designs on tribal lands within New York State by negotiating treaties with the three central Iroquois tribes in the months between the State's July 26, 1788 ratification of the federal Constitution and its formal inception at high noon on March 4, 1789. The preemption rights to almost all "Indian lands" occupied by the Senecas had been assigned to Massachusetts in 1786, in exchange for Massachusetts recognition of New York State's western boundary claims. The easternmost Iroquois tribe, the Mohawks, fled to Canada during the Revolution, and very few returned. This left the lands occupied by the centrally-located Oneidas, Onondagas and Cayugas potentially at issue between New York and the new federal government.

New York State's Treaty with the Onondagas was signed September 12, 1788, that with the Oneidas on September 22, 1788. The Cayuga Treaty was delayed, and not finally completed until February 25, 1789, just days before the Constitution limited treaty-making to the federal government. The three Treaties began with almost identical words; that with the Oneidas read, "The Oneidas do cede and grant all their lands to the people of the State of New York, forever." New York State then "appropriated" for the "use" of each tribe a portion of the lands ceded. Prior to the inception of the Constitution, "all" lands occupied by these three vulnerable tribes were thus separately acknowledged by each to be State-owned lands on which they enjoyed a State-regulated use right.[3]

The tracts "appropriated" by New York State for the "use" of the three central Iroquois tribes were located within the historic homelands of these tribes but were not contiguous, all three being surrounded by territory designated for settlement by U.S. citizens, and thus in Jefferson's words "encircled within our line." The State hoped these tribes would adopt a quiet life of yeoman farming and abandon hunting and warfare. This plan proved more acceptable to the missionary-influenced, pro-U.S. Oneidas than to the Onondagas and Cayugas, most of whom chose not to move from their Wartime settlements under British military protection onto confining State-granted lands. But the Onondagas and Cayugas still thought of their State reservations as assets, and hoped to sell them rather than simply walk away from them. Federal Treaty Commissioner Timothy Pickering, who met annually with the Iroquois between 1790 and 1794, and the resident temporary deputy U.S. Agent to the Iroquois, General Israel Chapin, fielded repeated requests from these British-allied tribes to induce New York State to buy or lease their reservations.

Pickering and Chapin supervised a rudimentary Iroquois aid program, comparable to modern-day foreign aid programs, but focused their primary energies on the continuing British military threat, and on Iroquois land claims within the federal Northwest Territory. In fact General Chapin, though he resided at Canandaigua in New York State, reported administratively to the federal Governor of the Northwest Territory. But the Iroquois insisted on airing grievances against the State to Chapin and Pickering, who felt obliged to respond as best they could. In 1791 for example, in the absence of any State representative, Pickering confirmed a lease of the Cayugas' State reservation on the basis of a Cayuga assertion that the February 25, 1789, New York State Treaty with the Cayugas allowed such leases, which it didn't. Pickering's well-intended intervention in a dispute between the Cayugas and New York State so alarmed President Washington and Secretary of War Knox that "by command of the President of the United States" Knox wrote an almost abject letter of apology to Governor Clinton, promising that Pickering "will personally wait upon your Excellency, to give you any further explanations which you may request."[4]

These difficulties could have been avoided had Governor Clinton chosen to attend U.S.-Iroquois conferences. But he declined, just as in 1784 at Fort Stanwix, though this time for a different reason. He told Pickering that Confederacy-wide Iroquois conferences were a mistake from his State's perspective, because he "doubted whether it was politic to call the Six Nations together, as it would give them an opportunity

Iroquois Diplomacy. In this 1793 drawing by British Colonel C.A. Pilkington, federal Treaty Commissioners seated in chairs listen to a Seneca at Buffalo Creek. Colonel Timothy Pickering leans forward, papers protruding from his pocket. Beverly Randolph rests on his cane. In the middle sits General Benjamin Lincoln, the most prestigious of the three. General Israel Chapin, federal Agent to the Iroquois, stands behind Pickering. British officers in plumed hats and missionaries in broad-brimmed hats observe. In the center stands an interpreter, probably Horatio Jones. From *Massachusetts Historical Society Collections*, Third Series, Fifth Volume, Page 177.

of forming a union at a time when we might wish them to continue disunited."[5] The State's strategy, adopted after the State was rebuffed by the assembled Iroquois Confederacy at Fort Stanwix, was to isolate each Iroquois tribe from contact with the others. Federal policy in contrast encouraged Iroquois reunification, to facilitate decision-making regarding matters of Confederacy-wide concern, such as their joint land claims in the federal Northwest Territory.

Pickering was a Federalist bureaucrat, who on August 12, 1791 became the nation's second Postmaster General. When first asked to visit the Iroquois, Pickering knew little about tribes, and accepted the Iroquois job because he needed the money. But having entered "Indian Country," he grew fascinated and met annually with the Iroquois from 1790 to 1794, stopping then only because he was appointed to succeed Henry Knox as Secretary of War, in which capacity he had charge of all federal tribal relations.

In his conferences with the Iroquois, Pickering became gradually aware of deep flaws in U.S. tribal policy. The federal government had taken ultimate responsibility for tribal relations, but with an agenda that was negative and complicit with states, and largely ignored what happened to tribes after they sold their "Indian lands" in "Indian Country" at a federal treaty. Ever an activist, Pickering attempted to nudge federal involvement with tribes beyond mere certification of the end of tribal use of "Indian lands" into a positive guardian-ward relationship. For several years, Pickering limited his efforts to modest initiatives, such as arranging for the education in Philadelphia of the Seneca chief Cornplanter's son Henry. But in the fall of 1794, while acting as sole federal Treaty Commissioner to negotiate the Treaty of Canandaigua, Pickering abruptly decided that the federal government must take direct charge of Iroquois lands, including those held under State grant.

Meeting with the Oneidas at Canandaigua on Saturday, October 11, 1794, Pickering learned that because they were authorized by New York to lease up to one hundred square miles of their State reservation for up to twenty-one years, the Oneidas had leased all one hundred square miles to a man named Peter Smith, for two hundred dollars annually. Appalled, Pickering spent his Sunday in deep reflection and on Monday informed the Oneidas that he had "thought a great deal of the condition of the natives of this land" hoping "some new path might be discovered in which they might walk with more safety." He now had the answer. "Among the whites," Pickering explained,

> the poor, the ignorant and the young, who cannot take care of themselves, are under the guardianship of the laws. Those laws mark out the path in which such helpless people are to walk; and persons are appointed as guides to keep them from losing the path, and to prevent people more knowing, but having bad habits from leading them astray. Now, *Brothers*, you the natives of this land...are in the condition of the helpless people just described; and need the guardianship of our laws... especially in the management of your lands.

The Oneidas had been under State legal restraint for some years, and found nothing surprising in Pickering's basic proposition. What was startling was his announcement that the *federal* government would henceforth be their guardian, and be prepared to function as a more active guardian than New York State presumed to be. Whereas the State merely restricted the Oneidas' ability to sell land and limited the length of any lease they might negotiate, Pickering suggested that the federal government could regulate the monetary terms of their leases. The Trade and Intercourse Act, Pickering told the Oneidas, "declared that no sale of Indian lands should be valid unless made at a public treaty held under the authority of the United States. Now, *Brothers*, it is my opinion that the lease of your lands to Peter Smith, is by this law made void."

Realizing the Oneidas were "struck" rather than persuaded by this argument, Pickering added,

> I have explained to you what I take to be the true meaning of the law: and I believe I am not mistaken. Perhaps some may tell you that the President and Great Council of the United States have no right to meddle with your lands, not even to keep you from being cheated out of them. But pay no regard to such men. Consider them as deceivers, who want to take your beds from under you. The makers of the law were wise and good men, who would not do what they had no right to do. Keep fast hold of your lands, therefore, and do not give up even those you have leased, until wise men, who understand all our laws, have examined into the matter and found who is right.

To launch a test case of the applicability of the Trade and Intercourse Act, Pickering recommended that the Oneidas "send a petition to the President, praying that he would cause it [i.e., the land leased to Peter Smith] to be restored. And if it should be restored, then I would advise you to lease it" on better terms at a full federal treaty. Pickering informed the Oneidas that unless negotiated in this fashion a lease "can no more bind you than a thread of rotten bark."

For years, New York had regulated leasing of State reservation land. Stirred by Oneida complaints about an ill-advised lease, Pickering suddenly announced that it might be invalid if not federally sanctioned. Moreover, declared Pickering,

> I now tell you further, that the State itself cannot buy it, unless the agents appear at a Council Fire kindled by the United States, and in the presence and with the approbation of the commissioners appointed by the President, agree on the price. And after this, the paper containing the articles of the treaty signed by the chiefs must be laid before the President and his Council of wise men, and be approved by them, before it can have any strength....I know you will be told the State has all the power over your lands, and that the President and his Council have nothing to do with them....But, *Brothers,* even if the right of the United States to interfere were doubtful, your own right is certain. The land is yours, and the State cannot take it from you without your own consent.

Pickering knew his attempt to expand the scope of the Trade and Intercourse Act to cover leasing of State reservation lands was a gamble. At a minimum, he trusted his exhortation would strengthen tribal vigilance. Whatever happened to their petition, Pickering assured the Oneidas that the United States would never forget them: "Speak strong and be not afraid. Follow this advice, and nobody can hurt you: for the United States will protect you."[6]

Before he left Canandaigua, Pickering was confronted with two additional Iroquois land matters, these involving future sales rather than an extant lease. British-allied Onondagas and Cayugas wished to sell portions of their State reservations but since New York officials had refused to come to Canandaigua, all Pickering could do was forward the tribes' requests. On November 15, Pickering recorded these words addressed to him by pro-British Cayuga and Onondaga chiefs:

> *Brother* Commissioner....Now listen to the mind of the two nations here present....This business we first desire should be laid before General Washington, and by him be sent to the York people; and we desire General Washington to request the York people to grant what we desire; and for them to let us know quick whether they will be so kind as to comply with our request.

Final discussion took place the next day, when Pickering presented the Cayuga and Onondaga chiefs for their approval an "expression of their minds" summarizing their various speeches to him. This read:

> *Brother*, it is the situation of our lands which makes our minds uneasy. We have but two small pieces left, and we are desirous of reaping from them all the benefits which they are capable of yielding. The York people have got almost all our country, and for a very trifle. They will not then deny us the liberty of disposing of the little that remains, in such manner as will do most good to our old women and children and children's children. For this reason we desire to dispose of our land for an annual rent, to be paid to us and our posterity forever....[A]ll they will produce will be but a trifle when divided among so many families: but it will at least relieve the poor, if we can obtain the just value of our land....We desire this business may first be laid before General Washington and by him be sent to the York people, and we request General Washington to ask the York people to grant what we desire....If they do, let them first inform General Chapin of their determination, and he will inform those at the westward as well as those at the eastward. We shall want his assistance, if our requests respecting our annual dues are complied with.[7]

This procedure alluded in non-technical language to the federal treaty process Pickering hoped would be used, if he could gain acceptance from the federal government for his proposed extension of the Trade and Intercourse Act to cover New York's State reservations as "Indian lands." Knowing this might not happen however, he devised a course of action for the Onondagas and Cayugas that paralleled the federal treaty procedure but stopped short of referring to it directly.

The federal Treaty of Canandaigua, completed November 11, 1794, consented to by the Senate on January 9, 1795, and proclaimed by the President on January 21, 1795, included in Article Two these words:

> The United States acknowledge the lands reserved to the Oneida, Onondaga and Cayuga nations, in their respective treaties with the State of New York, and called their reservations, to be their property;

> and the United States will never claim the same, nor disturb them or either of the Six Nations, nor their Indian friends residing thereon and united with them, in the free use and enjoyment thereof; but the said reservations shall remain theirs until they choose to sell the same to the people of the United States, who have the right to purchase.

The "United States" here meant the federal government. The Treaty's reference to "the people of the United States" on the other hand acknowledged that the federal government did not have "the right of purchase" which was held by New York State. The Treaty did however declare the tribes' State-granted reservations to be the "property" of the "Oneida, Onondaga and Cayuga nations" and implied that the federal government intended in some manner to supervise their "free use and enjoyment thereof." The Treaty thus stopped short of stating that federal treaty regulation would be required for future sales, but Pickering evidently hoped that such an understanding of the Treaty would in time be accepted, along with his interpretation of the Trade and Intercourse Act. Narrowly read, Article Two of the Treaty was nothing more than a statement of things as they were, but an expansive reading implied new federal guarantees.

Pickering employed the word "property" to describe not only the valuable State reservation lands of the Oneidas, Onondagas and Cayugas but also the "nearly worthless" hunting ground use right or "Indian title" possessed by the Senecas in "Indian Country" in western New York State. Pickering was well aware that the Iroquois thought of themselves as a sovereign confederacy of tribes, each of which claimed to be the outright owner of its ancestral lands. So Pickering ingeniously inserted the word "property" in the Treaty, which the various Iroquois tribes and the federal government could interpret according to their respective predilections.

On January 2, 1795, Pickering succeeded Henry Knox as Secretary of War. In this new capacity, Pickering prepared a letter "by direction of the President" informing Governor Clinton of the desires of the Onondagas and Cayugas to sell some of their reservation lands, and attached it to a copy of the speech he had drafted for them.[8] Pickering also sent Clinton a request from the Mohawks for consultations with the State regarding their tribal land claims. Pickering's January 30, 1795 communication was little more than a cover letter, because the chiefs' speeches themselves outlined the procedure Pickering implicitly recommended to Governor Clinton. By the time Pickering transmitted the chiefs' request on, the approval of President Washington had been obtained. Beyond this, the only federal involvement mentioned in the chiefs' speech was that of General Chapin. But Pickering apparently hoped that Governor Clinton would assume the speech alluded "Indian-style" to the federal treaty procedure. Unsure whether the listing of the State reservations in his Treaty meant that the federal treaty procedure was legally required, Pickering confined himself only to hinting strongly that Governor Clinton apply for appointment of a federal treaty commissioner to supervise sale of the Cayuga and Onondaga State reservations.

On March 7, 1795, General Chapin died. On April 6, Pickering appointed his son Captain Israel Chapin, Jr., to succeed him as federal Iroquois Agent. Captain Chapin had assisted his father and possessed a day-to-day familiarity with the job, but he proved not up to managing the events that followed.[9]

On April 9, 1795, the New York Legislature passed "An Act for the better support of the Oneida, Onondaga and Cayuga Indians," designating Philip Schuyler and three others as State Commissioners to negotiate land sales with these three tribes. The Act made no mention of Pickering's January 30th letter, and instead listed a number of other justifications for initiating land sale negotiations, among which was an Oneida request that their old Revolutionary War adviser General Schuyler be appointed to confer with them regarding how best to utilize their lands productively.[10] The inclusion of the Oneidas, not mentioned by Pickering, and omission of the Mohawks, whom Pickering did mention, indicated that the Legislature was not tailoring its actions to Pickering's request but rather was acting in its capacity as legal guardian of the welfare of the Oneidas, Onondagas and Cayugas—though not of the Canada-based Mohawks.

The State Commissioners began making arrangements to negotiate with the Oneidas, Onondagas and Cayugas, but Pickering in Philadelphia heard nothing until he received a letter (now lost) written on May 22, 1795, by Captain Chapin, giving what the Captain no doubt considered a routine report of actions he had taken to help arrange State meetings to be held at Cayuga Lake with the Cayugas and Onondagas. Chapin knew that the desire of the Cayugas and Onondagas to sell portions of their reservations to New York State had been discussed with Pickering at Canandaigua the previous fall, and assumed that Pickering approved of what was now proposed. A second letter dispatched by Chapin on June 13 reported in an equally perfunctory fashion that his assistant Jasper Parrish "is now at Buffalo Creek to bring forward the Cayugas and Onondagas to the treaty respecting their lands."[11]

Neither of Captain Chapin's letters conveyed a clear picture; from them Pickering ascertained only that something was going on regarding the State reservations of the Onondagas and Cayugas. So Pickering made inquiries of Thomas Morris, a member of the New York Legislature and son of Robert Morris, the celebrated Revolutionary financier. Intentionally or not, the younger Morris left Pickering with the impression that the New York Legislature had directed Clinton to petition the federal government to convene a treaty session. Assuming that the Legislature's Act said what he thought it should say, Pickering concluded that the contemplated land purchases were in violation of New York State law. Still anxious about whether federal law in fact required use of the federal treaty procedure, Pickering was drawn to the idea that it might have been made obligatory by the New York Legislature.

Pickering resolved to force a showdown. His first step was to request on June 13 an Opinion from U.S. Attorney General William Bradford on whether New York's State reservations were or were not subject to the provisions of the 1793 federal Trade and Intercourse Act. On June 16, Bradford supplied the desired Opinion

> Whether the State of New York has a right to purchase from the Six Nations or any of them the lands claimed by those nations and situate within the acknowledged boundaries of that State, without the intervention of the general government.
>
> By the Constitution of the United States, Congress has power to regulate commerce with the Indian Tribes, and by the act of 1 March 1793, it is expressly enacted, That no purchase or grant of lands, or of any title or claim thereto, from any Indians or nation or tribe of

> Indians, within the bounds of the United States, shall be of any validity in law or equity, unless the same be made by a treaty or convention entered into pursuant to the Constitution....The language of this act is too express to admit of any doubt upon the question unless there be something in the circumstances of the case under consideration to take it out of the general prohibition of the law.
>
> Nothing of this kind appears in the documents submitted to the Attorney General. It is true, that by treaties made by the State of New York with the Oneidas, Onondagas and Cayugas, previous to the present Constitution of the United States, those nations ceded all their lands to the people of New York, but reserved to themselves and their posterity forever for their own use and cultivation, but not to be sold, leased or in any other manner disposed of to others, certain tracts of their said lands, with the free right of hunting and fishing etc. So far therefore as respects the lands thus reserved the treaties do not operate further than to secure to the State of New York the right of preemption: but subject to this right they are still the lands of those nations, and their claims to them, it is conceived cannot be extinguished but by a treaty holden under the authority of the United States, and in the manner prescribed by the laws of Congress.

Bradford accepted without challenge the 1794 Treaty's conflation of two radically distinct forms of tribal "property," and thus was able to conclude that New York possessed only a right of preemption to the State-created Oneida, Onondaga and Cayuga reservations, which could therefore be said to be comprehended by the language of the Trade and Intercourse Act, just as certainly as were the aboriginal "Indian title" lands occupied by the Senecas in the still-British-controlled western region of New York State. Bradford concluded that the Oneidas, Onondagas and Cayugas had actively "reserved to themselves" the State lands "appropriated" for their "use" by New York State, thereby likening these State-regulated lands to aboriginal Seneca lands. Bradford implicitly acknowledged the existence of the Iroquois Confederacy (the "Six Nations") as an organized entity, which made it easier for him to conclude that the several Iroquois tribes possessed similar land rights.

More than two hundred years after it was written, this Opinion remains the basis of numerous federal court decisions, including two Supreme Court decisions rendered in 1974 and 1985.[12] But Bradford's Opinion is fundamentally deficient. By Bradford's own admission, his Opinion—completed three days after Pickering's request—was based solely on documents supplied him by Pickering. While it is not known what these were, it is certain that Bradford was not given the most recent and authoritative expression of New York State's position, the Legislature's April 9th Act, because Pickering himself did not see it until July at the earliest. The April 9th Act declared repeatedly that the lands occupied by the Oneidas, Onondagas and Cayugas had been "appropriated" by New York State for the "use" of these tribes. Instead of analyzing and refuting this State contention, Bradford seems to have been unaware of what New York's position was. But even with access only to the 1794 federal Treaty of Canandaigua and the 1793 federal Trade and Intercourse Act, Bradford might well have concluded that it was a stretch to extend the legal definition of "Indian lands" requiring federal treaty supervision to State reservations which were clearly within what Jefferson called "the limits of our society." [13]

Armed with Bradford's Opinion, Pickering placed the New York State reservation matter before President Washington, who on June 23 authorized him to proceed. The next day Pickering fired off a letter to New York's Governor Clinton, enclosing Bradford's Opinion. Then on June 29, an energized Pickering sent Captain Chapin a scorching letter insisting that he give

> no countenance to this unlawful design...as it is repugnant to the law of the United States made to regulate trade and intercourse with the Indian tribes....[Y]ou are to tell these tribes of Indians that any bargains they make at such a treaty as that proposed to be held...will be void; and as the guardian of their rights you will advise them not to listen to the invitation of any Commissioners unless they have authority from the United States to call a treaty.
>
> The conduct of this Commissioner is the more extraordinary seeing, as Mr. T[homas] Morris informs me, the act of the legislature of New York expressly instructed the Commissioners they appointed to apply to the General Government to call the treaty; but Governor Clinton, denying the authority of that Government in this matter, would not make the application.[14]

As of June 29, Pickering clearly still had not seen the April 9th Act. Moreover, "guardian of their rights" was quite an enlargement of Captain Chapin's job description as a federal Agent, since these were State-granted rights, and Chapin was expected to guard against their abuse *by the State.*

Governor Clinton completed his term on June 30 without replying to Pickering's letter of June 24 enclosing U.S. Attorney General Bradford's Opinion. So on July 3 Pickering wrote another letter to Clinton's successor reiterating his contention that the State could not negotiate with the Cayugas, Onondagas and Oneidas until federal treaty commissioners were appointed.[15] As it happened, Clinton's successor was none other than John Jay, one of the three authors of the *Federalist Papers* and first Chief Justice of the U.S. Supreme Court, as well as having himself served with distinction as a federal treaty commissioner; he negotiated the important "Jay Treaty" with Great Britain signed November 19, 1794. On July 13, 1795, Governor Jay replied in words calculated to remind Pickering he was accustomed to reaching his own conclusions on matters of law, and that the Opinion of a U.S. Attorney General was far from being the last word. "Whether the Constitution of the United States warrants the act of Congress of the 1 March 1793," Jay wrote Pickering, "and whether the act of this State respecting the business now negotiating with the Onondaga and other tribes of Indians, is consistent with both or either of them, are questions which on *this* occasion I think I should forbear officially to consider and decide." Observing dryly that Pickering "doubtless" had a copy of the State's April 9th Act, Jay added,

> As to any intervention or concurrence of the United States the act is silent and I do not observe any thing in it which by implication directs or authorizes the Governor to apply for such intervention or which implies that the Legislature conceived it to be either necessary or expedient.[16]

Receipt of Jay's letter was Pickering's first intimation that he had been mistaken in assuming that the New York Legislature had directed the Governor to request appointment of a federal treaty commissioner. Pickering replied apologetically to Jay on July 16 conceding he had erred.[17]

Governor Jay made no attempt to halt the negotiations authorized prior to his assumption of the governorship. But five days later he did act in the way Pickering preferred, requesting that a federal commissioner be appointed to preside at a Mohawk treaty conference.[18] Like the Cayuga and Onondaga land sales, the Mohawk transaction had been initiated at Canandaigua the previous fall, and mentioned in Pickering's letter to Governor Clinton dated January 30, 1795. It was however considered distinct by New York State because the Mohawks had not put themselves under State protection by a pre-Constitutional treaty, and Jay's request for appointment of a federal treaty commissioner to preside at the Mohawk negotiation thus did not imply repudiation of the procedure authorized by the New York Legislature for dealing with the Oneidas, Onondagas and Cayugas, formally under State protection. In reporting receipt of Governor Jay's letter to President Washington on July 21, 1795, Pickering noted that

> By the Act of the Legislature of which an extract is enclosed, and the Governor's letter referring to the subject of it, a distinction seems to have been taken between the lands...claimed by the Saint Regis [Mohawk] Indians and those of the Oneidas, Onondagas and Cayugas. With respect to the latter the intervention of the general government has not been thought requisite; but in regard to the former Governor Jay has resorted to it; as the Act of the Legislature of New York authorized him to do.

Pickering rejected the Legislature's "distinction" but at least he was now aware that New York made one. And he responded with satisfaction to Governor Jay's Mohawk request, advising the President to give "facility to every measure of a state government, which conforms to the regulations prescribed by the laws of the Union."[19]

Pickering's July 21st letter reported both that Governor Jay desired appointment of a federal treaty commissioner to supervise negotiations with the Mohawks and that federal efforts were underway to halt negotiation of the three sales of State reservation land set in motion before Governor Jay took office. On July 27, Washington replied from Mount Vernon. Regarding Pickering's attempt to halt the three State reservation transactions, Washington cautioned that they might have already been completed, in which case "any further sentiment *now* on the unconstitutionality of the measure would be received too late." If on the other hand it turned out that these land sales had not been completed, Washington affirmed, "It is my desire that you would obtain the best advice you can on the case and do what prudence, with a due regard to the Constitution and laws, shall dictate." Washington lacked Pickering's zeal for partisan confrontation, but authorized him to move forward on the understanding that he seek further advice and exercise restraint. Veiled exchanges of this sort had characterized the relationship of the impetuous Pickering and the supremely self-controlled Washington ever since 1780, when Pickering became Quartermaster General of the chronically under-supplied Continental Army. In the context of their long, always-strained relationship, Pickering would have recognized in Washington's charged word "prudence" an emphatic signal of concern that Pickering might have once again gone too far. Washington did wholeheartedly endorse Pickering's desire to applaud the contrasting initiative of Clinton's successor:

> With respect to the meeting which is proposed to be held with the Saint Regis [Mohawk] Indians the proposition of Governor Jay is regular; and I can think of no better character than Colonel Wadsworth or Mr. Boudinot to attend it on the part of the United States. If both should decline the service any other respectable and well known disinterested character would meet my approbation equally.[20]

Washington had reason to be concerned that the tribal land sales Pickering wished to halt might have already been completed. The first State conference began on July 19, with agreement concluded July 27, the very day on which Washington expressed this doubt.

In his opening speech to the Cayugas and Onondagas assembled at Cayuga Lake, New York's principal negotiator, Philip Schuyler, recalled that while the New York Legislature

> was deliberating on the most effectual mode of carrying into effect their humane and benevolent intentions towards you, they received from the President of the United States, a copy of your speech made to Colonel Pickering on the 16th day of November last, relative to the subject in question. And our Great Council was exceedingly happy to find that your intentions and theirs perfectly coincided on the subject. For you requested, that your reserved lands might be so disposed of as to produce an annual rent to be paid to you and your posterity forever.[21]

Schuyler expressed pleasure that the federal government had forwarded the Cayuga and Onondaga requests, but made clear he did not consider any federal participation legally indispensable.

After cautioning that no transaction would be completed unless all factions could agree, Schuyler requested that the Cayugas indicate how much of their reservation they wished to give up. The tribe's British-allied majority then confessed that they had been "endeavoring to unite in sentiment with our brethren who live on the reservation" behind a proposal that their entire New York State reservation be leased, with the fifty Cayugas still at Cayuga Lake moving west to join with them under British protection near Niagara. But having failed to win over the reservation-dwellers, the emigrant Cayuga majority proposed

> to reserve one mile square for the use of such of our nation as now live on the reservation...[and] another mile square on which we think there is a silver mine. This we wish to reserve forever; and when we open it we shall share with those who may work it for us.

Additionally, by the pre-Constitutional State treaty with the Cayugas completed in early 1789, the Cayuga leader Fish Carrier had been guaranteed a personal square mile, whose location was now specified for the first time. This tract was to be leased to provide Fish Carrier with personal income, wherever he might choose to live. The Cayugas also requested that one square mile be transferred to the private ownership of a Mr. Harris who operated a ferry and had "been useful to both you and us." As for the remaining ninety-six square miles, "You know the value of lands when divided into farms; we will lease you the lands for twenty-two years and then we will confer on the subject." Clearly the Cayugas supposed the "property" they possessed adjoining Cayuga Lake was more than a "nearly worthless" use right to hunt!

In reply the following day, Schuyler accepted the British-allied Cayuga majority's proposals as a basis for discussion. But he recommended quadrupling the area reserved for the Cayugas who would be staying at Cayuga Lake, in the hope that "neither those who reside at Buffalo Creek nor those who remain on this ground shall have cause to complain of our candor and justice....[A]nd as there are thirteen families who now live here we think one mile square of land is not sufficient for them." Indicating his understanding that the Cayugas' State reservation was far more valuable than mere "Indian land" as then defined by the federal government, Schuyler agreed to the proposed silver mine reservation. "*Brothers*," he told Fish Carrier's majority faction,

> you also wish to reserve a mile square on which you think there is a mine. We have already informed you that we were willing to purchase

> only such part of your reservation as you were willing to sell, we therefore have no objection that you should reserve that mile square to you and your posterity forever to use it as you like, either to cultivate or to work any mine which may be thereon. But...you must not sell or lease it to any white inhabitant or other person without the permission of our Great Council.

To a twenty-two year lease arrangement, Schuyler was however firmly opposed, "because at the end of a lease for a short time a controversy would arise between you and those who might be willing to settle for so short a time." Schuyler also refused to consider making the special provision requested for the ferryman Harris, but was more receptive to the Cayugas' proposal that a square mile of the land they would relinquish then be deeded by New York State to federal Agent Chapin.

Having resolved how much land the Cayugas would be selling, Schuyler offered them $1800 annually forever. He also assured them that "if you do not choose to part with your lands (for a longer term than twenty-two years) on the terms we have mentioned we can do no more and the negotiations must terminate. But whether we ultimately agree or not we shall part with you as friends who wish you well."

On July 25, the British-allied Cayuga majority reiterated their desire to have no more than one square mile reserved for the reservation-dwellers at Cayuga Lake. "Our people cannot live happily in the neighborhood of your people," Fish Carrier's deputy Hanging Face informed Schuyler.

> We wish for this reason that a small reservation only may be kept. We have lands at Buffalo Creek and we love our brothers and wish them to come and live with us. You know...that spiritous liquors are injurious to us and that taverns are plenty among you. We wish that care might be taken to prevent our people from being imposed upon.

Hanging Face did accept a permanent arrangement. He told Schuyler, "You proposed to take a lease forever, we agree to this and will give you a lease to last as long as the world endures....By these means our children and children's children will always receive....This is very pleasing to us." Schuyler welcomed this offer but again insisted that four square miles rather than one be reserved for the Cayuga Lake Cayugas. Two days later, an agreement was concluded, with the understanding that the Legislature's confirmation would be necessary because the Cayugas had insisted on terms that went beyond the Commissioners' instructions.[22]

The next day, the Onondagas also agreed to terms. The pro-British majority of this tribe had come to Cayuga Lake eager to renegotiate the agreement reached by New York State two years earlier with the tribe's minority still resident at Onondaga, an agreement by which the bulk of the Onondagas' reservation was relinquished in exchange for an annuity of $410 payable at Onondaga. Subject to Legislative assent, Schuyler and his colleagues agreed to increase this annuity to $800, and that this amount would be distributed by the federal Agent, an arrangement the tribe's majority (based at Buffalo Creek near British-held Fort Niagara) felt was more likely to insure they received a large share. New York's Commissioners agreed to send payment through Chapin, but warned the Onondagas that the federal government might soon abolish the "temporary" office Agent Chapin held. Already insecure, he could not have relished this prediction.[23]

Secretary of War Pickering's June 29th letter instructing Chapin to halt these negotiations arrived at his Canandaigua home after he had left to attend the negotiations at Cayuga Lake, and it was not until he returned to Canandaigua that he realized for the first time that his rambling reports had stirred up a hornets' nest in the nation's capital, Philadelphia. Two of the three tribal agreements were now completed. The Cayugas had moreover requested that Chapin himself be given a square mile of the land they were relinquishing, and the New York Commissioners had agreed to pass along this request to the Legislature. Writing on July 31, Captain Chapin tried hard to convince his boss that he had not been remiss:

> Commissioners for the State of New York...have purchased the Cayuga reservation for $1800 to be paid to them annually excepting reserving to the Cayuga Nation six square miles to them and their children forever....I was knowing to the law of the United States respecting holding treaties with the Indian nations, and not having any directions from you, I have endeavored to not interfere in the business as I supposed the Commissioners were fully authorized by the Government of the United States as well as that of their own with full power to transact the business. I have petitioned them to send me the law of the State whereby they were authorized to hold the treaty, but

> they have been backward to do it, or even to show it to me when at the treaty and which I have not as yet seen. The Indians all requested me to go with them to the treaty which I according did but have not used my influence with them as I very soon see they were determined to manage the business as a separate interest from the United States. I inquired of General Schuyler how he construed the law of Congress in regard to holding treaties with the Indian tribes? He made very little reply by saying it was very well where it would correspond with that of an individual state. Had I received your letter I could have managed the business more to your mind but as I had supposed the Government of the State of New York had applied to the General Government and had obtained sufficient power to call the Indians to the treaty, and in that it would have been an imprudent act for me to persuade the Indians not to adhere to their invitation, as the business first originated at this place and delivered to your charge in order that Commissioners properly authorized might come forward to make the purchase before recited. And as they have presumed to make the purchase who were well acquainted with the law whereby they were authorized will plead an excuse for me who have not had opportunity to hear a word of information respecting the business....I shall set out for the Oneida tomorrow and will engage the treaty will not take place there under the present Commissioners. I shall be there in season as General Schuyler is going first to Oswego Falls to view them for the purpose of pleasing looks. I have been cautious to not furnish the Indians who have been to the treaty out of the United States property or in any way to have it appear on the part of the United States as I had no special directions and therefore attended as a private individual without speaking or having any thing to do in their Council more than another individual.[24]

His pretense at competence notwithstanding, Captain Chapin clearly was no master of the federal Trade and Intercourse Act. And Chapin floundered into incomprehensibility when he moved from the fact that he did not dispense federal supplies to the pose that he had acted "as a private individual." By his own admission, prior to and during these negotiations he perceived his function as an official one, "as the business first originated at this place," in other words stemmed from consultations between his father and Pickering at Canandaigua the previous fall. Nor could federal Agent Chapin bring himself to tell his superior that "as a private individual" he anticipated receiving in due course a square mile of the land relinquished by the Cayugas through this transaction that purportedly violated federal law.

From Chapin's July 31st letter, Pickering learned that two of the three planned State negotiations were now completed. Having been instructed by President Washington not to try to undo these transactions if they had been completed, Pickering felt obliged to pass this word along. But since the Oneida conference might still be halted, Pickering composed what must have been a painful letter to write, acknowledging his receipt of Chapin's report that

> Commissioners of New York purchased the land of the Onondagas and Cayugas; and that you proposed to go to Oneida where you supposed that tribe might be influenced to avoid a sale. Seeing the Commissioners were acting in defiance of the law of the United States, it was entirely proper not to give them any countenance; and as that law declares such purchases of the Indians as those Commissioners were attempting to make, invalid, it was also right to inform the Indians of the law and of the illegality of such purchase. But having done this much, the business might there be left. The negotiation is probably finished ere now: if not, you may content yourself with giving the Oneida the information above proposed, and there to leave the matter.[25]

The normally crisp, self-assured Pickering here sounded listless and resigned. Why bother to "inform" the Oneidas that they might be making an "invalid...illegal" sale if Pickering was willing to accept such sales after the fact? In addition to receiving President Washington's word of caution, Pickering had by now also learned from Governor Jay that the New York State Act of April 9, 1795, said nothing about federal involvement, and that Jay saw no reason to halt the negotiations it authorized. Perhaps Pickering had concluded that opposition was futile, but could not quite bring himself to *say* this.

For the better part of a year, Pickering had followed a course he hoped might bring about federal regulation of New York's State reservations. He began cautiously in his consultations with Iroquois chiefs, not wishing to raise unrealistic expectations. Then he became excited when he believed New York's Legislature was cooperating, and triumphant when Attorney General Bradford produced the desired Opinion. But after Governor Jay and President Washington expressed skepticism, Pickering reluctantly—and somewhat incoherently—

abandoned his attempt to extend federal treaty regulation to the State reservations of the Cayugas, Onondagas and Oneidas.

A second opportunity to reject the "illegal" Cayuga transaction was presented by a letter from Chapin dated September 7, 1795. It read,

> A party of the Cayugas from the reservation came to me with a complaint that the western Cayugas at the late treaty sold their land from under them and crowded them into the lake, as they term it. Their complaint in the first place was that Governor Clinton had confirmed the Cayuga reservation to them that resided upon it, treaty after treaty, and that Commissioners had come forward from the same Government and purchased the whole of their reservation excepting a small piece, which is much too small to make them comfortable. Secondly, they said that...[New York State] treated with the Indians from under the British Government who were not subjects of the [United] States, that those people had taken the sole prerogative of their lands and confined them to a small tract....This they conceived to be a grievance and insisted I would make it known to you and if it could be in your power to help them in the business their minds would be more at ease.[26]

In relaying this complaint to Pickering, Captain Chapin offered no endorsement of it. Even so, his letter gave Pickering an opening to say outright that in his opinion the entire one hundred square mile reservation had not been legally sold and therefore still belonged to the Cayugas. But neither of these federal officials tried to resist the completed Cayuga land sale.

What happened at Oneida was equally contentious. Though no doubt terrified, Captain Chapin informed General Schuyler that he was violating the 1793 federal Trade and Intercourse Act. Schuyler—Revolutionary War General, U.S. Senator, father-in-law of President Washington's Treasury Secretary Alexander Hamilton and co-author of the 1790 federal Trade and Intercourse Act—begged to differ. Then in opening remarks, Schuyler endeavored to rise above the controversy. "*Brothers*, Sachems and Warriors of the Oneida Nation," he began,

> We rejoice that the great Spirit has again afforded us an opportunity to meet you our *Brethren* in health, and that peace prevails in the country. It affords us particular pleasure that our Great Council has deputed us for the benevolent purpose of trying to render the situation of our Oneida *Brethren* more comfortable and we doubt not but that the good will of the State will meet with corresponding

sentiments on your part. *Brothers,* attend: Let your ears be erect that you may distinctly hear, and settle your minds in peace....*Brothers,* we must remind you of your repeated complaints that the income from the large tract of land reserved to your use was small, and not adequate to your support, and you intreated our Great Council to take measures to render it larger and more productive. *Brothers,* whilst our Great Council was deliberating on this business, and devising the means to accomplish your desire, and to provide you a greater annual rent for your lands, Colonel Pickering by order of the President of the United States sent us a speech delivered by the Onondaga and Cayuga Nations at the treaty held last year at Canandaigua, in which those nations, as you had done to our Great Council, requested that their lands might be made more productive of an annual income. In consequence therefore of your request, and of that of the Onondagas and Cayugas transmitted by order of the President, our Great Council determined to afford the relief which was requested and passed an Act authorizing us to stipulate the payment of an annual rent for so much of the lands reserved to your use and to the use of the Onondagas and Cayugas as you or they should determine to have so appropriated and thus our Great Council substantially acquiesced in what appeared to be the intention of the President of the United States, in sending us the papers already mentioned. But they did not order us to apply for the attendance of an Agent, on the part of the United States, as they... conceived it unnecessary, having always heretofore negotiated treaties with you and with the Onondaga and Cayuga nations without the interference of Congress, as with a people residing within the known and acknowledged limits of the State of New York. But if it had been necessary, the President's message appeared to have superseded it. Then, *Brothers,* you see that Colonel Pickering has been misinformed or has misapprehended the business in supposing that Governor Clinton expected to apply for an Agent. That Governor was not authorized to make such an application, nor is the present Governor authorized to do so by the Act of the State of New York under which our power to treat with you is derived, and therefore the communications made to you by Captain Chapin ought not to impede the business of this treaty, and the accomplishment of so good an object to you as we are sent upon, and especially as we act perfectly agreeable to law.[27]

General Schuyler's assurances sufficed to avert immediate collapse of the negotiations. But a combination of Captain Chapin's warning that they should not agree to anything and dissatisfaction with the rate of remuneration offered resulted in an impasse, and Schuyler declared the talks ended and returned to Albany. After Schuyler and Chapin had both left, the Oneidas decided to sell after all, and in September a specially deputed group of Oneida chiefs traveled to Albany to contract a land sale agreement with Schuyler, on better terms than Schuyler had first offered but well below the full market value originally demanded.[28]

Each of the 1795 New York State tribal negotiations presided over by General Schuyler presented unique problems, raised by tough tribal bargainers, and all three agreements contained provisions insisted on by tribal chiefs that went beyond the Legislature's instructions. Follow-up action was therefore required, and on April 1, 1796, the New York Legislature formally approved Schuyler's handiwork. Governor Jay acquiesced, once again rejecting Pickering's view that New York State's tribal reservations should be considered "Indian lands" as that phrase was used in the 1793 federal Trade and Intercourse Act.[29] Throughout his six-year governorship, Jay supervised implementation of Schuyler's 1795 tribal transactions, which required annual appropriations.

A 1798 treaty may provide the best indicator of Jay's thinking about the applicability of the federal Trade and Intercourse Act to New York State's tribal reservations. Up to a point, events in 1798 proceeded as they had in 1795. The Oneidas sent word that they wished to sell another portion of their State reservation. Governor Jay referred the matter to the New York Legislature, which approved the Oneida request. The next day, Jay appointed three State Commissioners who quickly entered into preliminary discussions with Oneida chiefs. Then Governor Jay wrote to Pickering, who was now U.S. Secretary of State, reporting on the progress of the negotiation and requesting

> Be so obliging, sir, as to lay these representations before the President, with my request that he will be pleased to appoint a commissioner to hold the said treaty, at the time and place before mentioned....I have the honor to be, with great respect, sir, your most obedient and most humble servant, John Jay.[30]

Pickering must have been overjoyed. A federal commissioner was quickly appointed, and a federal treaty expeditiously completed.[31] Governor Jay in 1798 evidently decided that battling Pickering again wasn't worth the trouble. But no one felt it necessary to redo the 1795 Oneida land sale simply because it had not been negotiated as an application of the Constitution's federal treaty procedure.

President Washington's perspective is perhaps best summed up by his description of Governor Jay's 1795 request for federal supervision of the Mohawk treaty as "regular" and by implication New York's refusal to make such a request prior to negotiating the 1795 Oneida, Onondaga and Cayuga land sales, irregular. For Washington—eighteenth century military man—following regular procedures was the essence of civility, and the treatment of tribes was no exception. As first President under the Constitution, Washington was preoccupied on a daily basis with establishing procedures that insured the primacy of the new federal government in its relations with the old state governments. Since states enjoyed largely unchecked freedom prior to 1789, it was incumbent upon the federal government not only to articulate but to gain respect for new procedures that curtailed state freedom. This seems to have been the focal concern that motivated President Washington in his criticism of the 1795 State-tribe transactions; they might, he feared, have an adverse effect on state respect for federal authority in tribal relations. But Washington also wished to enhance tribal respect for both state and federal governments, and evidently believed a public assault on New York State would prove counter-productive. Some such calculations must have lain behind his decision to attempt to halt the New York State transactions if this could be done quietly, but to let them stand if they had already been completed.

Washington as President desired not only "regular" dealings with tribes but also harmony among his Cabinet advisers. Washington conducted his administration rather like a seminar on the brand-new, often enigmatic Constitution. Almost everyone had an opinion about what was and was not Constitutional, in these days before the Supreme Court took up questions of such moment. Washington encouraged uninhibited expressions of opinion from his diverse Cabinet regarding the appropriate relationship of the federal government to states and tribes. No mere presiding officer, Washington moreover sought synthesis incorporating elements from numerous perspectives. But where the Constitution or federal law was clear, Washington enforced it. Regarding the applicability of the Trade and Intercourse Act to state reservations, Washington saw no clarity, and consequently authorized

Secretary of War Pickering to seek further advice and proceed cautiously to explore his hypothesis, but only if this could be done non-divisively, and in a manner that would lead to a future rule that could be beneficially applied. Washington was not against expanding federal protection for tribal land rights in the manner Pickering advocated, but apparently did not feel that Pickering and Bradford had made an unanswerable legal case that such expansion was required by the federal Trade and Intercourse Act.

Washington heard no one in his administration argue that New York's State reservation transactions violated federal price guidelines, which assumed that tribes would be paid no more than one or two cents an acre for relinquishing their "Indian lands." The price paid by New York State, roughly fifty cents per acre, exceeded the prevailing federal norm many times over. Today's standard of "conscionable consideration" linked to market value payment does not originate, as courts and scholars commonly suppose, in early federal assurances of "fairness" to tribes. On January 22, 1795, Washington for example called urgently for "*fair* treaties with the savage tribes, (by this I mean, that they shall *perfectly* understand every article and clause of them, from correct and repeated interpretations)."[32] Washington's administration prided itself on offering tribes a kind of notary service intended to "prevent all deception and fraud." Tribal assent to any sale of "Indian title" land was to be openly obtained, but free tribal assent to a level of payment far below market level was presupposed because of the way in which the transaction was defined, as the sale of a "nearly worthless" hunting right to the only purchaser with whom tribes were permitted to deal. Federal willingness to accord tribes a right of occupancy to many millions of acres was conjoined to an assumption that purchasing most of this land from tribes in due course would not entail heavy expenditure.

To his first meeting with the Iroquois in November of 1790, Pickering took with him a copy of the first Trade and Intercourse Act, which he interpreted to them as

> intended for the mutual advantage of the United States and of the Indian tribes. In times past some white men have deceived the Indians; falsely pretending they had authority to lease or purchase their

> lands, and sometimes they have seized on more lands than the Indians meant to sell them; again falsely pretending that those lands were comprehended within their purchase. Such fraudulent practices have made our *brothers* angry; and sometimes occasioned hostilities, war and bloodshed. Yet Indians will always be exposed to such deception and imposition while they continue to sign and seal papers which they cannot read. Now, *Brothers*, to prevent these great evils in future, the Congress declare, That no sale of lands made by any Indians to any persons or persons, or even to any state, shall be valid, unless the same be made at some public treaty held under the authority of the United States. For at such public treaty, wise and good men will be appointed by the President to attend, to prevent all deception and fraud. These wise and good men will examine every deed before it is signed and sealed; and see that every lease or purchase of the Indians be openly and fairly made.[33]

This explication was endorsed by President Washington in remarks made to the Seneca chief Cornplanter on December 29, 1790. "For the particular meaning of this law," said Washington, "I refer you to the explanations given thereof by Colonel Timothy Pickering at Tioga." Even more clearly than Pickering, Washington stressed that federal officials could not bargain for tribes. "When you may find it your interest to sell any part of your lands," the President explained, "the United States must be present by their Agent and will be your security that you shall not be defrauded in the bargain you make.[34] Since many chiefs were illiterate, Washington thought it proper to insure they fully understood the terms of written contracts. Washington did *not* conceive it his duty to insure tribes were paid full market value for hunting lands they relinquished. Nor was this required by federal law. Only tenacious lobbying by the Iroquois and other tribes, sustained over many decades, forced a shift to the standard of "conscionable consideration" now insisted on by federal courts.

At Canandaigua in 1794, Pickering attempted to establish federal guardianship over the valuable New York State reservations of the Oneidas, Onondagas and Cayugas, as a way to help them maximize their return on these assets. But Pickering assumed that the game-based, use-right federal theory of compensation did apply to the Senecas, who still resided in "Indian Country" beyond the frontier of U.S. settlement, which then was located near Canandaigua. During bargaining sessions with the Cayugas, Onondagas and Oneidas in 1795, New York Commissioner Schuyler—who had himself devised the U.S. government's game-based payment theory for tribal land rights in 1783—didn't invoke it, because New York didn't consider it applicable to State reservation lands. Tribal rights to State reservation lands were deemed much more desirable than tribal hunting rights on the federally-protected "Indian lands" of independent tribes. The reservation-dwelling Oneidas, Onondagas and Cayugas were no longer politically independent, in the view of both Pickering and New York State. The Oneidas, Onondagas and Cayugas had therefore been assigned lands by New York as a form of "outdoor relief" for a class of State welfare "dependents." From the earliest days of seventeenth century settlement, England's colonies had assigned to needy persons tracts of land on which they could be expected to subsist. In this tradition, the Oneidas, Onondagas and Cayugas were allocated State reservations, which they might either till directly themselves or turn to monetary account in one fashion or another, by having tenants till it for them, allowing wood to be harvested on it or by leasing or selling some portion of it, either for an immediate cash payment or in return for a long-term annuity. Since it was obviously not in the State's interest to allow a permanent class of State residents to become destitute or homeless by squandering their assets, the New York Legislature placed restrictions on the ability of reservation-dwelling tribes to lease or sell these land rights. But while they required State supervision, leases and sales of portions of the tribes' reservation lands were understood by New York State to be routine events, occurring whenever these tribes needed a little cash, and (*pace* Pickering) scarcely the occasion for a federal treaty ratified by the U.S. Senate. The welfare of tribal wards was an acknowledged state responsibility, altogether unrelated to the valid federal interest in the extinguishment of aboriginal title to "Indian lands" and the transfer of such hunting grounds utilized by autonomous tribes to ordinary state jurisdiction. Pickering's eighteenth century advocacy of *federal* guardianship for tribal wards was an idea whose time had not yet come.

Perhaps most indicative of the fact that New York did not consider the State reservation lands of the Oneidas, Onondagas and Cayugas federally protected "Indian lands" was an exchange that took place between Governor Clinton and the New York Legislature in April of 1795—two months before Pickering's intervention—about the appropriate valuation of these tribal assets. The Legislature authorized Schuyler and his fellow negotiators to offer Oneidas, Onondagas and Cayugas annuities amounting to six per cent of a sum that assumed the value of the land rights to be acquired from the tribes would be four shillings an acre. The Act then further specified that after being acquired from the three tribes this land was to be sold at no less than sixteen shillings per acre. The Legislature in other words directed that these three State-protected tribes were to be paid only one quarter of the current value of the land they relinquished. Presented with this Act, New York's Council of Revision consisting of Governor Clinton, Chief Justice Robert Yates and Justice Egbert Benson pronounced it inconsistent with assurances given by the New York Legislature on February 13, 1794, that any modifications in the tribes' State reservations would be for their "sole" benefit. The Legislature's 1795 Act contemplated, in the Council's words, a "*disposition* three fourths of which at least will be for the benefit of the *State*, and consequently not a *disposition* for the sole benefit of the Indians" which was therefore "inconsistent with the *assurances*...made to the Indians by his Excellency the Governor" in 1794. Unfortunately this well-reasoned veto was overridden by a two-thirds vote in both houses of the New York Legislature.[35]

Transparently, the Governor's Council of Revision was right and the Legislature wrong. A small differential to cover handling costs might have been allowed between the price paid the tribes and the price for which their State reservation lands would be sold, but not four hundred per cent. Equally clearly, what was at issue was not the "nearly worthless" tribal hunting land then protected by federal law. New York's State reservations were assets held by needy tribes, to be sold only for their benefit. The State in supervising the sale of these restricted lands was acting as fiduciary trustee for these tribes and therefore, as affirmed by the Governor's Council of Revision, had an obligation to insure that tribes were not cheated in the transfer of their assets from land into cash. No one can argue that New York State in 1795 did well by the Oneidas, Onondagas and Cayugas. But the State's dismal performance as a trustee of tribal assets was not the issue before the Supreme Court in 1974 and 1985. In 1795, despite Pickering's assertive efforts, the federal government was not yet acting as a trustee conscientiously endeavoring to maximize the value of tribal assets. New York State in contrast was performing this role, albeit badly. It is highly ironic that the Supreme Court in 1985 should have belatedly decided to penalize New York State for its malfeasance as a fiduciary trustee of tribal assets, long before the federal government was prepared to assume any such responsibility.

In 1974, the Supreme Court held unanimously that the 1793 federal Trade and Intercourse Act applied to "Indian land" sales in New York State. In 1985, the Court then ruled that the 1795 sale of State reservation land by the Oneidas was indeed a sale of "Indian land" of the sort for which a federal treaty was required, as Secretary of War Pickering and Attorney General Bradford had futilely argued.[36] On the principle of deciding no more than is necessary to the case at hand, in 1974 the Court ruled that New York State in 1795 had not been altogether exempt from the 1793 federal Trade and Intercourse Act. Since New York State itself accepted the Act's applicability to Mohawk and Seneca land transactions, this was not a surprising decision. While certainly correct, the Court's majority Opinion in this 1974 case, written by Justice White, did however give unfortunate sanction to the now-pervasive misnomer "Nonintercourse Act" to describe the land sale section of the Trade and Intercourse Act, a misnomer which misleadingly implies that the purpose of this section was to prevent land sales, rather than to *regulate* land sales. Use of the term "Nonintercourse Act" for a section of the broader Act also suggests the separability of this section from the full Act's "Indian Country" setting, which has induced federal courts to find federally protected "Indian lands" in places far more unlikely than New York's three State reservations, which were at any rate enumerated in a federal treaty.

In 1985, the Court next decided—this time by a vote of five to four—that New York State had violated the 1793 Act by terminating Oneida rights on their State reservation without federal treaty authorization. In his Majority Opinion, Justice Powell argued, "Despite Congress's clear policy that no person or entity should purchase Indian land without the acquiescence of the federal government, in 1795 the State of New York began negotiations to buy the remainder of the Oneidas' land." To Justice Powell, the Oneidas' State reservation was without question "Indian land" within the meaning of the 1793 Act. Justice Stevens' Dissent also presupposed that "the Oneida plainly knew or should have known that they had conveyed their lands to the State of New York in violation of federal law." Like Powell, Stevens concluded that the 1795 Oneida-New York State transaction had indeed violated the 1793 Act, and merely protested the fact that litigation regarding such a very old violation had been allowed into court.[37] All nine Justices agreed that New York State had terminated Oneida land rights illegally, outside of federal procedures laid down for acquisition of "Indian land."

Like U.S. Attorney General Bradford in 1795, the Supreme Court in 1985 ignored entirely New York's theory that State reservation lands "appropriated for the use" of the Oneidas, Onondagas and Cayugas were not the kind of "Indian lands" subject to regulation by the 1793 Trade and Intercourse Act. The Court's 1985 position is in accord with modern-day federal law. But in using a retrospective legal lens, the Court missed the distinction drawn at the time by New York State, and thereby dismissed as culpably lawless conduct what was in fact part of a state-federal jurisdictional dispute resolved without litigation in New York's favor.

The strange chain of events that began in 1790 when Timothy Pickering first conferred with the Iroquois is nowhere near an end. Because he came to respect the Iroquois, and did not want to see them fade into penury as abused State wards, Pickering took up their cause. But while Pickering precipitated a Federalist-Jeffersonian crisis on their behalf, the real instigators were the Iroquois themselves, successfully reviving in new circumstances their historic strategy of finding strength in combination, and then playing off one outside force against another. When New York State's Jeffersonian Governor attempted to isolate individual tribes and establish welfare relations with each separately, the Iroquois revived their Confederacy, and lobbied persistently to establish relations with the new federal government, confident they would be better off if not wholly subordinate to any one jurisdiction.

Six

Coming to Terms in "Indian Country"

PRESIDENT WASHINGTON'S FIRST PRIORITY in tribal affairs was peace. Only after amicable treaty ties were fashioned could attention be directed to the myriad other mutual concerns of federal, state and tribal governments. Even so, by the end of his second term Washington had delineated sensible patterns for the conduct of day-to-day relations with tribes, encompassing issues ranging from absconded criminals to the fur trade.

Almost all tribes with which the federal government concerned itself resided in "Indian Country," the perimeter-bounded zone where U.S.-allied tribes might anticipate living much as they had before, making only whatever modifications in their customs they themselves came to think were in their own best interests. This understanding of "Indian Country" underlay the series of Indian Trade and Intercourse Acts passed in 1790, 1793, 1796, 1799 and 1802, as well as President Jefferson's 1803 draft of a Constitutional amendment setting aside the region of the Louisiana Purchase above the thirty-first parallel for exclusive tribal occupancy.[1] The document that spells out most elaborately what "Indian Country" meant in these pivotal decades is probably the 1795 Treaty of Greenville, which established a "general boundary line between the lands of the United States and the lands" of twelve different tribes in the federal Northwest Territory. No intertribal boundaries were specified for these twelve tribes, which were to control jointly what was termed "their country" as well as "the Indian lands." The Treaty further declared that all the various "Indian tribes who have a right to those lands, are quietly to enjoy them, hunting, planting, and dwelling thereon, so long as they please, without any molestation from the United States." The relative emphasis to be given hunting and planting was a choice for these tribes to make, because Washington's "plan of *civil*-ization" designed to shift the tribal economy away from hunting toward agriculture was a recommendation, not a requirement. The Greenville Treaty moreover provided

> if any citizen of the United States, or any other white person or persons, shall presume to settle upon the lands, now relinquished by the United States, such citizen or other person shall be out of the protection of the United States; and the Indian tribe, on whose land the settlement shall be made, may drive off the settler, or punish him in such manner as they shall think fit.

On this basis, the Greenville Treaty anticipated that "a friendly intercourse shall take place between the said United States and Indian tribes ...which will be beneficial to both parties."[2] With perfect parity, the Treaty also provided that

> for injuries done by individuals, on either side, no private revenge or retaliation shall take place; but, instead thereof, complaint shall be made by the party injured, to the other; by the said Indian tribes, or any of them, to the President of the United States, or the superintendent by him appointed; and by the superintendent, or other person appointed by the President, to the principal chiefs of the said Indians tribes, or of the tribes to which the offender belongs; and such prudent measures shall then be pursued, as shall be necessary to preserve the said peace and friendship unbroken, until the Legislature (or Great Council) of the United States shall make other equitable provision in the case, to the satisfaction of both parties. Should any Indian tribes meditate a war against the United States, or either of them, and the same shall come to the knowledge of the beforementioned tribes, or either of them, they do hereby engage to give immediate notice thereof to the general, or officer commanding the troops of the United States, at the nearest post. And should any tribe, with hostile intentions against the United States, or either of them, attempt to pass through their country, they will endeavor to prevent the same, and in like manner give information of such attempt, to the general, or officer commanding, as soon as possible, that all causes of mistrust and suspicion may be avoided between them and the United States. In like manner, the United States shall give notice to the said Indian tribes of any harm that may be meditated against them, or either of them, that shall come to their knowledge, and do all in their power to hinder and prevent the same, that the friendship between them may be uninterrupted.

These were new patterns, but most chiefs were more than willing to make adjustments in tribal ways of life, so long as federal officials for their part acknowledged the importance to tribes of maintaining the greatest possible tribal autonomy consistent with prevailing conditions.

Perhaps the most astute early advocate of U.S.-tribal coexistence was U.S. Colonel Louis Atayataghronghta, the talented French Catholic Mohawk chief, who discovered to his regret that most Revolutionary leaders—even Washington—did not accord tribal rights high priority, and would not necessarily safeguard tribal interests if not compelled by tribes to do so. In 1788, frustrated by being whipsawed for years between the Continental Congress and New York State, Atayataghronghta told New York's Governor Clinton,

> *Brother* Governor! You counseled us to industry and care, so that thereby we might be made happy in the enjoyment of our country, and not be going out here and there, and wanting everything. But *Brother*, what shall we do? You have the control of our land, although it is said to be ours. Had you given us a writing to confirm it as our property, as the French Governor used to do, we should have been in the quiet enjoyment of it.[3]

Having grown up under French colonial rule, Atayataghronghta knew what was admirable about the old French imperial and inadequate in the new Revolutionary way of dealing with Native American land rights. In the initial post-Revolutionary system, even U.S. Army officers were obliged to fight again for their lands, simply because they were tribal Native Americans, while white veterans were awarded bounties of land seized from tribes.

In 1796, Atayataghronghta laid out these guidelines:

> Let justice take place betwixt you and us, in place of arbitrary power: for that, *brothers*, you very well know, is a thing that never gave contentment to any people or nation whatsoever.... Formerly we enjoyed the privilege we expect is now called freedom and liberty; but, since the acquaintance with our *brother* white people, that which we call freedom and liberty becomes an entire stranger to us; and in place of that comes in flattery and deceit, to deprive poor ignorant people of their properties, and bring them to poverty and, at last, to become beggars and laughing stocks to the world.
>
> *Brothers*: This is what we have already seen; but, however, we wish never to reflect on what is past, but trust in the Great Spirit that made us all to so order it that justice may take place, and that better is to come....We pray you to take this matter into good consideration, and do by us as you would wish to be done by.... that every *brother* might have their rights throughout this continent, and all to be of one mind, and to live together in peace and love, as becometh *brothers*; and to have a chain

> of friendship made between you and us, too strong ever to be broke, and polished and brightened so pure as never to rust.
>
> *Brothers:* We wish, likewise, to enjoy our own laws, and you yours, so far that, if any of our people, Indians, should commit a crime to any of their *brothers*, the white people of the United States, that he may be punished by his own nation, and his chiefs to make good all damages; and likewise on the other part, if any white person should commit a crime to any Indian, that we, the Indians, are not to take revenge on the person but to resign him up to justice, and there let him be punished according to the laws of his nation.[4]

Colonel Atayataghronghta remained nostalgic for the "good old days" under French rule prior to 1763, but considered the Revolutionary Americans at least preferable to the imperial British, and working out a future basis for peace distinctly preferable to lamenting the past. In 1796, the Colonel's Saint Regis Mohawk tribe occupied (as they still do occupy) land on the southern shore of the Saint Lawrence River where the international U.S.-Canada border shifts from following the Saint Lawrence to being the 45th parallel, which therefore arbitrarily divides this tribal territory in two. With one foot in the United States, the other in Canada, the Colonel's community was more than willing to come to terms with the United States if tribal autonomy, mobility, and commercially vital international ties were secured.

Washington's administration acknowledged these concerns in its treaties with tribes, and in non-tribal treaties with Great Britain signed November 19, 1794, concerning the northern U.S. border, and with Spain signed October 27, 1795, concerning the southern U.S. border. Both these borders ran through "Indian Country" and both treaties took note of the fact that tribes engaged in international trade. The Treaty negotiated by Thomas Pinckney with Spain provided for example that

> The two high contracting parties shall by all the means in their power maintain peace and harmony among the several Indian nations who inhabit the country adjacent to the...boundaries of the two Floridas; and...both parties oblige themselves expressly to restrain by force all hostilities on the part of the Indian nations living within their boundaries: so that Spain will not suffer her Indians to attack the citizens of the United States, nor the Indians inhabiting their territory; nor will the United States permit these last mentioned Indians to commence

Peace Medal, 1792. In this Washington-era medal (pierced so that it could be worn in the manner of the "half-moon" gorget depicted), a tribal chief has dropped his war tomahawk and hands a peace pipe to a U.S. military officer. Cultivated fields exemplify the future that the officer will suggest to the chief. Courtesy, National Museum of the American Indian.

> hostilities against the subjects of his Catholic Majesty, or his Indians....
> And...in future no treaty of alliance or other whatever (except treaties of peace) shall be made by either party with the Indians living within the boundary of the other; but both parties will endeavor to make the advantages of the Indian trade common and mutually beneficial to their respective subjects and citizens observing in all things the most complete reciprocity.

While tribal chiefs might defer to the federal government's desire to curb tribal war-making across international borders, chiefs also insisted on military autonomy within U.S. "Indian Country." In 1802, Creek chief Efau Hadjo explained to federal officials what this implied for relations among the major southern tribes:

> There are four nations of us. If we should fall out, quarrel, and dispute about anything, you must look upon them as two *children* quarreling and fighting....It may be some years before any disturbances and quarreling may take place, or it may be more. If we should quarrel, you, our white friends and *brothers*, are to be neutral, and not to interfere on either side. There is, among us four nations, old customs, one of which is war. The young have grown up to manhood; if they want to practice the ways of the old people, let them try themselves at war, and when they are tired, let the micoes, as they all have such, interpose and stop it; we want you to let us alone.[5]

This same year, a visitor encountered Efau Hadjo

> mounted on a small...horse about twelve hands and a half high. His dress consisted of a linen shirt, a pair of blue cloth trousers with yellow and scarlet flaps sewed down the outward seams: over this he had an old full-dress uniform of the English footguards. The lace very much tarnished; a very large tye-ing on his head, one ditto gold-laced uniform hat, cumberland-cocked; a large gorget round his neck; a sword, in a belt hung over his shoulders; a tomahawk and scalping-knife in his girdle; rings in his nose and ears; his face and breast which was quite open, painted various colors, and a musket on his shoulder.[6]

The U.S. official with whom Efau Hadjo routinely dealt was former U.S. Senator Benjamin Hawkins. For a variety of reasons, personal as well as patriotic, Hawkins decided in 1796 to accept President Washington's request that he become Agent in charge of federal relations with all tribes south of the Ohio River. Later Agent only to the Creeks, Hawkins continued in this capacity until his death in 1816. For twenty years Washington's "man in Indian Country," Hawkins more than any other individual made U.S.-tribal collaboration viable.

Washington and Hawkins didn't always agree, but Washington had a genius for enlisting in national service highly motivated persons with whom he managed to work effectively even when they differed. In 1792, Hawkins had for example opposed sending troops against tribes in the Ohio region. Writing confidentially to the President, Senator Hawkins earnestly reminded him that during the Revolutionary War tribes had been called *brothers*, and "assured...that when success crowned our efforts they should be partakers of our good fortune: They were then acknowledged to be the possessors of the soil on which they lived." Yet

> At the close of the war, being anxiously desirous of paying...our officers and soldiers...we seem to have forgotten altogether the rights of the Indians. They were treated as tenants at will, we seized on their lands, and made a division of the same as possessing allodial rights [i.e., underlying fee title], allotted certain portions to the Indians for hunting ground, and did not even think of offering them compensation for any claims they might pretend to have to those reserved for other purposes of the government. This doctrine it might be expected would be disliked by the independent tribes. It was so, and was complained of by them.

Because of tribal pressure, the tribes' "boundaries were recognized and established by a *principle of purchase*." Even so, reasoned Hawkins, tribes remained mistrustful of U.S. intentions, and this suspiciousness underlay the current troubles with tribes northwest of the Ohio. Would it not therefore be prudent, he concluded, to make one more friendly overture to these tribes?[7]

In an animated response to the would-be peacemaker, Washington questioned whether the motivation of tribes then on the warpath was as defensible as Hawkins seemed to feel. Were they genuinely in need of reassurance or merely attracted by opportunities to ravage and loot? "May it not rather be said, that while they could war with impunity, they were better pleased, and found it more profitable to plunder, than to hunt." Be that as it may, Washington bluntly informed Hawkins, the time for soul-searching was long past: "We are involved in actual war!"[8]

As their 1792 exchange of views indicated, tribal policy was only one of Washington's worries, whereas for Senator Hawkins stabilizing tribal relations was of paramount concern. To his credit, Washington found ways to take constructive advantage of Hawkins' energy and idealism. When Hawkins was defeated for re-election to the Senate in 1794, in part because he incurred the wrath of frontier constituents by his solicitude for tribal rights, Washington courageously commissioned him to negotiate a new treaty with the Creeks to replace the 1790 Treaty which Georgia had declared un-Constitutional, provoking the Creeks to repudiate it as well.

Just as he had in 1785 on behalf of the Continental Congress, Hawkins politely invited Georgia to attend the 1796 federal-Creek treaty to be held at Colerain. Georgia did send the requested representatives, along with a large contingent of militiamen who sailed up the Saint Marys River to the treaty site in a ship named *Fair Play*. "The people of this State are very thick settled," maintained a Georgia spokesman,

> and on the Oconee they are in such numbers that they have not land enough to maintain their families. They are like a river, so very full that its bank cannot contain it, so that it overflows the neighboring grounds. They must go somewhere to settle.

The combined slave and free population in Georgia counties at this time was less than ten persons per square mile. But the Creeks, with a population of 20,000 and a territory ranging some four hundred miles east-to-west and two hundred miles north-to-south above the Spanish Florida line, possessed more than four square miles of land per person. Overcrowding in eastern Georgia was (in a word) relative. The pressure that Georgians felt unable to control was determination to expand, not simply to "maintain their families." Hawkins believed Georgia would be better off if its population remained consolidated. And Creek rights had to be respected. After the Colerain negotiations, Hawkins sternly notified the Governor of Georgia, "The expectations formed by your State...are frustrated." Moreover, he warned, unless Georgians modified their unruly conduct, future "attempts to acquire land...by fair and open purchase, will be ineffectual." Georgia's militiamen sailed home aboard the *Fair Play* empty-handed.[9]

At Colerain, Hawkins respected Creek desires and resisted Georgia's machinations, convinced he was doing what President Washington wanted done. Indeed Hawkins' failure to acquire additional Creek land in 1796 was described by Washington in his Eighth Annual Message to Congress as a confirmation of his policy rather than as a setback. Washington reported that

> The meeting of the deputies from the Creek Nation at Colerain, in the State of Georgia, which had for a principal object the purchase of a parcel of their land, by that State, broke up without its being accomplished; the Nation having, previous to their departure, instructed them against making any sale; the occasion however has been improved, to confirm by a new Treaty with the Creeks, their pre-existing engagements with the United States.

Washington in other words affirmed that the Creeks in declining to sell had acted within their rights, and portrayed as appropriate Hawkins' conduct in acquiescing. Washington emphasized that the frontier was roiled at least as much by the provocations of U.S. citizens as by the vagaries of "savage" tribes. Preserving peace required that care be

> taken to guard on the one hand, our advanced settlements from the predatory incursions of those unruly individuals, who cannot be restrained by their tribes, and on the other hand, to protect the rights secured to the Indians by treaty.[10]

First among these treaty rights was undisturbed use of their lands; yet, confided the President to Edmund Pendleton, tribes

> are very much irritated by the continual pressure of land speculators and settlers on one hand; and by the impositions of unauthorized, and unprincipled traders (who rob them in a manner of their hunting) on the other. Nothing but the strong arm of the Union, or in other words, energetic laws, can correct these abuses; but here! jealousies, and prejudices (from which I apprehend more fatal consequences to this government than from any other source) aided by local situations, and perhaps by interested considerations, always oppose themselves to efficient measures.[11]

Moreover, Washington warned Congress in 1795,

> the provisions heretofore made with a view to the protection of the Indians, from the violence of the lawless part of our frontier inhabitants are insufficient. It is demonstrated that these violences can now be perpetrated with impunity. And it can need no argument to prove, that unless the murdering of Indians can be restrained, by bringing the murderers to condign punishment, all the exertions of the government to prevent destructive retaliations, by the Indians, will prove fruitless; and all our present agreeable prospects illusory.[12]

Orderly frontier settlement could not be anticipated while

> our citizens, in violation of law and justice, are guilty of the offences I have mentioned, and are carrying on unauthorized expeditions against them; and when, for the most atrocious murders, even those of whom we have the least cause of complaint, a jury on the frontiers can hardly be got to listen to a charge, much less to convict a culprit.[13]

Washington's personal engagement with these questions was clearly evidenced by his appointments of Hawkins to be Treaty Commissioner, and then Agent. In 1783, General Washington had questioned the practice of employing agents among the tribes. British agents were notoriously corrupt, Washington noted, and a "recurrence of the conduct of these people" seemed all too probable.[14] Hawkins was one of the five members of Congress to whom General Washington addressed this warning, and thirteen years later Hawkins may well have recalled it when he accepted President Washington's invitation to demonstrate personally that U.S. Agents could improve upon the bad British example.

Despite their occasional differences, Hawkins and Washington were in such fundamental agreement about the need for honorable treatment of tribes that the President could speak of Hawkins as a person doing a job he would under other circumstances have been happy to do himself. Introducing Hawkins as his "general or principal Agent...for the four southern nations" in a letter to the Cherokees dated August 29, 1796, Washington explained, "I have chosen him for this office because he is esteemed for a good man; has a knowledge of Indian customs, and a particular love and friendship for all the Southern tribes." Washington then confided,

> What I have recommended to you I am myself going to do. After a few moons are passed I shall leave the great town and retire to my farm. There I shall attend to the means of increasing my cattle, sheep and other useful animals; to the growing of corn, wheat, and other grain, and to the employing of women in spinning and weaving; all which I have recommended to you, that you may be as comfortable and happy as plenty of food, clothing and other good things can make you.[15]

The 1790 appointment of Alexander McGillivray as U.S. Agent to his own Creek nation had not been a success. The next U.S. Agent to the Creeks, James Seagrove, resided in coastal Georgia and during his one

Tallassee Mico. Pencil sketch by John Trumbull, 1790. Fordham University Library. Photo, Courtesy Frick Art Reference Service.

extended visit to Tuckabatchee on the Tallapoosa River managed to annoy the chiefs so thoroughly that the Tallassee Mico sent a raiding party to harass him. Seagrove was "run out of his bed from a young Indian lady he had had with him" and obliged to flee "into a pond of water." After the Tallassee Mico's men left laden with loot, Seagrove's "lady with a torch of light-wood in one hand and his breeches in the other went to look for him, and at last found him almost perished to death with cold."[16]

Hawkins was confident he could advance U.S.-Creek understanding more effectively than either of his predecessors. But like them, Hawkins found the unpredictable Tallassee Mico a resourceful adversary. The two first conferred—and disagreed—during Continental Congress treaty negotiations in 1785. Out of step with McGillivray because he preferred to cooperate with Georgia traders, the Tallassee Mico had then joined McGillivray in approving the 1790 Treaty of New York, probably because by its terms the federal government permitted the continuation of Creek trade to Europe through a Georgia port. But the war chief of Tallassee never lost his love of provocation, as he would demonstrate again many times until he was finally slain in 1813 fighting General Andrew Jackson.

Like McGillivray, the Tallassee Mico saw little merit in unilateral Creek adoption of Washington's "plan of *civil*-ization" until the United States itself became more *civil.* Washington and Hawkins conceded this point, and worked hard to promote societal compatibility by encouraging *civil*-ization on both sides of the line separating "Indian Country" from U.S. settlements. The best way forward, in the opinion of both the President and his Agent, was through face-to-face exchanges between leaders in tribal and U.S. societies, epitomized by the meeting between McGillivray and Washington that Hawkins helped arrange. Popular animosities could be dealt with by leaders encouraging the educable and restraining the incorrigible on each side. Having devoted so much thought and effort to reforming their own central government to facilitate this process, both Washington and Hawkins believed they could be helpful in making tribal governments more progressive as well.

The Creek Confederacy of more than fifty towns was dominated by five or six large towns, notably Coweta and Cusseta among the Lower Creeks, and Efau Hadjo's Tuckabatchee and the Tallassee Mico's Tallassee among the Upper Creeks. The Confederacy's Presiding Chief came normally from one of these principal towns. Being a young chief from a smaller town, Alexander McGillivray in the 1780s was ineligible to become Presiding Chief of the Creek National Council, and therefore had established an ad hoc national executive of his own invention. Bypassing town micos, he urged town head warriors to take orders directly from him. As Caleb Swan, a 1791 visitor, put it, McGillivray

> effected a total revolution in one of their most ancient customs, by placing the warriors in all cases over the micos....The micos resisted this measure...until, finding the Georgians aimed at them indiscriminately

> ...they dropped their internal disputes, and united all their efforts, under the great chief, against the frontiers.[17]

But McGillivray's innovations died with him, and Creek recollections of them may have complicated Efau Hadjo's more modest efforts to centralize authority with Hawkins' backing.

Under Efau Hadjo, the Creek National Council met only when specially summoned to discuss matters beyond the power of clans and towns, for example to "punish great delinquents, regulate internal policy [or] form plans for hunting or war the ensuing season....All propositions are debated until they are agreed to or postponed," recorded Hawkins; "the agreement is called the will of the nation."[18]

The National Council was summoned by announcing the "Broken Days." A bundle of twigs was dispatched by messenger to town chiefs. Each day thereafter, "One of the sticks is thrown away at sunrise, to the last which is the day appointed." Council sessions were inaugurated by imbibing *White* (what whites called Black) Drink, after which the Creeks would deliberate continuously, talking, sleeping, eating and drinking in and around the meeting ground until consensus was achieved. "The Council, when convened, sit night and day," Hawkins explained;

> the public buildings is their place of lodging as well as business, and they debate as much in the night as in the day. They lie down when they are sleepy; when hungry they eat; and when anything important is under debate they attend to it.

During one such Council session, Hawkins reported, "we have Black Drink and talks during the day, and dancing at night. I go to bed about twelve and rise pretty early; the remainder of the time is claimed by the Indians." The Creeks accorded Hawkins the privilege to "enter and speak when he pleases," though not to remain "constantly in the Council during their sitting." Hawkins reciprocated by contributing quantities of supplies: "The Agent furnishes beef, corn, beans, and salt," he reported proudly, "and the town where the Council meets, furnishes butchers, cooks, and waiters." These may have included Creek-owned African American slaves; Efau Hadjo personally owned five.[19]

Hawkins believed that in time the Creeks' National Council could become an entirely adequate legislative assembly. Building on existing strength, he encouraged improvements similar to those recommended to the Cherokees by President Washington in 1796:

> The wise men of the United States [wrote Washington] meet together once a year, to consider what will be for the good of all their people. The wise men of each separate state also meet together once or twice every year, to consult and do what is good for the people of their respective states. I have thought that a meeting of your wise men once or twice a year would be alike useful to you. Every town might send one or two of its wisest counselors to talk together on the affairs of your nation, and to recommend to your people whatever they should think would be serviceable.[20]

To further parallel reforms among the Creeks, Hawkins made discreet efforts to encourage the chiefs to enhance the regularity and predictability of their proceedings. He hoped for example that a more definite system of voting and representation could be established, and informed President Jefferson in 1801 that "The number of deputies who attend" could not currently be "restrained to a given number," but that gradually a convention was developing that a proper representation was no more than "five or six from a town." He similarly urged holding annual meetings at fixed times, and that the council adopt a few "general regulations" which might be enforced by an appointed executive. When Hawkins arrived in 1796, no authority could make decisions in the intervals between National Council sessions, and unanimity offered the only security that a decision would be carried out. Even when war was declared, each town had to agree to send its warriors with the rest. On the other hand, as Efau Hadjo countered with gentle sarcasm, "when we do make a law we believe we can execute it."[21]

Hawkins also sought to divert annuity payments being made to individual town chiefs into a national treasury which "would enable them to do justice to those who faithfully exerted themselves for the honor and interests of their country." Efau Hadjo responded by accepting the full amount "on behalf of the nation" and then dividing it among the towns. Hawkins enjoyed better success in promoting a more modest change, by which towns were grouped into regional "classes" with "a warrior over each class, denominated the warrior of the nation."[22] Such comprehensible changes in their inherited institutions, innovations that were thoroughly discussed and amicably agreed upon, were not opposed just because they were advocated by the U.S. Agent, who was obviously trying hard to reform the behavior of his own countrymen as well.

Most Creeks felt no need for a more centralized government because within their own society informal controls were highly developed. The Creek tradition was intensely participatory, and every able-bodied male Creek was expected at one time or another to function as an enforcer. While growing up, a Creek boy would often be scratched with snake teeth or other sharp objects to accustom him to the sight of blood on his body. Two small boys who "sneaked under the peach trees and knocked green peaches down with a stick" were for example punished by their father who held each boy upside down by the feet with one hand, while scratching him with pine sticks held between the fingers of the other hand "from the stomach...to the sole of his feet until he was covered with blood." After the boys' "bad blood" had been purged, "the blood was washed off with cold water."[23]

Whether to defend the honor of his extended family, town or nation, a male Creek was expected to fight throughout his active life. Even when far from home, a lone warrior would be greeted with a request to name his town and clan. The forests of "Indian Country" were free for all to roam in, but if a warrior did misbehave, his kin would suffer. At any time a raiding party could be dispatched to punish his relatives, even if he successfully absconded. Since every clan contained members able to inflict vengeance, no resort to national authority was presumed necessary to deal with ordinary crimes. Adultery for example was "punished by the family or tribe of the husband. They collect, consult and decree." Although the Creeks considered pre-marital "fornication as a *faux pas* or venial crime at most" both persons involved in an adultery were severely punished. "If the proof is clear," Hawkins recounted, family members would go in search of the adulterers,

> beat them severely with sticks, and then crop them. They cut off the hair of the woman, which they carry to the square in triumph. If they apprehend but one of the offenders, and the other escapes, they then go and take satisfaction from the nearest relation. If both offenders escape, and the tribe or family returns home, and lay down the sticks, the crime is satisfied.[24]

This was deliberately ferocious, so quarreling really would end when the sticks were laid down.

Adultery as well as many other crimes could also be "satisfied in another way, if the parties offending absent themselves till the Booske-tau is over." The Creeks permitted extended family retaliation for family injuries only if completed before the annual Boosketau or Festival of the New Corn. "This happy institution," exulted Hawkins,

> ...restores man to himself, to his family and to his nation. It is a general amnesty, which not only absolves the Indians from all crimes, murder only excepted, but seems to bury guilt itself in oblivion.[25]

In Creek understanding, individuals literally belonged to their extended families, which were self-interested groups that could take revenge on other extended families without damage to the nation. The perpetrator's motive made little difference to the victim or the victim's family; what mattered when a crime was committed was not whether the culprit planned to cause injury but that an imbalance had been created. As a child of the Enlightenment, Hawkins deplored such vengeance-based punishment, and imagined that a rational government ruling over a society of discrete individuals could be rendered both disinterested and discriminating in the punishment of crime. If all crimes were considered injuries to society, motive might be impartially weighed by courts which could consider the character and motives of each criminal and devise punishments designed to educate rather than simply inflict equivalent loss.

In defense of Creek justice, Efau Hadjo explained to Hawkins how he dealt with an incident in which "two promising boys were playing and slinging stones. One of them let slip his sling, the stone flew back and killed his companion." Relatives of the boy who had been killed seized his hapless friend, determined to bury them both in the same grave. "I took the uncles to my house," Efau Hadjo recalled,

> raised their spirits with a little rum, and told them, the boy was a fine boy, and would be useful to us in our town, when he became a man; that he had no ill will against the dead one; the act was purely accidental; that...taking away his life would not give it to the other. The two uncles, after some reflection, told me, as you have advised us, so we will act; he shall not die, it was an accident.[26]

In such cases involving Creek against Creek, traditional patterns moderated by thoughtful leaders still made sense. Trouble resulted when Creek retaliatory procedures were extended to U.S. citizens. In Creek reckoning, special courage was displayed when a Creek abducted wrong-doers or their relations (including women and children) from their own homes, since this could be done only by invading hostile territory. U.S. women and children thus abducted were considered by the Creeks to be the "property of the captor and his family." Hawkins arranged for the return of a number of these captives by compensating their Creek captors. Other U.S. citizens, some of whom had been with the Creeks for many years, declined to be ransomed. Carried off as "a prisoner from Georgia when about eleven or twelve years old," Hannah Hales had "married the head man" of one of the smaller Upper Creek towns and borne him five children. The family had "some property ...one Negro boy, a horse or two, sixty cattle, and some hogs." Hawkins satisfied himself that Hannah Hales had truly "made her election...to reside in the nation" and presented her with a spinning wheel and loom.[27]

What happened to Hannah Hales years earlier was not supposed to happen under President Washington's policies, according to which each nation was to be responsible for punishing its own members for crimes committed against persons of the other nation. In theory, each nation would also be free to punish its own malefactors according to its own laws or customs. In practice, tensions developed because of national differences in defining just punishment. In 1799 for example, a U.S. surveying team arrived to demarcate the northern border of Spanish Florida, as defined by the 1795 Pinckney Treaty between the United States and Spain. The value of marking with blazed trees, stones and earthen mounds that sector of the U.S.-Spanish border running through the Creek nation was at best questionable, and the Creeks liked neither the line nor the team marking it, headed by surveyor Andrew Ellicott who had just finished laying out the District of Columbia.

Hawkins considered Ellicott's equipage top-heavy: his flatirons alone totaled one hundred fifty pounds, and in all it took "four horses to move Mr. Ellicott's washerwoman." The Creek National Council debated urging the Spaniards to halt Ellicott. Meanwhile the Tallassee

Mico took direct action. His warriors advanced at sundown to within two hundred yards of Ellicott's camp proclaiming, according to Ellicott, "their object was to plunder the camp, scatter the people, and let them go home what way they pleased." Summoned to deal with this crisis, Hawkins advanced to within twenty yards of the Creek marauders and announced that if the Tallassee Mico's "party presumed to march one step nearer, it should be instantly fired on." Menacing exchanges continued well into the night, when Hawkins finally returned to camp with assurances that no plundering would be attempted prior to the resumption of talks in the morning. Instead, recounted Ellicott,

> The hostile Indians kept moving about in small parties the whole night.... They threw down the contractor's bullock pen, and let his cattle out, and opened the pen which contained the Spanish horses, and haltered four of them; but were driven off with but two. Three of the horses belonging to my party broke loose, and ran without the camp, and though every exertion was made to bring them back, they were mounted by some Indians, who rode off on them.

When the night marauders also failed to show up in the morning for the promised discussions, Ellicott "thought it best to retreat" to a small schooner moored in the Gulf of Mexico. But during the night, as he next discovered, the schooner's sails had been methodically "cut to pieces, and the running rigging carried away." No one had been killed or apparently even injured but, "The master and other persons on board had been robbed of all their clothing, even their handkerchiefs from their necks and heads." Also taken were "twelve or fifteen guns which wanted repairing, a case of claret, a small quantity of brandy, a chest of axes with other tools, and a few blankets." Ellicott managed to limp away in this maimed vessel, and the boundary line project was abandoned.[28]

Hawkins felt he must insist on severe retribution for the discomfiture suffered by the nation's most prominent surveyor. In response to Hawkins' demand for appropriate punishment, the Creek National Council conferred at length and finally singled out not the Tallassee Mico but a lesser perpetrator named Mankiller. As the chiefs reported back to Hawkins in due course, "We pulled down and set fire to his house, we beat him with sticks until he was on the ground as a dead man." They then presented the sticks to Hawkins, explaining it was customary among the Creeks "when they punish any people to do it with sticks; and then to send them to those interested in the punishment." Accentuating the positive, Hawkins thanked the chiefs for their attention to his demand, but also expressed the hope that Mankiller's pursuit and execution might be viewed as a public rather than partisan act. Hawkins offered the chiefs this friendly advice:

> If the sticks are used by the Law of the whole nation and a man dies, it is the Law that killed him, it is the nation who killed him. If anyone complains and asks for satisfaction, this is your answer: Your relation was a rogue and a mischief maker, the Law says such people must have the sticks, and that is their pay....It is the pay of the nation.[29]

As a student of the traditional Creek attitudes and practices he was attempting to modify, Hawkins understood that unless accepted as impartial enforcement of justice, the National Council's action could be considered an unprovoked assault needing to be itself avenged.

Reluctantly or not, the chiefs often obliged when Hawkins requested that they pursue Creeks who had assaulted U.S. citizens, though it was sometimes unclear whether in doing so they were trying to implement justice in a new way or using Hawkins' requests as excuses to settle old scores. Then in the spring of 1802 a revealing incident occurred. After a U.S. citizen was murdered by a Creek, warriors went in pursuit of the culprit. They returned to inform Hawkins that they had been unable to capture the murderer because he had been "concealed and protected," and inquired whether it would be acceptable since the actual murderer was "out of reach" to give "according to the Indian rule, one of the family, a bad man and somewhat instrumental in his escape." The chiefs explained that "this man is now here, and can be executed immediately" but admitted that they made this offer "with some apprehension from the doctrine of Colonel Hawkins on guilt and innocence, that it will not be approved of." As an alternative, they proposed keeping the murderer's relative "closely confined in iron" meanwhile announcing that he had been killed in retribution for the U.S. man's murder. The real murderer would then feel free to reveal himself, whereupon "they will put him to death." By this plan, punishment would be inflicted on the individual culprit and not simply on a member of his family. As for himself, Hawkins replied, he was "a man of plain dealing and despise[d] duplicity." But he appreciated the effort of the chiefs to depart from strict extended family accountability, and was prepared to accept the ploy.[30]

By virtue of the 1796 Treaty of Colerain, the Creeks possessed the right to seize and punish all U.S. intruders into Creek territory, but as a courtesy the chiefs authorized Hawkins to deal with U.S. citizens and slaves who committed crimes in Creek territory. As Hawkins informed President Jefferson in 1806, he could "dispense justice among white and black people according to the authority vested in me by" the Creek chiefs. He had for example recently sentenced "two white men, part of a banditti forming in this quarter to live by theft" who had been found guilty of "stealing a valuable mare from a traveler...to receive twenty lashes each on their bare backs, which was carried into effect publicly."[31]

In one case believed to be "the first known in this land" a U.S. slave who caused the death of a Creek woman was allowed by his white master to be tried by the Creeks. After what Hawkins deemed a "fair trial" the slave

> was condemned to die, and executed the same day. The order being given for his execution, the warriors took him to the river bank, the brother of the deceased knocked him down with a stake, stabbed him and threw his body into the river.[32]

Nevertheless, all too often U.S. culprits succeeded in escaping from Creek territory. Once when a Creek hunter was "shot through the body and robbed of the property at his camp by a white man" the Creek victim came to Hawkins and "stated the injury received and property lost which was verified by his companions, all red men." After conferring with the victim's town elders, who vouched for his character, Hawkins sought through U.S. channels to bring the perpetrator to justice in Georgia. But since the testimony of Native Americans was not acceptable as evidence in the State courts of Georgia, Hawkins was eventually informed that a charge could not be brought "for want of *legal proof.*" So Hawkins paid the Creek victim compensation out of federal funds at his disposal.[33]

In earlier days, a Creek raiding party would have gone straight to the white perpetrator's Georgia home and carried off him or a family member, as had been done with Hannah Hales. Hawkins hoped to halt not only such retributive border-crossings by Creek avengers but even casual border-crossings by Creek hunters. Hawkins supplied "tickets to all the hunters who will be on the frontiers of Georgia. They are in parties each with a chief to be answerable for their good conduct." One year Hawkins gave such tickets to "twenty-eight parties, numbered from one to twenty-eight."

U.S. citizens were meanwhile refusing to keep within *their* bounds. Even where the border was a major river such as the Ocmulgee, U.S. citizens persisted in "building fish traps...hunting with dogs, cutting cedar and other timber...on the Indian side of the Ocmulgee." An imitation of Creek-style retributive justice was even practiced by some U.S. citizens. As Tennessee Territorial Governor William Blount lamely explained in 1792, when a U.S. citizen believed that a horse had been stolen and driven into tribal territory,

> The only thing I can do is to give passports to the sufferers to go into...[tribal territory] in search of their horses....It is a subject on which the whites are very sore, and with difficulty restrain themselves from taking what they call satisfaction, that is, from killing some of the Indians.[34]

The working relationship developed by Hawkins and Efau Hadjo nonetheless enabled them to resolve many controversies resulting from such frontier frictions. To reduce their frequency, Hawkins and Efau Hadjo both favored stationing U.S. troops on the border, to ward off intruders and allow the Creeks time to introduce needed changes in their institutions of government. As Efau Hadjo put it,

> the heads of the white people, who can govern their people, should take the necessary precautions on their part, to keep their young people in bounds, and we will do the same on our part, as well as we can.

Specifically, Efau Hadjo advocated stationing U.S. troops "on our frontiers; and that there may be horsemen as well as foot, to repress the evil doing, as well of my own people, as the white people."[35]

Such a federal border patrol had been proposed as early as 1789 by Secretary of War Henry Knox, who advised President Washington that "The angry passions of the frontier Indians and whites are too easily inflamed by reciprocal injuries, and are too violent to be controlled by the feeble authority of the civil power." Washington was skeptical, believing "scarcely anything short of a Chinese wall, or a line of troops, will restrain land jobbers, and the encroachment of settlers upon the Indian territory." Though not averse to turning federal guns on citizens of the United States, Washington knew a line of troops (not to mention a Chinese-style Great Wall) was far beyond the financial capabilities of the fledgling federal executive. Because "people have got impatient," Washington concluded, the federal government could not even if it wanted "stop the road" west, but might honorably "mark the way."

Following up this hint of flexibility, Knox recommended stationing a total of five hundred federal troops in small outposts scattered along the border.

> By this arrangement...the Indians would be convinced of the justice and good intentions of the United States, and they would soon learn to venerate and obey that power from whom they derived security against the avarice and injustice of lawless frontier people.

To do nothing at all, Knox argued, would be a mistake because

> The Indian tribes can have no faith in...imbecile promises, and the lawless whites will ridicule a government which shall, on paper only, make Indian treaties, and regulate Indian boundaries.[36]

Unlike Efau Hadjo however, Knox proposed that these garrisons "be without the limits of jurisdiction of any individual state, and within the territory assigned to the Indians." Even federal troops, he feared, would be subject to strong pressure from their fellow citizens if stationed among them to restrain them. Hawkins was also concerned about bonds of sympathy between federal border guards and frontier whites but believed posting troops within tribal territory instead of enhancing their discipline by isolation as Knox hoped would only make these troops more dangerous. Like Efau Hadjo, Hawkins urged stationing a border force "not in their country but in our own; as long as we attempt to go into their country or to remain there, we shall be at war." Professional soldiers, Hawkins reasoned, would suppose their careers benefitted by war, and identify with bellicose frontier politicians.[37]

As it turned out, Knox's view prevailed. At Colerain in 1796, Hawkins was assigned the task of persuading the Creeks to accept a federal garrison on their soil, and under pressure the Creeks reluctantly agreed. A tract on the Oconee River five miles square was placed under U.S. jurisdiction with the understanding that title would revert to the Creeks if and when the base was abandoned.[38] In addition to its federal troop contingent, Fort Wilkinson housed a federal trade goods depot, part of the federal effort launched in 1796 to woo tribes away from British and Spanish traders. Concerned lest any federal involvement in trade be seen as an unfair intervention in free U.S. enterprise, Congress imposed such severe limits on federally-operated trading houses that they had little chance of becoming profitable or even effective. Trade goods sought by Creek hunters in exchange for their deerskins could be requisitioned only from federal headquarters in Philadelphia, and Fort Wilkinson's local depot manager also had to ship all skins acquired back to Philadelphia even when higher prices for them could be secured in Savannah. The federal tribal trading operation exemplified all the classic failings of state-run commerce—without captive consumers. Rates were better and goods more plentiful in Spanish Pensacola. In 1799, Creek chiefs scornfully asked Hawkins "how you expected to get skins for goods when you had no powder? how you expected to trade with Indians if you had no powder, salt, blankets or flints?"[39]

Nor was this the only problem. On August 22, 1798, Edward Price, manager of the federal depot at Fort Wilkinson, wrote woefully to Hawkins from a Georgia jail. "I am in the custody of the Sheriff of this County at the fort of J.W. Devereaux," he lamented, "for a [U.S. depot] debt sworn to be upwards of $1300." Price later informed the Secretary of War,

> I hardly ever pass the lines to Georgia but what I am arrested. I was dragged to the County jail [in] the hottest weather...and put in a dungeon of the place with only a hole of communication with the surrounding atmosphere which I was obliged to stand up with my mouth to or be in danger of suffocation from the effluvia of filth from within—this on the oath of a man who was in debt to us on this side.[40]

Georgia harassment of federal trading operations was aggravated by the presence of U.S. troops in Creek territory. On August 14, 1797, Price asked Corporal Clark and Privates Cary, Couch, Spikkard and Sharp to help move a shipment of goods destined for the Creeks. One hogshead of salt slipped out of the soldiers' hands and rolled down a slope into the river. Price was willing to concede this might have been an accident but took a harsher view when they towed a bale of blankets headed for Creek country across the river "like a piece of lumber" and left it sitting in the water.[41]

Sabotage by enlisted men extended even to the pillaging of Price's warehouse supplies, whenever he was fortunate enough to have any. "Insubordination and dissipation are carried to great excess," Price wrote Hawkins on October 15, 1798.

> I don't think the public property safe....We are robbed at all points: cattle, pigs, poultry, trade provisions out of the stores, furs, peltry—in short, everything. No law. No address. We are almost getting to be free plunder.[42]

Twenty years later, Price's successor operating at a post farther inland similarly complained that "the military here have frequently broken [the stores] open and ransacked everything." After years of frustration, the Creek trading house was finally "sold to the Indians" for about $4,000 in 1820.[43]

Fort Wilkinson's federal troops proved to be tools of Georgia's frontiersmen, not a curb on them. Georgians even offered enlisted men bribes because by law only federal employees or federally licensed agents could do business on Creek soil. The result, complained Price to Fort Wilkinson's commanding officer, Major Constant Freeman, was that enlisted men

> in opposition to the public interest...collect large stocks which interfere with our trade of stock from the Indians by totally destroying the range adjacent to the garrison....Many private soldiers have large stocks under their charge which on well-founded [evidence] are the property of the citizens of the state of Georgia put over under this cloak to evade the law. I made an estimate sometime since of several hundred individuals' property.[44]

As Efau Hadjo observed in 1802,

> The Oconee is a large river, half was ours; it was a stopping place; but we see cattle over...[which] have eaten all the food of our black game [i.e., bears]. We were told that people were set to prevent it, and to protect our rights, but they cannot prevent these things; they are over, and we see they cannot be prevented.[45]

Fort Wilkinson was intended to draw Creek trade away from Spanish

Florida, and to encourage the Creeks to rely on federal border guards rather than on Creek war parties. Both these objectives were sabotaged by federal enlisted men corrupted by Georgians. The regular federal army in these post-Revolutionary War years was poorly paid and poorly educated. A garrison payroll of 1799 reveals an enlisted strength of five sergeants and corporals, thirteen privates. The sergeants and corporals signed their names to acknowledge having received their pay, but all thirteen privates signed with an "X" witnessed by the clerk.[46]

Federal troops located in tribal territory rather than squarely on the border served only to blur lines, not to enforce them. As it turned out, "the feeble authority of the civil power" wielded so assertively by Agent Hawkins was a far greater deterrent to provocations by both sides.

Once while explaining the significance of the Creek ritual of White (or Black) Drink, Efau Hadjo pointed out that U.S. officials were by no means the first to have been thus instructed. "This is not a new thing," he elaborated, indeed "our first acquaintance commenced with the English at Charleston" in the seventeenth century when Creeks

> first took them by the hand...and this ceremony was in use then and has been repeated on all like occasions; after the English, our next acquaintance was with the French, then the Spaniards, and lastly with the United States.[47]

Efau Hadjo's Creeks stood for continuity in their region, and believed they possessed knowledge that could benefit the upstart United States. The Creeks also desired to preserve trade ties with Europe, and cultural ties with other tribes. For its part, the United States desired land for expansion. Was there no basis for a compromise enabling both Creeks and U.S. citizens to realize their objectives peacefully? Hawkins and Efau Haufo felt sure that tensions could be eased and mutually acceptable solutions worked out, in time. Reducing daily frictions came first. This seemed to presuppose clearly marked borders and curtailment of territorial intrusions by both sides, especially "private revenge," and Hawkins and Efau Hadjo spent much of their time negotiating clear boundary lines, as well as attempting to compel their respective countrymen to observe them. As Presiding Chief of a consensually governed tribal confederacy, Efau Hadjo wielded little independent authority but was an effective leader because of his skill in devising realistic solutions. As U.S. Agent, Colonel Hawkins functioned within bureaucratic limits, but made a difference because of his personal ties to a succession of U.S. Presidents, from Washington to Madison, as well as his certainty that the Revolution could be rendered compatible with tribal dynamism. The Chief and the Agent were from different worlds, but discovered a surprising array of overlapping concerns. Their extemporized remedies for daily crises were more successful than their efforts to reach longer-range goals, but in their way of addressing both they demonstrated that constructive dialogic relationships between Native American and U.S. leaders could be achieved.

George Washington Resigns as Continental Commander-in-Chief, December 23, 1783. Detail of oil painting in U.S. Capitol Rotunda by John Trumbull, 1822-24. Among those shown in addition to General Washington are Benjamin Hawkins, in chair with cloak over back; Thomas Jefferson, seated across table from Hawkins; James Madison, standing beside doorframe; James Monroe, seated with legs crossed; and Colonel David Humphreys, standing behind Washington, with hand on chest. Photo, Courtesy Library of Congress.

Seven

President Jefferson's Creek Choice

IN THE U.S. CAPITOL ROTUNDA IS A LARGE PAINTING by John Trumbull, of General Washington resigning as Revolutionary War Commander-in-Chief. Assembled to hear Washington's December 23, 1783, farewell are thirty of the nation's leaders. In their midst, eyes turned toward Washington, Thomas Jefferson and Benjamin Hawkins sit near each other. Both sons of slave-owning plantation aristocrats, leaders in their neighbor states and common nation, Jefferson and Hawkins were colleagues within the circle of recognized American Revolutionary leaders. More than that, they became friends, at ease with each other discussing everything from the embarrassment of slavery to Venus Fly-Traps.

Soon after hearing General Washington's farewell words, Hawkins and Jefferson departed in opposite directions: Hawkins to "Indian Country" to negotiate treaties with the southern tribes, Jefferson to France. Yet Hawkins still came frequently to Jefferson's mind because of the many intellectual preoccupations they shared. In a letter from Paris dated August 13, 1786, Jefferson asked Hawkins to send him seeds of the Venus Fly-Trap, "called also with you, I believe, the Sensitive Plant."[1] Hawkins did better: he sent Jefferson a number of plants in "earthen pots" all addressed to Count Buffon, Superintendent of France's Royal Garden. Jefferson and the world-renowned naturalist Buffon divided these exotic North American specimens.[2]

Eighteenth century European intellectuals such as Buffon wished to encompass the whole known world in their theories, and eagerly sought details about the natural history of North America. Jefferson did his best to supply Buffon with accurate information, and in the process to correct conclusions Buffon had drawn questioning the healthfulness of North America's climate and citing as evidence the supposed poor health of Native Americans. Jefferson considered it imperative to defend North America's reputation for salubriousness, and sought Hawkins's assistance to confirm his personal impression that Native

Americans were as healthy as Europeans living similar lives. This impression proceeded "somewhat from my own knowledge," Jefferson explained, but primarily from "the information of others better acquainted with [Native Americans]...and on whose truth and judgment I can rely." Hawkins was among those asked by Jefferson to comment on "Buffon's character of Indians."[3]

Jefferson also urged Hawkins to collect information for him about Native American languages, and on June 14, 1786, Hawkins replied that he had passed this request along to (among others) the Creek leader "Alexander McGillivray...a man of good sense" who, Hawkins assured Jefferson,

> will be particular in his information respecting his nation as his large possessions in the heart of his country will afford him leisure to attend to the queries, and his taste for natural history with a good library which he has collected will make that attention amusement for him.[4]

Hawkins and Jefferson resumed face-to-face contact when Jefferson returned from Paris to become the nation's first Secretary of State in 1789 and Hawkins became a U.S. Senator in 1790. Hawkins left the Senate in 1795 and in 1796 settled in the Creek nation, while Jefferson in 1797 became Vice President and leader of a party of "Republicans" antagonistic to the "Federalist" President, John Adams. Political parties were just beginning to emerge in the United States, and by departing when he did for "Indian Country" Hawkins missed much of this process. So when Jefferson in the summer of 1800 wrote him excitedly anticipating the Republicans' imminent electoral triumph, Hawkins replied courteously that he had

> been so much occupied with the affairs of this Agency, that very little of my time is taken up with the political occurrences alluded to by you. I shall never change my old friendships, nor the men of the times of our first acquaintance, whom I esteem and venerate, for new ones. If the new are better, I am not displeased, but for me to know this, requires proof that is not within my reach.[5]

One would like to know what thoughts passed through Jefferson's mind as he read this polite letter. Hawkins' own feelings commingled nostalgia and personal respect for Jefferson with a determination to insulate tribal affairs from partisan politics. Nine months later, on March 1, 1801, Hawkins sent Jefferson a vocabulary of the Creeks'

Muscogee language (Hawkins' own work, Alexander McGillivray having not taken up the project), and invited such additional questions from Jefferson "on the state of our Indians as philosophy may require," adding wistfully, "This request is not made to the Vice President or I expect to the President of the United States but to the man placed as first in science and philosophy in our country."[6] Would this Jefferson survive elevation to the Presidency?

After the election, Hawkins expressed the belief that frontiersmen were mistaken in imagining that Jefferson would become their partisan. In a letter to Jefferson's Secretary of War Henry Dearborn, Hawkins voiced concern that "The exultation of the frontier citizens on the election of the President produced a belief that the President would favor the views of those deemed by Indians inimical to their rights." In consequence, southern tribes were displaying "distrust of the President and everything proceeding from him."[7] Hawkins remained hopeful that Jefferson would be honorable enough to safeguard tribal rights. But the expectations stirred up by his triumph were real, and Jefferson could not avoid taking them into account.

Jefferson's talent for maneuvering amongst these countervailing currents was called into vigorous action on February 14, 1803, when he received a letter from a regionally popular thirty-six-year-old Tennessee politician and plantation owner named Andrew Jackson, questioning Hawkins' patriotism. In his February 16th reply to Jackson, Jefferson staunchly affirmed that "No man has ever obtained more influence than Colonel Hawkins" over tribal counsels. Indeed, "Towards the preservation of peace, he is omnipotent; in the encouragement of agriculture, he is indefatigable and successful." Jefferson attributed the "doubts ...entertained by some whether he is not more attached to the interests of the Indians than of the United States" to Agent Hawkins' reluctance "to destroy his influence by pressing what he knows can not be obtained." But Jefferson also cannily assured Jackson that he would "always be open to any proofs" of Hawkins' disloyalty; and that he was henceforth to be placed under stronger "pressure from the executive to obtain cessions" of Creek land. In short, concluded the President, Hawkins "shall be made sensible that his value will be estimated by us in proportion to the benefits he can obtain for us." Showing he meant business, Jefferson added, "I shall myself write to Colonel Hawkins, and possess him fully of my views and expectations."[8]

Two days later in accord with his promise to Jackson, Jefferson sent Hawkins what was ostensibly a casual effusion provoked by a happy accident. "Mr. Hill's return to you," Jefferson began, "offers so safe a conveyance for a letter, that I feel irresistibly disposed to write one, though there is but little to write about." Jefferson then expressed sympathy for Hawkins' persistent gout, assuring him that gout "is considered as a security for good health otherwise." His own health, he confided, was excellent, apart from a "troublesome headache, and some slight rheumatic pains." The President reported also that "Mr. Madison enjoys better health," and that Browse Trist, a mutual friend, was thriving but "Mrs. Trist, his mother, begins to yield a little to time."

Jefferson's affectionate warmth here contrasted noticeably with the official tone of his reply to the young Tennesseean. But Jefferson also wove into this informal fabric a clear note of warning. Apologizing for his chatty gossip, Jefferson confessed uncertainty whether "You have been so long absent from this part of the world, and the state of society so changed in that time, that details respecting those who compose it are no longer interesting or intelligible to you." Following up this hint that Hawkins might be out of touch, Jefferson noted that unlike the administration of his Federalist predecessor John Adams, his own was "bottomed on popular election." Furthermore

> The preceding administration left ninety-nine out of every hundred in public offices of the federal sect. Republicanism had been the mark of Cain which had rendered those who bore it exiles from all portion in the trusts and authorities of their country.

Inevitably officials unresponsive to "popular" aims had found themselves replaced. In this indirect way, in the manner of an old friend relaying the latest news, Jefferson made clear he could not shield Hawkins indefinitely, should he prove insensitive to the new public mood.

Jefferson then revealed how this mood had modified his thinking about the future of tribes. "In truth," he confided,

> the ultimate point of rest and happiness for them is to let our settlements and theirs meet and blend together, to intermix, and become one

> people. Incorporating themselves with us as citizens of the United States, this is what the natural progress of things will, of course, bring on, and it will be better to promote than to retard it. Surely it will be better for them to be identified with us, and preserved in the occupation of their lands, than be exposed to the many casualties which may endanger them while a separate people. I have little doubt but that your reflections must have led you to view the various ways in which their history may terminate, and to see that this is the one most for their happiness. And we have already had an application from a settlement of Indians to become citizens of the United States. It is possible, perhaps probable, that this idea may be so novel as that it might shock the Indians, were it even hinted to them. Of course, you will keep it for your own reflection; but, convinced of its soundness, I feel it consistent with pure morality to lead them towards it.

Jefferson felt an offer of U.S. citizenship, while in their best interest, might "shock the Indians" because of their preference for being a "separate people." On this, as on so many other questions—including notably the future of slavery—Jefferson was as brilliant at stating paradoxes as he was ineffective in resolving them.

Concerning the immediate question of Creek land sales, Jefferson urged Hawkins to produce results that would

> relieve us here from a great pressure, and yourself from the unreasonable suspicions of the Georgians which you notice, that you are more attached to the interests of the Indians than of the United States, and throw cold water on their willingness to part with their lands. It is so easy to excite suspicion, that none are to be wondered at; but I am in hopes it will be in your power to quash them by effecting the object.

Jefferson deftly pointed his finger at Georgians rather than at the Tennesseean, but he cannot be accused of failing to deliver Jackson's message.

Jefferson's letter was meticulously crafted throughout, except at one point where he introduced a problematic image. Should the Creeks yield up more land, he wrote, they would be displaying "the wisdom of the animal which amputates and abandons to the hunter the parts for which he is pursued." Perhaps aware he had said too much, Jefferson added, there was "this difference, that the one sacrifices what is useful, the other what is not."[9]

Hawkins responded vigorously because Jefferson's friendly warning not only raised the question of his own continuance in office but addressed issues to which he had devoted decades of effort. Hawkins expressed entire satisfaction with the national political scene as outlined by Jefferson, and criticized the "bitterness" of "the Federal sect" which reflected "their disappointment and their deadly hatred to those who administer the government." This said, Hawkins turned quickly to tribal specifics. Extending U.S. citizenship to members of tribes, Hawkins reminded Jefferson, was "not a novel" idea, indeed as far back as 1785-86 (while Jefferson was in Paris) there had been talk of admitting the Cherokees "into Congress as a state, but instead of this it was provided in the treaty with the Cherokees that they might send a deputy of their choice to Congress." Nothing came of this plan either, and Hawkins doubted whether the Creeks, who were much less amenable than the Cherokees to U.S. influence, would be interested in citizenship even if it were offered, since they "adhere rigidly to their ancient customs in most things." As for intermarriage, Hawkins recalled that he had arrived among the Creeks enthusiastically "in favor of the idea of forming amorous connections with the women, [and] had in contemplation to set the example myself....[But I] found it would not do."[10]

Hawkins was here summing up for Jefferson seventeen years of rumination about intermarriage with Native Americans. In 1785-86, Hawkins had found his treaty negotiations with the southern tribes so compelling that he resolved to give his life an entirely new direction. As he had then confided in a letter to McGillivray,

> I shall remove from the northward into Georgia this year and I mean to settle on the frontier of that state, as near your nation as I can; and I must request the favor of you to choose for me a young damsel, out of one of your most reputable families, let her be handsome and agreeable, skilled in the customs of her own country, and of a mind that will feel the station I shall support her in.

Hawkins' hope of going to live in stately comfort on the Georgia frontier with a Creek lady of quality hand-picked by McGillivray, and thereby promoting harmony between Georgians and Creeks, apparently failed to impress the sardonic chief. McGillivray received Hawkins' letter and referred to other passages from it, but never mentioned Hawkins' naive marriage proposal.[11]

When he finally came to reside in Creek country ten years later, still single at age forty-two, Hawkins was as eager as ever to meet the Creek "damsel" of his dreams, and paid close attention to eligible Creek women. His favorite, as he recounted to his mentor in such matters, Jefferson's friend Mrs. Eliza Trist, was "the Queen of Tuckabatchee," a widow "about twenty-three years of age, plump built, not tall, of copper color, full breasted, her face regular, with the appearance of neatness in her dress." She wore moccasins "without stockings," a skirt reaching "just below the knee," a blouse held together in front by brooches, so designed that

> by raising it an inch or two the child could be put to the breast; she has eight *hutscotalcau* (ear bobs) around the rim of each ear, and a *cunnauwau* (necklace), all of silver beads and bobs, and a *hatchetau* (mantle), her hair was clubbed and tied with *tucullowau chate* (red binding).

Hawkins obviously had plans to communicate with Creeks in their own language.

"Very early one morning," Hawkins confided to Mrs. Trist, this young woman "came to my bedside and sat down." Rousing Hawkins from slumber,

> she accosted me: "My visit is to you, I am a widow. I have a son so high (holding her hand three feet from the ground). I have a fine stock of cattle, I wished them to be secured for my use and for my son. I know you are *Istechatelige osetat chemistechaugo* (the beloved man of the four nations). My relations are not careful of my interest. If you will take direction of my affairs, the chiefs have told me you may settle my stock where you please and it shall be safe. When you go to Tuckabatchee you will have a home. Maybe I am too old for you, but I'll do anything I can for you. I shall be proud of you if you will take me. If you take a young girl into the house I shall not like it, but I won't say one word; maybe I can't love her, but I won't use her ill."

Such directness, Hawkins assured Mrs. Trist, was characteristic of Creek women, who had "a great propensity to be obscene in conversation, and...call everything by its name." Hawkins was delighted.

Just prior to the arrival of the "Queen of Tuckabatchee," Hawkins claimed, he had been so "sorely afflicted with the gout or rheumatism" that "I could not turn in my blankets." Now all thoughts of gout vanished. "I immediately rose up in my bed and took her in my arms and hugged her, my hands wandered to certain parts the most attractive and she resisted not. Which were they? The milk pots."

Neither Hawkins nor his visitor lost track of the business side of their relationship. Before they parted, Hawkins

> replied to her, hugging her in my arms, you shall be gratified. You may return home. I will have your cattle put out at a proper place. I will take care of them and your son. If you have any desire to call me *chaehe* (my husband) do so. But you must not forget, I have not yet determined to set up a manufactory of babes, in either of the four nations. But you are at liberty as you have one, and know the trade, to carry it on under my name, and to choose any assistant you may deem suitable. The children will be mine and I will attend to you and them. I know the Creeks are jealous of their wives, and I am sorry for it. I am not a jealous man...[but] your assistant must leave me the house, if I direct him to do so, on my arrival.[12]

Hawkins made a limited commitment to her, and sought a limited commitment from her. A widow with a son seemingly solved the problem he had been made aware of in the course of an earlier marital negotiation with a Creek woman who recommended her daughter "for her cleanliness and attention to white people." Hawkins responded positively, but Hawkins' prospective mother-in-law "would not consent that the women and children should be under the direction of the father, and the negotiation ended there." Under Creek law, Hawkins learned, "marriage gives no right to the husband over the property of his wife; and when they part she keeps the children and property belonging to them."[13] A Creek woman married to a foreigner expected to control her children and raise them as members of Creek society. This was why Lachlan McGillivray's son Alexander had grown up as a Creek leader, not a Scotsman. And why Hawkins decided to share living arrangements with a widow who already had a son, and explained to her that he was undecided about setting up his own "manufactory of babes."

Even so, Hawkins soon concluded he was being ill-served by his Tuckabatchee paramour. Fourteen months later, "having obtained from my own observation this degrading fact, that a white man by marrying an Indian woman of the Creek nation so far from bettering his condition becomes a slave of her family," Hawkins reversed direction and proclaimed that "no assistant in the Creek department shall be suffered to commit himself with a Creek woman as a wife." Hawkins vowed to fire assistants who subsequently acted as he had, although honorable prior commitments were to be respected.[14] He

> prohibited all amorous intercourse between red and white people at the Agency. My young men were permitted to go to town after girls, and to have white girls, who, if they were clean, neat and usefully instructive to the Indian women, were permitted to reside at the Agency and to be at my table.

Regarding the longer run, Hawkins was somewhat more optimistic:

> Indian women were invited to dine at the Agency, treated with the most friendly attention, and on the footing of the daughters of the house. This banished jealousy and gives a considerable degree of influence over them and their conversations. Experience in this line has brought the Indian women to reflect on and form proper ideas on the subject. They have recently made propositions to me to submit themselves and children to be governed by white men if I will rescind the order. I have some young girls of good families raised under my own roof to usefulness, with whom I shall begin the experiment anew, with the smiths and strikers in the public service.[15]

Based on his experience, Hawkins warned Jefferson, eliminating tribes through intermarriage with whites was at best a remote possibility, and could scarcely be anticipated in one generation. This dose of cold water may have influenced Jefferson's decision later the same year to shift from racial amalgamation as a strategy for dealing with the southern tribes to the idea of removing them to the just-acquired Louisiana Territory, a cynical plan which Jefferson toyed with, and Jackson as President implemented with disastrous consequences.[16]

Jackson's accusations notwithstanding, Hawkins *was* promoting U.S. interests, along with his distinctive version of the European Enlightenment's progressive agenda. Hawkins admired many Creek customs, and preferred their religious outlook to conventional Christianity. He also believed the Creeks needed urgently to modify their economic and legal systems. But since he was dealing with independent people possessing rights in U.S. law, he ruled out coercion and confined himself to promoting reform by argument, and above all by example. In a very literal sense, Hawkins aspired to *exemplify* the Revolutionary United States among the tribes, to be a living *example* of what the Revolution could offer U.S. citizens and their neighbors. "The plan I pursue," Hawkins affirmed in 1807,

> is to lead the Indians from hunting to the pastoral life, to agriculture, household manufactures, a knowledge of weights and measures, money and figures, to be honest and true to themselves, as well as to their neighbors, to protect innocence, to punish guilt, to fit them to be useful members of the planet they inhabit....I set the example in all things myself.[17]

The Agency compound he created was in effect a teaching plantation. With the Creek chiefs' approval, Hawkins selected a two-hundred-acre site on the east bank of the Flint River where he gradually brought into being a bustling world of agricultural activity reminiscent of his parents' North Carolina plantation, Pleasant Hill, but adapted so as to promote pursuits congenial to Creeks. Hawkins could see innumerable ways to improve the productivity of such traditional Creek crops as peaches, grapes, squash and corn. Like the Iroquois apple orchards of New York State, Creek peach orchards were older than the U.S. republic, and in Hawkins's view only needed enhancement. For this purpose, "nearly five thousand" new peach trees had by 1801 been started in a nursery at the Agency and distributed to Creeks.

An 1810 plan of Hawkins' Agency shows dwellings and workshops arrayed close together on either side of a rudimentary street, with the overall effect more reminiscent of a small company town than of a showy ante-bellum plantation. Hawkins' own house at the head of the street by the riverside was no more than four or five times larger than the other buildings, which all appear to have been about the same size, and in which African Americans, whites and Native Americans lived interspersed. Twelve "Negro houses" for the seventy-five slaves Hawkins brought from North Carolina were in three clusters, alongside a weaver's shop, blacksmith, joiner and halter shops, and an "Indian tavern." Below the main compound, a stream was dammed up to create a millpond to power saw- and grist-mills and a cotton gin, a recent (1793) invention. Also included were kitchen gardens, an orchard and cornfields, stables, spring house, smoke house, tanyard, fish traps in the river, and a bear pen. "We are clothing and feeding ourselves," Hawkins recorded proudly in 1808.

> The tinware we use; and hats; shoes and boots, and the saddle I ride on, are made in the Agency; and all the leather we use or want is tanned at the Agency. My family of eighty persons are all clothed in homespun.

An 1816 inventory of animals at the Agency listed 291 cattle, 81 pigs, 59 goats, 58 sheep and 20 horses. Milk was "measured by barrels and churned by machinery."[18]

As U.S. Agent, Hawkins was obligated to press for the return of runaway slaves to their legal owners in the southern states. But he also dealt routinely with free African Americans, and happily certified the freeing of slaves. He was gratified that a community of free African Americans was emerging in the United States, and he applauded (indeed practiced) racial mixture. A young African American slave woman named Rachel, owned by Edward Price who managed the U.S. trading establishment at Fort Wilkinson, became briefly Hawkins' mistress. When Rachel gave birth to a son, affectionately called by Hawkins his "young Muscogee," Hawkins put Rachel in touch with friends in Philadelphia, helping her and her son gain freedom in the north.[19] Slave-owner Hawkins could not bring himself to marry Rachel, even though the Creeks would have found such an arrangement entirely acceptable.

In his various legal proceedings as U.S. Agent, Hawkins proclaimed that "the evidence of any person, red, white, or black, shall be allowed and admitted in all cases."[20] Like Washington, Jefferson and numerous other comparatively progressive slave-owners of this era, Hawkins seems to have assumed that the long-established, widespread American colonial practice of slavery could not be immediately eradicated in the post-Revolutionary United States, even though it was inconsistent with the Revolution's fundamental affirmation of human dignity and rights. But while Hawkins accepted slavery as a short-term necessity, he anticipated its gradual elimination for economic as well as political and moral reasons. Hawkins was consequently disturbed by indications that instead of gradually dying out, the nature of slavery might be changing in ways that, he believed, could menace the country's future stability. Informed by Jefferson that their young mutual friend Browse Trist wished to move to the Mississippi Territory to get rich quick growing cotton, Hawkins replied on October 28, 1801, that to him the idea seemed ominous:

> [T]he crop arising from a well chosen and cultivated field has produced three to five hundred dollars profit per hand. One disagreeable circumstance attending this business is the keen desire generated by such great profit to accumulate slaves by any and every means...regardless of future consequences and it is more than probable that the period cannot be very distant when the black people of the north kidnaped and thrust into the severe labor of the south will make an effort to regain their liberty.[21]

The optimism of the Revolution's first phase induced many liberal thinkers to imagine that U.S. slavery might gradually disappear without forcing a violent showdown. Young Browse Trist had other ideas.

"I want an assistant who can spin and weave," Hawkins informed Rachel's owner Edward Price. "Eliza or Lavinia or someone else."[22] Lavinia Downs, a white woman of humble origins then living at Fort Wilkinson, accepted Hawkins' offer of employment and proved so valuable an assistant that after Rachel's departure she became Hawkins' mistress, the mother of seven children fathered by Hawkins, and eventually his wife. Long before they were formally married, Lavinia was referred to as "Mrs. Hawkins" and Hawkins told friends that while not "married to my wife according to the laws of the United States," he had "lived with her according to the customs of *this* land" and "always considered, recognized, and acknowledged her as my wife."[23]

Hawkins first planned to marry a Creek "damsel," then contracted with a Creek mistress, then slept with an African American slave who may have borne him a son, then married according to Creek custom a white woman, with whom he raised a family that turned out to be as *exemplary* as most of his other creations. Hawkins' hope for regional harmony under benign federal guidance was projected with disarming directness in the naming of the seven children Lavinia bore him. Two, a daughter and a son, were named for the Presidents Hawkins knew best, three daughters were named for southern states and two daughters were named for tribes. The children's names were Jeffersonia Hawkins, James Madison Hawkins, Virginia Hawkins, Carolina Hawkins, Georgia Hawkins, Cherokee Hawkins and Muskogee Hawkins.[24] In a very literal sense, Benjamin Hawkins thought of everyone in his region, slave and free, as part of his extended family, and relished all its diversity. In 1800, not long after coming to reside among the Creeks, Hawkins contentedly informed Jefferson,

> I am now in the woods like an Arab chief in tents, with my stock and family around me, and at the moment I am writing I hear the language of Scotch, French, Spanish, English, Africans, Creeks and Yuchis, and all in peace, considering themselves as forming one family.[25]

In addition to managing the Hawkins household, Lavinia continued in her original role, teaching Creek women to spin and weave. Looms for their use were constructed by a Moravian from Denmark, Brother Karsten Petersen. In past years a frequent visitor to the Moravian settlement at Salem, North Carolina, Hawkins won their gratitude when he defended them from attacks provoked by their pacifist neutrality during the Revolutionary War. On November 9, 1796, while on his way to take up his post in "Indian Country," Hawkins stopped at Salem, and the Moravians asked whether he would permit them to assist him. Hawkins welcomed the offer but urged that they "first establish themselves as craftsmen." Ten years later, two qualified Brothers arrived. Brother Petersen was a "joiner and turner." Brother Johann Christian Burckhard, originally from Germany, worked as a cooper and also followed "the tinner's trade."

Brother Petersen and Brother Burckhard acquired some proficiency in the Creeks' Muscogee language, but their proselytizing seems to have been limited to showing "a picture of the crucifixion" to Creeks who visited their workshops. Such modest acknowledgment of their own faith, combined with respect for the beliefs of others, was fine with Hawkins, who identified himself with the Creek approach to religion, as he understood it. When Dolly Madison inquired in 1811 about the Creeks' spiritual welfare, Hawkins asked President Madison to "Tell Mrs. Madison we are all Quakers in the Indian Agency." Hawkins called the annual sessions of the Creek National Council "as silent, as grave and circumspect" as any Quaker meeting in Philadelphia. And he sketched for Madison how Creeks might characterize their religious outlook, as follows:

> We [Creeks] are under the guidance of reason, and they [the Quakers] under the light of the gospel, in pursuit of the same object, content and a complacency in this life, and neighbors for hereafter. We are more solicitous for the first than the last, believing it more immediately concerns us, and that our faculties are limited to our sphere of action

> here. If our doctrine of hereafter is unsound, in the opinion of our white friends, we will exchange our *guide* for their *light* and subscribe to whatever they recommend, provided they will assist us here to preserve the birthright portion of the planet we inhabit. To this end the little that we require is, that the followers of the meek and humble Jesus will believe we are their neighbors, and treat us accordingly.[26]

Whether or not Hawkins' imagined Creek *philosophes* had a basis in reality, they did express how Hawkins himself felt about efforts to convert the Creeks.

Ironically, the most aggressive challenge to Hawkins' "Quaker" opposition to missionizing came from one of his own slaves, a fire-and-brimstone Christian named Phil, who sought to proselytize other slaves. Hawkins complained that Phil "damned all of the Negroes to hell" and "did not know how to point the way of a sinner to Christ." Sermons preached by Phil terrified one fellow-slave, who had to be confined in chains. Lavinia Hawkins suspected that Phil was primarily motivated by a desire to "take the women in his lap."[27] Phil's version of these events is not recorded.

The emergence at the Agency of this slave-preacher illustrates how difficult it was to control which aspects of southern U.S. culture would reach the Creeks. Hawkins intended to display for Creek emulation a model of disciplined, productive slave management. Phil was brought from North Carolina for this purpose but had a mind of his own. Hawkins' plan was doomed anyway, because Creeks approached slaves in a quite different manner.

In the sixteenth century, Africans had been a startling apparition to Native Americans. Two centuries later, African Americans were a familiar presence in tribal territory, where they occupied a greater range of social roles than in the southern states. A good many runaway slaves married Native Americans, others established separate settlements of their own. Quite a few of the African Americans who became Creek slaves had been captured during the Revolutionary War by the British, who then turned them over to pro-British tribes "in payment for their services." These slaves referred to themselves as "King's gifts" and in fact were treated more like adopted tribal members of low status than as human property. Beyond the reach of southern U.S. society, a composite Native American-African American culture was gradually forming. Alexander McGillivray's sister Sophia Durand, who owned "near eighty slaves," was married to a man who was himself at least part African. Each Christmas, African Americans from far and wide gathered at the Durand plantation "where there lived more of the black people than in any other part of the [Creek] nation" to attend a "proper frolic of rum drinking and dancing" in which all races joined.[28]

Creek slaves, complained Hawkins, "do nothing the whole winter but get a little wood, and in the summer they cultivate a scanty crop of corn barely sufficient for bread."[29] While Hawkins felt Mississippi's greed-driven slave system was inhumane and dangerous, he considered the Creeks' way of employing their slaves too casual, and recommended North Carolina's medium-sized plantations utilizing trained slave labor, as better suited to promote Creek agricultural development.

With or without slave help, the Creeks' country seemed to Hawkins

> fine for hogs, but the want of fences, [and] scarcity of corn...necessary to keep them from running wild, and being too much infested with wolves, tigers, and wildcats, is for the present a bar to their increase.

Unfenced hogs were further menaced by the fact that "the ponds and swamps abound with alligators." On the other hand, some indigenous Creek manufactures currently produced appeared already suitable for export, including "coarse earthen pots and pans, garters, ornamented with beads, basket sifters, and fans, ingeniously made, of split cane, and moccasins."[30] Hickory nut oil seemed to have the most immediate market potential. To produce this staple of the Creek diet, hickory nuts were "dried and pounded up...put into boiling water, stirred up for a while, [then] set by, from the fire." When oil rose to the top, it was "brushed off with feathers, and...boiled." Deciding to test its viability as an export, Hawkins in 1797 offered seventy-five cents a quart for hickory nut oil. That year "only a few bottles" arrived. In 1798 the quantity offered increased to eight gallons, in 1799 to thirty. By 1801, three hundred gallons were "actually delivered for market" and Hawkins lowered the price paid to one dollar a gallon. This permitted him to send a quantity to Mobile for sale at two dollars a gallon.[31]

Hawkins sought to combine incentives for manufacturing and commercial agriculture with disincentives to continued Creek reliance on hunting. Thus, when the chiefs expressed a desire for blacksmiths,

Hawkins provided them, along with the stipulation that they should "do all work appertaining to agriculture free of expense, but...make the hunters pay for their guns and traps." Before long, several Creeks learned blacksmithing, and the Upper Creek chiefs employed one of them at "the same pay as the public smith" to repair Creek guns.[32]

Hawkins sometimes spoke of Creek hunting as if it were little more than an amusement, and its boisterous side was more visible to U.S. citizens than its rationale. The most strenuous activities of Creek men—war, crime retribution and hunting—all involved prolonged periods of abstinence and intense concentration, followed by the ritual of release. Like sailors hoving into port after a long voyage, hunters made up for many weeks of taut discipline by allowing themselves several days of delirious holiday, often in towns where they came to trade. This was regarded by whites as evidence of how much Creeks enjoyed hunting. But hunting was also important in their economic calculations. On June 11, 1802, Efau Hadjo responded to what he termed Hawkins' attempt to "make it the fashion to plant" by noting

> as yet, we have a little hunting; it was what we have been brought up to; it is an old custom, we cannot lay it aside, and we must attend to that too. Whenever our young people find a skin, if it be but one, we wish a place where we may carry it, and get something for it. The hunters they have liberty to work or hunt. This day we tell you, we do not throw away cropping, stock, or weaving; we will attend to them all, and will attend also to hunting; if we get a little by the latter, it will be something to add to our chance in the former; if it be but a little, it is something.

According to Efau Hadjo's sources, the Cherokees "have found a good price for raccoons, foxes, and wildcats; for large ones, they have a chalk (quarter of a dollar) and when they are small, they put two on each other."[33]

Efau Hadjo was almost apologetic about the Creeks' adherence to hunting. But he could not resist pointing out that it made no sense to him to give up an activity that paid even a little. Contemporary Creek hunting was profit-driven. Indeed the Creek economy had been less weighted toward hunting before European contact, when both hunting and farming were pursued to maintain a subsistence way of life. The Creek shift to intensive hunting resulted from responsiveness to large profit opportunities created by the European market, as well as from

Creek willingness to adopt new forms of self-discipline and specialization; in short, from mastery of entrepreneurial skills. Hawkins' attempt to discourage hunting was directed ironically at that activity in Creek society which was most highly commercialized. In these years, Creek hunters annually delivered over one hundred thousand deerskins to market, an average of twelve per man per year. Only a quarter of this output reached the federal trade depot, since the bulk of Creek trade still went through Spanish Florida.[34] The Creeks were experienced hunters with an established position in the international market. They also served as brokers, buying for resale from tribes further inland. Markets were found not only for "deerskins, furs [and] hides" but also for processed by-products such as "tallow, oils, honey [and] wax."[35]

Contrastingly, Creek production of agricultural commodities involved a late and disadvantageous entry into a strongly resistant market. "When the Indians undertake to...till the earth," observed Alexis de Tocqueville, who visited the Creeks in 1832,

> they are immediately exposed to a formidable competition...[The Indian] is isolated in the midst of a hostile people, with whose customs, language, and laws he is imperfectly acquainted....Thus, when the Indian wishes to sell the produce of his labor, he cannot always find a purchaser, while the European readily obtains a market.[36]

In attempting to constrict hunting and promote tilling, Hawkins was discouraging an industry that was distinctive, complementary and lucrative in order to replace it with one that had been successfully developed by others, was now controlled by them and from which Creeks could hope for a scant return at best. Because no market was readily available for the sale of agricultural commodities, exclusive reliance on farming could only lead the Creeks back to the level of subsistence.

Tribes hunted and practiced agriculture; U.S. citizens practiced agriculture—and hunted. Both groups wanted exclusive control of land, and the freedom to exploit it employing whatever mix of uses seemed best at any given time. No one was asking U.S. citizens to choose between hunting and tilling. Indeed the major threat faced by Creek hunters was that their game supply might dwindle, not because of an inexorable dynamic of evolutionary societal development by which hunting was destined to make way for agriculture, but rather because of wanton slaughter by U.S. poachers. In 1796, Creek chiefs complained,

> The white people come over [the Oconee River] hunting; they hunt by night, with fire; they go even to the creeks of Ocmulgee, they encamp, and tarry days and nights on the heads of those waters; they carry fish by loads, and when the Indian hunters come into these lands, they find the whites there, taking their deer and other game; and this they do constantly.[37]

According to General Schuyler's 1783 theory, tribes would want to retreat west along with the game they hunted. Tribes were to be paid if necessary for the game remaining on the lands they left, but so little payment would be expected that tribes might well leave before being paid. Revolutionaries of a more positive disposition than Schuyler, including Knox, Jefferson, Hawkins and pre-eminently Washington, assumed that tribes might well stay and thrive on their ancestral lands, even if game became extinct, by taking up agriculture. Since this would require less land than hunting, tribal land sales could in theory still be elicited voluntarily. But placing additional land under cultivation didn't presuppose eagerness to sell off surrounding woodlands, and tribes refused to see a connection between shifting more of their efforts into agriculture and sale of their hunting grounds.

After outlining to the Iroquois an aid program designed to encourage them to abandon hunting in favor of settled agriculture, federal Treaty Commissioner Timothy Pickering expressed misgivings in a 1791 report to Secretary of War Knox. "The introduction of the art of husbandry, in its improved state," he warned, would deter tribes from selling land "*altogether*, unless those improvements, by showing the Indians how small a portion of their lands, under proper cultivation, will suffice for their ample support, should induce them to part with the residue."[38] Was this at all likely? Moreover, was it honorable for the United States to encourage tribes to improve their land and then ask them to sell it for a pittance? As Pickering noted, "Every proposition made by me...for introducing among them the...most useful improvements of civil life ...leads to a *separate occupancy* and enjoyment of land." Theoretically, this could have slowly transformed tribes into individual agricultural entrepreneurs, leading to loss of the tribes' collective capacity to control large territories. But so long as tribes were deemed political entities, and conceded the right to make free decisions, federal officials could not take for granted that tribes would wish to dispose of currently unused land rather than retain control of it for recreational use or future development or as security for poorer tribe members. Hawkins for example was unsure

> whether the division of land among the individuals would tend to their advantage or not. In such an event, the long and well tried skill of land speculators might soon oust a whole tribe, whereas the whole country being a common, each of the community having exclusive property in their own farms, only, the combined intelligence of the whole might be sufficient to resist such an evil, and secure at all times land for the cultivation of the indigent and improvident.[39]

If General Schuyler's theory that tribes would willingly and cheaply surrender land proved flawed, could it not be modified? During Washington's administration, tribal chiefs such as Efau Hadjo and Colonel Atayataghronghta did make some headway in explaining to federal officials such as Benjamin Hawkins and Timothy Pickering why the till-and-sell-excess-lands-for-next-to-nothing theory made no sense. In Washington's administration, tribal perspectives were attended to, and officials committed to working faithfully with tribes received his strong backing. Though pressure from tribes and advocates for tribes was only one factor he weighed in making decisions, which therefore often went against tribal interests, Washington was an attentive listener. Tragically, Jefferson as President proved to be a poor listener who was unwilling to hear that his tribal policy was based on a fallacy, waved aside objections from advisers such as Hawkins, and sought to save incoherent policy by coercing tribes into conforming to it.

In 1802, Jefferson's administration finally prevailed upon Georgia to cede its claims to the regions that became Alabama and Mississippi. But the price exacted by Georgia was steep. The federal government acquiesced in Georgia's pre-Constitutional treaties, despite the fact that the Creeks considered them invalid, and agreed to attempt to persuade the Creeks to vacate the lands covered by these State treaties "as early as the same can be peaceably obtained on reasonable terms."[40] James Madison, who represented the Jefferson administration in the 1802 negotiations, actually committed the federal government to "extinguish the Indian Title to all...lands within the State of Georgia" in due course. Federal officials were to have a free hand in diplomatic efforts to induce the Creeks to come to terms, but Georgia clearly expected results sooner rather than later.

To pressure the Creeks, Jefferson appointed the erratic, politically ambitious General James Wilkinson to "assist" Hawkins in negotiating the next land purchase. In formal remarks at the Creek treaty ground, General Wilkinson told the chiefs led by Efau Hadjo he was angered that they

> put our talks aside, and you offer to your *Father* a small strip....You tell us you are poor and ignorant, and that you look up to your Father for help and for advice. Open your ears and your hearts then....When the *child* turns a deaf ear to the voice of his *father*, and throws away his advice, what can such a *child* expect?...You cannot suspect the sincerity of our dispositions to provide for your wants....You cannot deny our superior knowledge of the manner and means by which this provision may be attained....Your *Father*, the President...will hang his head when we tell him you have refused his request for a small part of your land, necessary to his white children, of little value to yourselves....He is under no obligation to extend his cares to a people, who withhold from others what they cannot themselves enjoy, and refuse to employ the means they possess, to promote their own happiness.[41]

Wilkinson here twisted beyond recognition the tribal concept of federal *fathership*.

While Wilkinson railed, Efau Hadjo and Hawkins worked on a compromise. Sale of a small tract of Creek land was finally agreed to, but only after Efau Hadjo rejected Wilkinson's insistent demands with the haunting words, "The thing that was asked us to part with, was like asking us to cut ourselves in two." Jefferson may have read a transcript containing these words prior to penning his 1803 letter to Hawkins suggesting that the Creeks emulate "the wisdom of the animal which amputates and abandons to the hunter the parts for which he is pursued."

Whatever he thought privately about the Jefferson administration's tactics, Hawkins could see the menacing frontier realities hinted at in Jefferson's letter, and hoped to persuade the Creeks that yielding on land sales was the only way to avert catastrophic consequences, even if disposing of additional land was neither welcome nor in their economic interest. In fact, long before Jefferson turned up the heat, Hawkins had been working to encourage Creek land sales. He meant it however when he said ingenuously "honesty is our best policy."[42] Like President Washington, Hawkins was willing to accept a Creek "No" as a reasoned answer. The Creeks, Hawkins wrote, were "an independent nation" and "unquestionably the rightful possessors of their own lands." And since land was the last thing any Creek wished to part with, "it requires that a man should be high in the confidence of the Indians to be able to mention the subject [of land sales] in the public square without being insulted."[43] One Creek insult directed at disorderly frontiersmen, and uttered often in these years, was *Ecunnaunuxulgee*: "greedily grasping after the lands of the red people against the voice of the United States." Hawkins called this "more expressive than any word I know, of what they and we mean when we speak of that class of our fellow citizens."[44]

After receiving Jefferson's 1803 letter, Hawkins made a renewed effort to push the 1802 boundary westward to the Ocmulgee River, which he thought might be a more confining and therefore hopefully more viable line of division. As Hawkins earnestly pointed out to the chiefs assembled at Tuckabatchee in 1804,

> A line of marked trees cannot be a line of peace; where the land is good and admits of thick settlements, stock will come over, our [Creek] young people will destroy it, the...owners will destroy them, and thus this source of confusion will overwhelm us with distress.[45]

The Presiding Chief was new. Efau Hadjo had retired and been replaced by Hopoie Mico. The independent-minded Tallassee Mico was absent, his faction having convened a "council among themselves." Of this, Hopoie Mico remarked wryly that "he did not understand [people of] his own color and he did not know how Colonel Hawkins should."[46]

Negotiations dragged on all summer, while the Tallassee Mico traveled to Spanish Florida to confer with Seminoles and British agents. Then in October of 1804 the chiefs gathered at the Agency on the Flint River. Hopoie Mico walked all the way there, "being unable from sores to ride." And this time, "the opposition chiefs were present" including the Tallassee Mico. Here indeed was, as Hawkins put it, a "combination of favorable circumstances."[47]

Hopoie Mico did the talking, having previously reached agreement with the Tallassee Mico. Hopoie Mico had been working for four months to put together consensus, and now having succeeded could speak with great authority. The tract he offered was not quite what Hawkins wanted, but fairly close. The Ocmulgee was to be the line, although not north all the way to its source because this would have given the Cherokees "bad neighbors." Solicitude extending beyond their own borders to take into account what would impact their three *brother* tribes—the Cherokees, Choctaws and Chickasaws—was characteristic of Creek chiefs, who also would "never agree to mark their boundary between them and those nations."[48]

Why had the Tallassee Mico agreed? Some reasons became apparent when Hopoie Mico outlined what the Creeks expected in exchange. He

> understood from some people who had been to the Northwest, the United States sold their land at two dollars per acre; and if they...give him enough to pay all the debts of the nation, and...[yield in addition] five hundred dollars to each town...forever, he would then bring the chiefs to accommodate the views of the President on this point.

Hopoie Mico wasn't asking for two dollars an acre. He simply pointed out what full market payment would have amounted to, as an argument for a price substantially higher than the government's one-cent-per-acre game-based formula allowed.

The "debts of the nation" to which Hopoie Mico referred included some to British traders in Spanish Florida with whom the Tallassee Mico had close relations. The prospect of a large capital payment the annual yield on which would be directly under town control must have also appealed to him. So the Tallassee Mico's faction had agreed to the compromise. But Hopoie Mico warned Hawkins that since "of all things, this of land selling was the most disagreeable to an Indian," the United States would be wise to accept his offer quickly, before it was withdrawn. Since Hawkins "knew the country and its value," he had better "take it at their offer...; if not," Hawkins recounted,

> they would see me again in the summer; that they should adjourn tomorrow, and some of them were going this evening; I replied that they must come down to a reasonable price, and I would close with them, but what they asked was out of all bounds; they persisted to the moment of departure, when I offered the sum mentioned in the treaty, and told them expressly, that it was not unlikely it would not be ratified, and we

should have the whole subject before us again; upon this we agreed, and I drew the treaty.[49]

Hawkins' instructions were not to exceed *"the usual rate of compensation,"* or approximately one cent per acre.[50] As a gamble, he took upon himself to offer ten cents per acre, and secured Creek acquiescence. In reporting this, Hawkins conceded it might sound excessive. But half of the two million acre tract acquired was "unquestionably the best land in this country," and ten cents an acre was therefore in Hawkins' view "far from being unreasonable." Of at least equal significance to Hawkins was the fact that a Creek consensus had been laboriously pieced together in support of the sale, with even the Tallassee Mico acquiescing.[51]

Negotiating this Treaty had been difficult, and whether to ratify it also presented Jefferson with a difficult choice, because tribal lands were supposed to be paid for based on a calculation of the commercial value of the game remaining, a calculation never actually made but which had come to be quantified arbitrarily at one or two cents per acre. If federal guidelines were violated in even one transaction, a precedent would be set that might cost the government time after time. Even when supervising private purchases from tribes, the federal government sought for the same prudential reason to keep the price paid tribes low. In 1805 for example, Jefferson's Secretary of War Henry Dearborn for example instructed U.S. Treaty Commissioner Charles Jouett regarding a purchase of land "bordering on the southerly part of Lake Erie" from the Wyandots, Ottawas, Chippewas and other tribes, as follows:

> The object of the proposed treaty being principally that of affording the Connecticut land companies (who hold the preemptive right, under the State of Connecticut, to a certain part of the land above described) an opportunity to purchase the Indian title to the lands claimed by the said companies, your duties will chiefly consist, in notifying the chiefs of the several nations, who are interested, of the time and place of holding said treaty; and in presiding thereat, for the purpose of seeing that any bargain, which the agents of the said companies may enter into with the proper representatives of the Indian nations, shall be fair and just, and well understood by the parties.
>
> You will use your influence to induce the Indians to make a cession of the lands claimed by the Connecticut companies, on reasonable terms, such as they, and their respective nations, will, or ought to be satisfied

with.

If this had been fair market value, no company would have bothered to make the trip west, let alone purchase the right to bargain for these tribal land rights in the first place. "The price usually given for Indian cessions, in different parts of the United States," Dearborn went on to explain,

> has not exceeded one cent per acre. And the Government of the United States is, in no case, except for some particular favorite tracts, inclined to give, at most, more than at the rate of two cents per acre. But if the agents on the part of the aforesaid companies should be disposed to agree to a higher price, there should be no such objection, on your part, as to prevent the bargain; although it would be the most advisable, that the price should not exceed what the United States usually pay or would agree to pay for lands similarly situated, and of equal quality. From one to two cents per acre would, probably, be a reasonable price for the lands in question[52]

While the Creek chiefs had in mind their land's market value of some two dollars per acre as they bargained Hawkins up to ten cents per acre, President Jefferson was aware that the federal government would have trouble keeping the price low in other parts of the country if the Creeks were paid what they asked. After mulling his options, Jefferson passed the Creek Treaty along to the Senate with a carefully worded message noting that though instructed to offer only what was *"reasonable, according to the usual rate of compensation,"* Hawkins had been

> induced to go beyond this limit, probably by the just attention due to the strong interest which the State of Georgia feels in making this particular acquisition, and by a despair of procuring it on more reasonable terms, from a tribe which is one of the most fixed in the policy of holding fast their lands.

Jefferson also ventured to suggest that "instead of giving them stock [notes], which may be passed into other hands, and render them the prey of speculators," it might be better if the Creeks were paid for their lands in a series of annual payments. Then "the price of these lands will become a pledge and guarantee for our future peace with this important tribe, and, eventually, an indemnity for the breach of it." Jefferson thought this modification would make the Treaty less objectionable, but ultimately made no recommendation as to whether it should be ratified, concluding, "On the whole, I rest with entire satisfaction on the wisdom and counsel of those whose sanctions the Constitution has rendered necessary to the final validity of this act."[53] With Jefferson disposed to second-guess particulars, the Senate rejected this Treaty so laboriously put together.

Though he attributed his opposition to transferring capital assets to his concern that the Creeks not become the "prey of speculators," in fact Jefferson sought to undermine Creek financial independence because this would make them harder to control and less amenable to further land sales. Jefferson consequently preferred annual stipends revocable for bad behavior. Applying the same logic, Jefferson wanted credit extended by government trading houses, which would put within the tribes' "reach those things which will contribute more to their domestic comfort than the possession of extensive, but uncultivated wilds."[54] Hawkins in contrast pronounced such credit manipulation "unquestionably prejudicial" to Creek interests, indeed "the ruin of every project to better the condition of these people" because credit "increases their extravagance while it lessens the means of supporting it." In 1799 he praised the Secretary of War's decision "excluding it altogether" and wrote, "I hope never to see credit introduced again into the nation." Hawkins wanted the Creeks to become "a free people under the guarantee of the government of the United States." Jefferson advocated debt ensnarement, to place the Creeks subtly under the control of the U.S. government.[55]

Despite the Senate's rejection of the 1804 Treaty, a settlement seemed close, with the remaining disagreement apparently between officials in Washington on the one hand and Hawkins and the Creeks on the other. So it was proposed that Hawkins and a Creek delegation come to Washington to complete the Ocmulgee land sale. Hawkins informed Hopoie Mico, who summoned the National Council to meet at Tuckabatchee on June 5, 1805.

Georgians were meanwhile already moving onto the land east of the Ocmulgee, acting as if it were no longer Creek territory. Hawkins wanted all squatters evicted by federal troops, believing these lands "should be delivered over without encumbrance to the State of Georgia and the sooner we interposed the better, to place things agreeable to law." The Secretary of War agreed, and in August of 1805 Hawkins ordered Captain William Boote, stationed at Fort Wilkinson, to "remove all intruders and destroy their settlements."[56] With the few men at his disposal, Captain Boote would find this a formidable task.

A further complication at this critical juncture was that Hawkins' principal Creek assistant, Alex Cornells, was found "guilty of an indiscretion in taking a married woman for a night or two from her husband" and consequently had to "conceal himself till the Boosketau" was over in late July. Cornells did hide successfully, but was not present for the discussions that convened at Tuckabatchee on June 5.[57]

With all factions in attendance, the chiefs conferred at Tuckabatchee for nine days, eventually deciding to send the requested delegation to Washington, empowered to settle final terms for the Ocmulgee land sale and even if necessary to allow a post road to be cut through their land. But without assigning a reason, Hopoie Mico refused to join the Creek delegation scheduled to depart September 1. Hawkins considered this ominous, and kept trying till the last minute to persuade him to change his mind. Alex Cornells, now safely returned from hiding, informed Hawkins that Hopoie Mico's "disinclination to going arises from an apprehension on his part that the warriors will blame him"; and that the delegation going to Washington would do so from "fears to offend the President and not from any inclination to grant a road through their land and make Ocmulgee their boundary."[58] The moment of opportunity had passed. The chance for unanimous acquiescence in the sale of the Ocmulgee lands, potentially laying the foundation for peaceful relations for years to come, was lost because of Jefferson's decision not to endorse unqualifiedly the consensual compromise laboriously achieved by Hawkins and the chiefs.

A replacement Treaty incorporating Jefferson's preference for annual payments but preserving the "high" ten-cent-an-acre price was expeditiously negotiated in Washington. For this supplemental negotiation, Hawkins and several second-tier chiefs (one was William McIntosh, prominent in later years) traveled to Washington, where Hawkins conferred with Secretary of State James Madison and also revived his sagging friendship with Jefferson. This new Treaty was soon ratified. Tragically, between the Creeks' agonized attainment of agreement in

1804 and their grudging consent to revised terms in 1805, the spirit had changed completely. Jefferson chose to reject not only the terms of a carefully constructed treaty but much more importantly the consultative premise of decision-making at the tribal meeting ground. From the Creek point of view, a treaty concluded in the wrong spirit wasn't worth the parchment it was written on.

Before long, Hopoie Mico was slain by "two men of Cusseta." Fear of blame had kept him at home but not saved his life. As Hawkins bluntly confided to Jefferson, "the young men" of the Creek nation were "not yet accommodated to the sale of the Ocmulgee lands." Even worse, Hopoie Mico's position as Presiding Chief could not be filled. The chiefs pressed Alex Cornells to accept but Cornells, who had made the trip to Washington and actually signed the Treaty, "alarmed by... threats for his personal safety" declined "repeatedly."[59]

The post road provided for by the 1805 Treaty was almost as unwelcome as the land cession, and for related reasons. In 1801 shortly after Jefferson's inauguration, Hawkins had been requested to secure Creek consent to the cutting of several roads through Creek territory. Hawkins dutifully raised the matter with the chiefs but was repeatedly rebuffed. In the 1804 negotiations, Hawkins dropped the road issue to foster good feelings about the more important land sale. But in 1805 the Creek delegation in Washington reluctantly consented to the cutting of a five-foot-wide "horse path" from Georgia to the west. Log bridges were to be built spanning small streams and Creek-managed ferries provided on large rivers. U.S. citizens would "at all times have a right to pass peacefully on said path," but the Creeks refused to permit U.S. citizens to set up "houses of entertainment" for the accommodation of travelers. The following year, Jefferson's Secretary of War Henry Dearborn devised a solution to this difficulty. He ordered Hawkins to issue, under authority he already possessed, trading licenses to U.S. citizens who desired to establish wayside taverns. Presents, Dearborn blandly suggested, could remove any objections the chiefs might raise. Technically defensible, this proposal was wholly at odds with any solicitude for bolstering tribal political autonomy. When Dearborn instructed Hawkins to secure assent to a second post road in 1808, he again "presumed that moderate presents to some of the most influential characters, will be deemed sufficient for so trifling a favor."[60]

Jefferson left the Presidency in 1809, burdening his successor with the consequences of his rejection of respect for tribal preferences. The philosopher-President was never discourteous in manner to tribal leaders, and always surrounded unwelcome choices with a rhetoric of benefit to tribes. But he allowed others, such as Dearborn and Wilkinson, to act and speak coercively, and Jefferson himself defined a long-range goal for Native Americans that presupposed the demise of tribes, which left him radically indifferent to what tribal leaders themselves said they wanted. This in turn convinced many that violence was the only possible way to communicate with U.S. leaders, and the War of 1812, though it did not begin as a tribal war, drew into it numerous Native Americans to whom Jefferson had turned a calculatedly deaf ear.

As initiator of the Constitution's reference to tribes, James Madison who succeeded Jefferson as President in 1809 might perhaps have been expected to be more conciliatory. But Madison was a less dominant President than Jefferson had been, and permitted others in his administration to manage tribal affairs. In 1811, Madison's Secretary of War William Eustis instructed Hawkins to obtain Creek permission to cut two new roads, respectively from Tennessee and Georgia, to Fort Stoddert above Mobile—roads not just for use by postal couriers on horseback. These roads were to be wide and level enough for wagons. The Creek reply came from none other than the venerable Tallassee Mico. "You ask for a path and I say no," he proclaimed.

> I am glad the President has asked us without doing it first....The white people are as difficult to be restrained as the red and are constant habitual intruders on Indian lands....Cattle, hogs and horses are put over and stray on our lands. Some [white men] will be marking trees, roads, paths. My young people, being about and seeing them, will be killing and doing mischief and our young people will say our old people are crazy and do not look into our rights....I hope you will see justice done to both sides, that we may live in peace and be friendly.
>
> I have a large family of people in the country and cannot govern all so as to preserve a good understanding. What land we have left is but large enough to live and walk on....I am an old man and speaker for our warriors. When we find a thing will not be good for us we must say it will not do. I although an Indian have a little sense yet. The great God made us and the lands for us to walk on. I hope the great *Father* our

> President will feel for us and pay attention. We hope he will pity us and not take from us our rights....I am speaking to our great *Father* the President of the United States. When he sees my talk in his great house of talks I hope he will take notice and give me an answer. When his answer returns to me if I am alive I shall see his answer and be contented....My *Father* the President knows the truth and [I] hope he will pay attention to it.[61]

Expecting no sympathy from the Secretary of War, the Tallassee Mico addressed the President directly. But it was Eustis who retorted, "The answer of the Creeks appears to be unreasonable, and is by no means satisfactory." He then wrote Hawkins that President Madison had concluded the roads must be built, so Hawkins should simply inform the Creeks of this decision. In the fall of 1811 at a meeting of the National Council which the Creeks had called for the express purpose of restating their opposition to the proposed wagon roads, Hawkins was obliged to tell them that the roads were already being cut.[62] The Tallassee Mico's response was to travel to Spanish Florida to send a message asking for help directly to Britain's King George III.

The wagon road from Athens, Georgia, to the west was completed within a few weeks and between October of 1811 and March of 1812, 233 vehicles and 3,726 people passed along it. At the same time, certain Creek "wild young men" began, in Hawkins' words, "taking toll."[63]

Eight

Andrew Jackson and the Creek War

SOON AFTER U.S. AGENT HAWKINS INFORMED the Creek chiefs at Tuckabatchee that despite their express opposition two wagon roads would be cut through Creek territory, Tecumseh arrived. Accompanied by twenty-four warriors painted red and black, each carrying "a rifle, tomahawk, and war-club," the eminent Shawnee leader was welcomed by Tuckabatchee's Big Warrior, newly elected the Creeks' Presiding Chief, who offered his pipe to Tecumseh and "pointed to a large cabin, a few hundred yards from the square...furnished with skins and provisions. Tecumseh and his band, in single file, marched to it...not a word being spoken."[1] On each of several succeeding days, Tecumseh sent word that "the sun had traveled too far, and he would talk next day." In the evenings, the Shawnee delegation "danced, in the style peculiar to the northern tribes, in front of...[their] cabin, and the Creeks crowded around." Finally Tecumseh made explicit his unwillingness to speak in the presence of the U.S. Agent. Hawkins accordingly "packed up and publicly left the ground, and rode twelve miles to the Big Spring." With him went a wagoner named Sam Dale who intended to transport families from Georgia to the Mississippi Territory along the disputed new road. Dale expressed a desire to return to hear Tecumseh, and Hawkins agreed to wait for Dale at Big Spring.

At noon the next day, Tecumseh and his companions emerged from their

> cabin...painted black, and entirely naked except the flap about their loins. Every weapon but the war-club...had been laid aside....Tecumseh led, the warriors followed, one in the footsteps of the other. The Creeks, in dense masses, stood on each side of the path.

Entering Tuckabatchee's square, Tecumseh presented a five-strand wampum belt to Big Warrior. Next "the Shawnee pipe...large, long, and profusely decorated with shells, beads, and painted eagle feathers and porcupine quills...was lighted from the fire on the center" and presented to Big Warrior who in turn handed it to other chiefs. Tecumseh began speaking "slowly and in sonorous tones; but soon...the words fell in avalanches from his lips...his voice...now sinking in low and musical whispers, now rising to its highest key." Tecumseh spoke in the Shawnee language. His oration was then translated into Muskogee, which Dale could follow.

At Tuckabatchee, as he had at tribal meeting grounds from the Great Lakes to Florida, Tecumseh urged that all tribal lands be considered the joint property of all tribes, and that they should unite to prevent any one tribe from selling land without the consent of all. Addressing the Creeks as "brethren of my mother" because his mother, though a Shawnee, had been raised among the Upper Creeks, Tecumseh declared

> the Muskogee was once a mighty people. The Georgians trembled at your war-whoop....Now your blood is white; your tomahawks have no edge; your bows and arrows were buried with your fathers. Oh! Muskogees..brush from your eyelids the sleep of slavery....The spirits of the mighty dead complain. Their tears drop from the weeping skies....The white race...seize your land...they trample on the ashes of your dead! Back, whence they came, upon a trail of blood, they must be driven![2]

Several Creek chiefs publicly disputed Tecumseh's arguments but there was no way to determine what ultimate effect his words might have.

When the Council finally dispersed, Dale hastened back to Hawkins' Big Spring camp, "reporting faithfully to him what had occurred." Dale was fearful of what the Creeks would do next, particularly since Dale noticed at various points during Tecumseh's speech Big Warrior's "huge hand clutch, spasmodically, the handle of his knife." Six-and-a-half feet tall and weighing possibly three hundred pounds, Big Warrior was described by U.S. General Thomas Woodward as "the largest man I ever saw among the Creeks." He also was "almost as spotted as a leopard" because of a splotchy discoloration of his skin.[3] A leading chief since at least 1796, Big Warrior after Efau Hadjo's death married his widow and in time succeeded him as Presiding Chief of the Creek National Council.

Hawkins urged Dale not to overestimate the importance of mere "show and ceremony," trying to calm him at least in part to prevent his spreading an alarm throughout Georgia that could make war inevitable, whatever the Creeks intended. Dale fell silent, suspecting Hawkins was "relying too much on his own influence" with the chiefs.[4]

In the months that followed Tecumseh's Tuckabatchee speech, a belligerent mood seemed to be spreading unchecked. While Tecumseh exhorted tribes, the British Navy were accosting U. S. vessels on the high seas. And the weakening of Spanish authority had sparked British interest in regaining political control of Florida, as well as an abortive attempt by Georgians to "liberate" Florida. Finally, on June 18, 1812, the United States declared war on Britain.

Hawkins still hoped the Creeks would remain neutral, and in letter after letter to his superiors in Washington and to the Governors of Georgia and Tennessee, Hawkins sounded his favorite theme that the Creeks "are, many of them, occupied in spinning, weaving, making new settlements, or improving those heretofore made." He assured Georgia Governor David Mitchell that the Creeks had a "national, as well as town government, and have found...it is efficient to a certain extent" and boldly insisted, "If my fellow citizens on the frontiers will withdraw their intrusions on Indian rights, and be honest, they have but little to apprehend."[5]

For nine months after the United States declared war on Great Britain, only scattered incidents disrupted peace in and around Creek country. Then in March of 1813, several white families were massacred near the mouth of the Ohio River by an eight-man war party led by two Creek chiefs sympathetic to Tecumseh. Hawkins immediately lodged a strong protest. "Of all the murderous acts committed by savages against the people of the United States, this is the most outrageous," Hawkins informed the chiefs at Tuckabatchee. These murders had not been committed "by thoughtless, wild young men, but deliberately, by a party under the command of two chiefs....The guilty must suffer for their crimes, or your nation will be involved in their guilt."[6]

After twelve days of deliberation, the Creek National Council decided to send warriors to seize the eight marauders. In several separate incidents, eight Creeks were then slain resisting arrest: seven of the eight marauders and one who was a brother of one of those slain as well as a brother of the one culprit still at large. Pursuit was then halted. During the night much talk took place in the town that was home to the three brothers, two of whom were guilty and two of whom had been slain. The next day the town's aged mico announced that his townspeople felt, "As there were but two guilty in the town, brothers, and one killed helping his brother...the debt was satisfied." The town therefore assisted the surviving guilty brother to make his escape. "The fellow got his gun and set out the morning after, to kill white people. The women hid the canoes" to frustrate pursuit, and the warriors who had been instructed to arrest him returned to Tuckabatchee.

With Hawkins insisting "It is not an equal number the white people want, it is the guilty," Big Warrior and his fellow-chiefs reluctantly decided they must punish the surviving brother. When he was finally tracked down, he defended himself with gun, knife and tomahawk until the warriors attempting to arrest him "shot three balls through him. He fell, retained power of speech till next day, and died. He said he had been to the Shawnees helping of them, and had got fat eating white people's flesh." Before dying, he "told the town people, the nation would be ruined for killing him."[7]

The next provocation originated on the U.S. side. In 1810, Hawkins had advised Secretary of War Eustis that the Creeks "have long claimed the jurisdiction of Coosa River" and this was "valid and conclusive." The prospect of Tennesseeans sailing up and down the Coosa—almost literally the artery of the Creek nation—was, Hawkins warned, "alarming, in a high degree, to the Creeks...as they are fearful [it] will bring ruin on their nation."[8] Ignoring this advice, Eustis ordered Hawkins to inform the Creeks that the United States had decided to abrogate unilaterally another understanding laboriously achieved at the tribal meeting ground. Hawkins did what he was told. Invoking grandiose abstractions, he wrote the chiefs,

> As we are now in possession of Mobile, you will soon see people from Tennessee coming down Coosa, with their produce, to market; when you see that, you will see you are friends, and you may go that water path together to trade, either to Tennessee or Mobile. It is a natural right you both have....Touch not the land of one another, but use your waters and roads as friends....All water courses were intended for the use, comfort, and accommodation of those who live on them: those who live at the mouth use them, those who live half way up use them, and those who live on the head use them; all can make use of them, without injury to the waters or to one another....It is time for us to understand these

things, and to act on them.

"Now, Colonel Hawkins," Big Warrior replied curtly,

> you say you are a friend to the nation, and one of the old chiefs. If any people of any nation should use the waters of the Coosa, it will bring trouble on us, and I hope you will inform the people of Tennessee...of these talks....If anything should happen, I shall tell you I told you of it. I have stated this to you; the nation was obliged to give up the public road, and they knew that would bring trouble on them, and since that, the nation have spilt blood, and we had to give satisfaction. If they have to give up the waters of the Coosa, it will hurt the feelings of the Creeks; it will not do. You thought you would mention this waters to them, to bring trouble on them, and destruction at once; you mean to destroy us, on these waters, in trying to make use of it, when we don't allow of it.

Tennesseeans were to have unregulated access to the interior of the Creek nation at the very moment that Creeks were being denied entry into Tennessee. "It appears," complained Big Warrior,

> as if all the frontiers is blocked up....We have poor people, some may have cow hides, and some have other things, such as small fur and beeswax, to change for clothing....The Upper Towns had rather go to Tennessee...by water and land, to trade. They have not got much to carry, only a little to buy some clothing and a little powder to carry about to kill a little game, even if it is birds, not to consider it to spill blood of no color.[9]

Big Warrior could neither speak nor write English. Alex Cornells who was paid by Hawkins to interpret could speak English but not write it. Hawkins had therefore assigned a U.S. citizen named Nimrod Doyle to reside at Tuckabatchee and write down Big Warrior's talks, as translated orally by Cornells. Now the irate chiefs decided to hire back Cornells and fire Doyle. Alex Cornells, who was a nephew of Alexander McGillivray and married to Efau Hadjo's daughter and thus a stepson of Big Warrior, had worked for Hawkins for fifteen years without losing his standing as a chief of the nation. He was now required to sever his ties with Hawkins and give the Creek nation his undivided loyalty. And Doyle had to go: "One Agent is enough for this nation," Big Warrior informed Hawkins. "I have now given you an answer on that." Since "we have got some of our people who have got learning from white people" a Creek literate in English would henceforth "write the talks of the nation."

Big Warrior's earlier effort to oblige Hawkins by slaying the eight Creek marauders was meanwhile breeding challenges from an opposite direction. In the Creeks' western region, recently disrupted by the two new wagon roads and the resulting influx of settlers around Mobile, visionaries using techniques learned from Tecumseh's Shawnees were inducing trances and seeing portents. Big Warrior sent for details:

> You say that the Great Spirit visits you frequently; that he comes in the sun, and speaks to you; that the sun comes down just above your heads. Now, we want to see and hear what you say you have seen and heard ....You have nothing to fear; the people who committed murders have suffered for their crimes, and there is an end to it.

The runner who carried this message had participated in the execution of the eight marauders. When he reached the Creek visionaries, "They instantly put him to death, and scalped him."[10]

To confront this new crisis, Big Warrior summoned yet another National Council, which several chiefs including the Tallassee Mico and his head warrior Peter McQueen refused to attend. Big Warrior then sent Alex Cornells to make Hawkins aware of what at least a few Creeks were plotting:

> First to put to death every chief and warrior who aided to execute the murderers, then the old chiefs, friends to peace, who had taken the talks of Colonel Hawkins, from whom the order for punishing the murderers came, then [Alex] Cornells, because he was the interpreter, and if they could at the same time to put Colonel Hawkins to death. But having killed all the others, if he escaped, it would be of no consequence, as then none would be left alive to receive and communicate his talks; and the nation could fix their affairs their own way. After this they would be ready for the white people, who could do them no injury if they came among them, as the prophets would draw circles around their abode and render the earth quaggy and impassable. If any Indian town refused their aid to the prophets, they should be sunk with earthquakes, or hills should be turned over them. They had also the aid of the lightning whenever they wanted.[11]

A Creek threat to the United States was now confirmed by the Creeks themselves. Hawkins notified Secretary of War John Armstrong that there appeared to be a "contest among the chiefs for power," and described Tuckabatchee as a "scene of confusion." Cautiously, he then suggested "it might be policy in us to look on, and let it be settled among themselves." But since future developments could bring on "hostility to us eventually," he concluded, "we must be ready to apply a military corrective in due time." What Hawkins had in mind was a "detachment of mounted infantry" from the regular federal army.[12]

True to their declared intent, the Creek insurrectionaries assaulted Tuckabatchee. The Tallassee Mico directed the attack, while his town's head warrior Peter McQueen traveled to Spanish Florida to buy arms. By July 26, 1813, Big Warrior was compelled to abandon Tuckabatchee and remove his headquarters eastward to the Lower Creek town of Coweta on the Chattahoochee River.

Civil war convulsed the Creek nation. Forces loyal to the Tallassee Mico controlled Tuckabatchee and were moving toward Big Warrior's new base at Coweta. Since every able-bodied male Creek was a trained fighter, opposing armies formed rapidly and immediately swung into action. The exact strength of either side was difficult to determine, but Big Warrior estimated that the Tallassee Mico commanded "at least two thousand five hundred" warriors, the majority of whom were Upper Creeks: "twenty-nine towns and villages of the Upper Creeks has joined the war party; there are but five towns of the Upper Creeks that are for peace." The Lower Creeks were only one-third of the total Creek population, and even Lower Creek towns could not be wholly counted on by Big Warrior. Although most Lower Creek warriors followed their pro-U.S. town chiefs, a minority defied them and fought for the young visionaries and the venerable Tallassee Mico. In all, roughly two-thirds of all Creeks answered the Tallassee Mico's call to arms.[13]

On July 9, 1813, Hawkins had only with great reluctance made a belated request for the readying of several hundred federal troops, because he feared that any request for aid would be answered instead by the arrival of large, land-hungry contingents of state militia from Georgia and Tennessee. In a letter dated July 13, 1813, to Tennessee Governor Willie Blount, Andrew Jackson offered to raise just such a corps of several thousand Volunteers to march against the Creeks and "crush all opposition...at one blow." Jackson rejected the idea that his Volunteers should "barely make an incursion through their towns, burn their houses, destroy their crops, and hastily return"—as General Washington had ordered done to the hostile Iroquois in 1779. Jackson in 1813 urged establishing "fortified places in the heart of the Creek nation" and preparing to "drive the Indians and their allies into the ocean" and even to take possession of Spanish Pensacola should events make this possible. He derided Hawkins' strategy of attempting to support one tribal faction against another because, argued Jackson,

> There is no instance within my recollection wherein an Indian tribe or nation has been invaded, but they united their whole force against the invaders; therefore...no calculation ought to be made on the division of the nation.[14]

Jackson's "recollection" was wrong, and his intent malign. But Governor Blount enthusiastically seconded "teaching these savages, of all colors, the impropriety of their conduct." As for the supposed "civil war said by the Agent to be raging among the Creek Indians," Blount applauded Jackson's contempt for Hawkins' arguments, calling them "altogether fudge—a mere tub for the whale—thrown out by the hostile party of the Creeks, through the contrivance and suggestion of the British and Spaniards, as a blind to the credulous." Blount also delineated glittering objectives for Jackson's Volunteers:

> The American people are composed of too pure materials, they have too noble pursuits in view...to permit themselves to be insulted with impunity, or to suffer their country, which is the only known asylum for freemen, to be overrun...by savages....I entertain the hope...that the administrators of our Government...feel too ardent a desire for the general improvement of...that delightful tract, at this time inhabited by... the hostile Creeks...to permit their longer residence thereon...any longer than they can be ousted by our arms....Five thousand men, and upwards, from this State, are under marching orders....If those troops do their duty [they may] soon become the cultivators of the rich soil, which they [win] by their valor....These objects once effected, each southern and western inhabitant will cultivate his own garden of Eden [and] rationally enjoy the comforts of life, as all Americans should be privileged to do.[15]

While Jackson was still recruiting Volunteers for Tennessee's planned seizure of Creek territory, some frontiersmen could not wait. On July 27, 1813, at a place called Burnt Corn, a mixed force of one hundred eighty pro-U.S. Creeks and frontiersmen from the Mississippi Territory led by the wagoner Sam Dale attacked the Tallassee Mico's head warrior Peter McQueen and his party as they returned with military supplies purchased in Pensacola. Dale's men were driven off but did succeed in carrying away some supplies.

After the Battle of Burnt Corn, Dale's men sought refuge at Fort Mims, the fortified focal point of a frontier enclave north of Mobile, the very people eager to be connected to Tennessee settlements by the Coosa River. Some two hundred white settlers and pro-U.S. Creeks and a number of their slaves were gathered for safety at Fort Mims, a crude stockade enclosing an acre of land. The Fort's occupants welcomed Dale's reinforcements. But on August 30, 1813, scarcely more than a month after the Battle of Burnt Corn, one thousand Creek insurrectionaries loyal to the Tallassee Mico, led by Peter McQueen and Alexander McGillivray's nephew William Weatherford, attacked Fort Mims. Finding the gate standing open, they "fired the houses with cotton matches fixed to arrows" and slaughtered all who offered resistance. Of the more than three hundred people inside Fort Mims, about two hundred and fifty were killed. The attacking Creeks "put all the white people to death" and "made prisoners only of some half-breed women and children." Several dozen African Americans were also spared.[16]

Here at last was what could be called a Creek declaration of war on the United States, and the cry to avenge Fort Mims was heard up and down the frontier. What had happened at Fort Mims also seemingly vindicated the insurrectionaries' claim to superhuman force, and more Creeks now rallied to their cause. On September 30, 1813, Hawkins acknowledged that their "boasted power...to take American forts with bows and arrows...and...determination to put to death every red man who does not join them, [have] given to many much terror." The Tallassee Mico announced his intention to destroy the pro-U.S. chiefs at Coweta and then head for Savannah; and to "give Colonel Hawkins a chase and take him, unless he was on a fleet horse."[17]

Responding to a plea from Big Warrior, two hundred pro-U.S. Cherokee warriors arrived to reinforce Coweta. But ammunition and guns were scarce because the federal government, abusively extending Jefferson's manipulative policy, withheld the Creek annuity in both 1812 and 1813 "without assigning any reason for it" even though Hawkins urgently insisted that the "chiefs were never in greater need of their funds than at present, to pay their warriors." On October 18,

1813, Big Warrior was compelled to pull his roving war parties back within Coweta's walls. But Big Warrior's forces held; and on October 23, the military situation at last stabilized, Big Warrior arrived in person for consultations with Hawkins at the Agency.[18]

State militias were meanwhile swinging into action. Units from Georgia, from the Mississippi Territory and from Tennessee under Jackson marched to avenge Fort Mims. In all, some 15,000 state militiamen, rather than the few hundred federal troops Hawkins had sought, confronted less than three thousand ill-armed Creek insurrectionaries. More than a thousand Creeks, belying Jackson's prediction, offered invaluable support to the state militias. The Tallassee Mico's warriors fought well but soon began to feel the effects of overwhelming odds. On November 29, 1813, the Tallassee Mico was "killed by a cannon shot" while defending his last stronghold at Autosse against Georgia militia. Two hundred Creek insurgents were slain at Autosse by heavy artillery fire, and the town was then plundered and burned.[19]

Since the Creek insurrectionaries obviously could not hold out much longer, discussions began concerning a post-war settlement. On March 17, 1814, President Madison appointed Hawkins and General Thomas Pinckney of the regular federal army to serve as Treaty Commissioners. Having negotiated the 1795 Treaty with Spain which established the Florida border, Pinckney like Hawkins was well-acquainted with the region and its problems. Pinckney and Hawkins informed the chiefs on both sides that they were prepared to offer peace terms that would compensate the United States for war costs, guarantee additional transit rights, and reinstate the pro-U.S. chiefs.

Jackson was infuriated by the selection of Pinckney and Hawkins, and strenuously protested the federal government's failure to appoint a frontier representative. At the same time he accelerated his military campaign, advancing quickly toward the last insurgent stronghold on the Tallapoosa River, determined, he wrote, "to exterminate" the one thousand Creeks gathered there and, in the Battle of Horseshoe Bend on March 27, 1814, well over six hundred were killed. Following this victory, Jackson marched down the Tallapoosa, burning Tuckabatchee and other undefended Creek towns along its banks, until he reached its confluence with the Coosa where he erected Fort Jackson. "The fiends of the Tallapoosa," he proclaimed,

> will no longer murder our women and children or disturb the quiet of our borders. Their midnight flambeaux will no more illumine their council house, or shine upon the victim of their infernal orgies. They have disappeared from the face of the earth.[20]

In response to the enormous popular elation resulting from Jackson's victory at Horseshoe Bend, President Madison canceled the appointments of Pinckney and Hawkins and named Jackson sole federal Treaty Commissioner to deal with the Creeks.

The Tallassee Mico was dead. Other insurgent chiefs, including Peter McQueen, had fled to Spanish Florida. Virtually the only Creek chiefs with whom Jackson could negotiate were U.S. allies. The Tennesseean summoned them—and Hawkins—to meet him in August of 1814 at Fort Jackson, where he had ready for signature a Treaty in which these chiefs were asked to acknowledge that they had been victimized by the "duplicity and misrepresentation of foreign emissaries" as well as by "imposters denominating themselves prophets." Jackson also insisted on a cession of approximately half the Creek nation, twenty million acres of fertile land in the shape of an L, comprising the nation's western and southern flanks. Much of the land demanded was the territory of the largely pro-U.S. Lower Creeks. Hawkins asked Jackson "upon what principles he took the lands eastwardly to Georgia, belonging obviously to the friendly Indians? The general answered," Hawkins reported, "he did it from political motives—to prevent an intercourse between the Indians and the Spaniards and English in the Floridas."[21] In the 1790s, the United States had sought to regulate such intercourse, but acknowledged its legitimacy in treaties with the Creeks, Britain and Spain; Jackson in 1814 peremptorily commanded that it must end.

Although Hawkins told Jackson he considered the Treaty's terms unjust, he encouraged Big Warrior and the other chiefs at Fort Jackson to place their marks on Jackson's document with the understanding that it was only a cease-fire agreement, and that their objections to it would be relayed to Washington. Hawkins advised the chiefs to consider their acquiescence an act of "capitulation" or military surrender only. He spoke of the land in question as having been for the moment "retained" by Jackson rather than "ceded" by the Creeks, pending clarification of the federal government's intentions. Even if the federal government did uphold Jackson, Hawkins believed, the Creeks could then decide independently whether or not to approve the Treaty.[22]

The Creek chiefs may have been less optimistic about a reversal than Hawkins. Shortly before the "capitulation" was completed, Big Warrior rose to speak. "The points now about boundary are pretty well settled," he said, "and we shall sign it; but, before we do it, and yield it up, we have something to say to you. We are a poor distressed people, involved in ruin, which we have brought on ourselves. It is not caused by a foreign people among us." Addressing Jackson he added,

> There is a man near you, Colonel Hawkins, the same, we give him three miles square. He has long been among us, helping of us, and doing good for our nation, and is their friend. He and I met at Colerain [in 1796], and were young men, and are now old; his children are born in our land. He is to select his land we give, where he chooses, on the land we are about to give up, and to sit down on it; and, if he dies, his children will have a place to live on. We do this as a token of the gratitude of the nation....Mrs. Hawkins must be put in, with her children, as she has had much trouble to teach the Indians to spin and weave.

The deed of gift which was then drawn up announced that

> Our nation feel under obligations to Colonel Benjamin Hawkins, our Agent, and to Mrs. Lavinia Hawkins, his wife, for the unwearied pains they have taken, both of them, for a long time, to introduce the plan of civilization among us.[23]

Shrewdly Big Warrior offered an equal tract to Jackson on the same terms, that he agree to live on it.[24]

On January 8, 1815, five months after his humiliation of the pro-U.S. Creeks, came Jackson's spectacular triumph over the British in the Battle of New Orleans. Hawkins spent this same five month period attempting to block a Creek-British military alliance in the Florida region, and to avert ratification of Jackson's Treaty. Immediately after the signing of the Treaty of Fort Jackson, Hawkins wrote Secretary of War Armstrong protesting that its terms were both unfair and dangerous because they would embitter the Creeks and render them receptive to British overtures. "As soon as our new line of limits for the Creeks is known," he warned, "it will rouse them and combine their whole force, in that quarter, against us." This is nearly what happened.

There had not been a significant British front in the Pensacola region prior to August, 1814, but now one emerged which included Seminoles, escaped African American slaves and uprooted Creeks. As many as two thousand Creeks, some previously friendly to the United States, fled in 1814 to Spanish Florida. Among them was a teen-aged boy named Osceola, from the Tallassee Mico's town. The British encouraged these Creeks to join them, called on African American slaves to defy their masters, supplied them all with ammunition and thereby maintained a credible military threat south of the Spanish border, though only a handful of Britishers were on the scene. Five of Hawkins' own slaves answered the British call. Even Big Warrior was prepared to take up arms against the United States, if the British supplied enough aid. To counter this threat, Hawkins managed to enroll more than a thousand Creek warriors in U.S. service under his own command. The War Department was uncertain what to think of Colonel Hawkins' Creek Regiment, with its U.S. Army-style titles but dressed and disposed in the customary Creek way. For better or worse, this unorthodox U.S. force was never tested in battle against Britain's unorthodox force.[25]

The British gave up in 1815, but Creeks and Seminoles sparked by Osceola vowed in 1816 to "resist as long as they have ammunition and a swamp to go to"—which is just what they did. Officially the Seminole Wars stretched from 1818 to 1858, and scattered survivors continued to hold out in isolated swamp regions for decades longer.[26]

No reply to either Hawkins' protests or Big Warrior's objections regarding Jackson's terms was made prior to the Treaty's formal ratification.[27] Indeed the first official word to reach the Creeks of what happened in Washington came in July of 1815 when a certain Captain Barnett, who had been appointed by the War Department to run the line specified in the Treaty, "addressed from Fort Stoddert [near Mobile] a letter direct to the Big Warrior inviting his attendance." Big Warrior replied that "he knew him not, and would not go one step."[28]

Hawkins was notified of the Treaty's ratification in letters written by the Acting Secretary of War on July 12 and 15, five months after the Treaty had been publicly proclaimed in Washington. On August 1 Hawkins replied, strongly criticizing the way matters had been handled by both Jackson and the War Department, and warning that the Creek chiefs "may refuse their ratification which...from the singular manner the capitulation is worded—the parties 'agree to ratify and confirm,' etc.—it appears they have a right to do." The Creeks who marked the Treaty, Hawkins further contended, had not been "a party and can only be viewed in the light of witnesses." Perhaps the Creeks could still be persuaded to ratify the Treaty when they next met at now-devastated Tuckabatchee although, as Hawkins caustically informed Jackson, "from what I hear we shall have much more trouble in perfecting your capitulation than you had in making it."

Captain Barnett was already trying to mark the boundary, Creek ratification or no. Relations between Hawkins and Barnett reached the breaking point, with Barnett making it clear he wanted to have nothing to do with Hawkins and Hawkins accusing Barnett of both "perversion of truth" and a "want of manners."[29] The informality in correspondence maintained by Hawkins and Presidents Washington and Jefferson and for a time also by Hawkins and President Madison had not survived the war. In his final years, Hawkins often found himself dealing with lower-ranking officials such as Captain Barnett who issued him orders, and scorned his advice. But Hawkins remained committed to rebuilding an improved working relationship with officers high and low.

Informed by Hawkins at Tuckabatchee that Jackson's "draft" Treaty had actually been ratified, Big Warrior ruefully observed,

> When the chiefs and General Washington met [in 1790], the talk [was that] they would hold each other fast. The treaty was if either party should do any murder, satisfaction should be given....I know the whites always told me, if there was anything I could not do myself my friends would assist me. When they told me they would assist me they never told me they would take away my land.

Having been appointed Agent by President Washington, and having begun working to promote good U.S. relations with the Creeks well before 1790, Hawkins would have found Big Warrior's reminiscence peculiarly painful.

"This is my answer to the President," continued Big Warrior.

> The Treaty with Washington is good with us. The Treaty at Fort Jackson is not straight....The chiefs of the whole nation did not meet together to hear the Treaty, it was in the woods, and not in a town house. Now this square is our appointed place. This we call a meeting. It is a place

> appointed as such. A talk which is made unless done here, is not of much force.... [At Fort Jackson] we were not settled in our minds. Now we are settled in our minds, and this is to be the talk....I told him [General Jackson] what little land I had, I loved....I told him he was taking all my land from me, he was going to leave us to suffer. The General's answer was if you will not sign the Treaty...you must go down to Pensacola and join your friends, Red Sticks [Creek insurgents] and British...[but] by the time I got to Pensacola he would be on my tracks and whip me and the British into the sea. I asked him if that was the way to treat a beloved friend. You know we are poor and you wish to leave us still poorer....I asked if it was the orders of the President to treat us in that way. After talking to the General I found out I was in distress. I found the General had great power to distress me. I told him it would not do to do a thing in a hurry.[30]

For Hawkins, the reason to consider the Creeks not bound by Jackson's Treaty lay in its technical legal language. For Big Warrior, the coercive negotiating process itself invalidated the Treaty. As Hawkins later reported, at Tuckabatchee it had not been "in my power to remove the impressions of unfair dealing on our part towards them"—impressions Hawkins himself shared.

The tribal tradition posited that nations would fight and then come together to bury the hatchet, in a ceremonial manner restoring good feelings and a willingness to cooperate once again. The 1814 Treaty of Fort Jackson did not even attempt to restore peace, and expressed contempt for tribal tradition. No acknowledgment was made that the United States shared responsibility for provoking this war, and no effort was made to be fair or courteous; General Jackson simply asserted that he was furthering U.S. strategic interests and expressed no interest in conciliating hostile Creeks, or honoring the assistance of pro-U.S. Creeks.

Captain Barnett was obliged to mark the line dictated by Jackson under armed guard and without any help from the Creeks. As Hawkins informed Jackson on April 21, 1816, "The friendly Indians...will not aid us."[31] Meanwhile Georgians began moving into the region demanded by Jackson long before the completion of legal formalities. In 1805 Hawkins was able to drive off such squatters. This time, Hawkins advised the Secretary of War, it was "not practicable to carry into effect your wishes relative to intruders in the recently acquired lands. The inroad of people moving from the southern states is much greater than I [have] ever known or heard of. Some days two hundred ten have passed and no day less than ten to fifty." Meanwhile, the Governor of the Mississippi Territory had proclaimed the western portion of these lands already under his control, having "prematurely" extended "the laws of the Territory over the lands, named the county Monroe, and appointed civil and military officers there."[32]

In April of 1816, a few weeks before Hawkins died, Big Warrior visited the Agency. "If you Colonel Hawkins had not advised me to sign Jackson's Treaty I never would have done it," he asserted, "and as I feel myself deceived and disappointed I am done with it and whatever relates to it. As it is, it is Jackson's, not mine." And he lamented,

> The white people suspected him, General Jackson threatened him and his own people were getting wrathful against him, charging him with consorting to his own use their annuities which had not been paid....For his part he could not account for the conduct of his white friends. It was not what he called just.

In reply, Hawkins

> entered much at large on our situation, the difficulties our nation have had to struggle with and ended with assurances that a delay to do them justice was not a denial and he might rest assured they would receive it ere long, that if I was not as certain of this as my existence I would not be Agent for Indian affairs....[Big Warrior] paused, sighed, and said it would come too late for him.[33]

In this final conversation between U.S. Agent Hawkins and the Creek Presiding Chief he first met in 1796, both men displayed remarkable candor and dignity. For years, each had represented his nation in negotiations with the other. In 1813-14, each had been shoved aside by militant forces in his own nation; and in 1816, each had to look far into the future to discern hope that consensual traditions would be revived. They had both lost, but neither lost respect for the other, or could see reason to pronounce their efforts irrelevant for all time to come. Big Warrior was right in his belief that an era had ended. Hawkins was also right in pronouncing the havoc Jackson wrought a perversion of the Revolution rather than the best one could expect from the United States.

Hawkins died on June 6, 1816, and was buried near the Agency on a bluff overlooking the Flint River. Less than a month after his death, the Agency compound was destroyed by fire. Lavinia Hawkins and the children escaped but "even their wearing clothes were burnt." Most of the manuscripts of Hawkins' scholarly researches concerning Creek culture were lost in the flames. In October of the same year, Hawkins' remaining effects including his five-hundred-volume library were sold at public auction. Scattered far and wide were copies of Blackstone's *Commentaries,* Jefferson's *Notes on the State of Virginia*, Adam Smith's *Wealth of Nations*, Chesterfield's *Letters*, Gibbon's *Decline and Fall of the Roman Empire*, Horace, Cicero and Xenophon, as well as books on bee-keeping and midwifery. Lavinia Hawkins was not skilled in financial matters and within a few years the family had little left. The distress of his family, the burning of his home and the dispersal of his library all bespoke the shattering of a cultural era, as well as family misfortune.[34]

The person appointed to succeed Hawkins as U.S. Agent to the Creek nation was not Captain William Hawkins, the able nephew who had been groomed for the job while serving as Hawkins' assistant, and who later became Governor of North Carolina. Hawkins' successor was an old opponent: David Mitchell, former Governor of Georgia.[35] In subsequent years, bribes such as those Hawkins had been pressured to offer in his final years became ever more common, and in 1824 federal officials privately approached several Creek chiefs seeking signatures on the Treaty of Indian Springs, by which the Creeks would have relinquished all their ancestral lands in exchange for western wilds. The aging Big Warrior stated that he would not listen even if offered "a houseful of money." He died soon afterward.[36] William McIntosh accepted a large bribe and signed the Treaty. An Upper Creek raiding party then murdered him. These avengers were led by Menawa, one of the few survivors of the final battle against Jackson at Horseshoe Bend. John Quincy Adams, just elected President, repudiated the corruptly negotiated Indian Springs Treaty, and the Creeks received a temporary reprieve.[37]

Given the methodical undermining of the tribal treaty process to which he himself had contributed, it is not surprising that in 1820 Jackson proclaimed it "high time to do away with the farce of treating with the Indian tribes."[38] By this date, meeting ground procedures had indeed often been made into farce by federal officials impatient with tribal treaty rituals and sarcastic about their presumption of reciprocity. The practice of signing treaties with tribes was however not formally abolished until 1871.[39]

After he became President in 1829, Jackson offered all the southern tribes a non-negotiable choice: either move west or become subject to the laws of individual states. The retention of tribal autonomy in their homelands was to be no longer an option. "You are within the limits of Alabama which is an independent State," Jackson's Secretary of War John Eaton advised the Creeks on May 16, 1831, and Alabama "is not answerable to your Great Father, for the exercise of her jurisdiction over the people who reside within her limits."

Jackson's administration read the Constitution in quite a new way. Under the Constitution properly construed, explained Jackson's second Secretary of War, Lewis Cass, any and all federal responsibility for tribal affairs was temporary, and extended only to situations beyond the capacity of individual states to cope with. The federal government was Constitutionally obligated "to provide for the common defense" by protecting the states from tribal depredations. But, Cass contended, when the "*posse comitatus* [an ordinary sheriff's posse] may be substituted for a military force, the respective states may safely assume jurisdiction ...without calling upon Congress." Federal responsibility

> will cease when danger is no longer to be apprehended, and when the ordinary civil power of the community is sufficient to govern and restrain the Indians. And the states must necessarily judge when this period has arrived....The portion of jurisdiction till that time entrusted to the general government may then be assumed, and the whole subject left to the state authorities.

Under the Constitution, according to Cass's reading, "jurisdiction over the Indian tribes...belongs to the several state governments, whensoever and howsoever they may choose to exercise it." In fact Cass believed a tribe that was no longer dangerous didn't deserve the name; with "the extinction of that portion of [federal] jurisdiction arising out of the duty of general defense...they will then cease to be tribes."[40]

Alabamians eager to have the first pick of vacated properties seized Creek lands on the assumption that their Creek owners would "choose" to emigrate. Creeks returning from treaty sessions found their farms occupied and their families turned out of their homes by U.S. citizens. Such actions provoked protests in Congress but coerced eviction moved forward slowly until the last year of Jackson's presidency when an intensive effort was made to complete the process. During this year, fourteen thousand Creeks, the bulk of those who had not yet fled or been forced from their homes, were escorted west in huge convoys.[41]

One such convoy of one thousand, nine hundred and eighty-four Creeks left the Tallassee Mico's town on the Tallapoosa, in the charge of Lieutenant J.T. Sprague. "From the first day's march," Sprague noted in his journal,

> I saw a disposition in the Indians, among both old and young, to remain behind. From their natural indolence and from their utter disregard for the future, they would straggle in the rear....I used every entreaty to induce them to keep up but finding this of no avail I threatened them with soldiers and confinement in irons.

Sprague's convoy was given little rest and the "lame, sick, and blind were left behind, dependent upon the charity of the country." Haste was demanded by the private contractors who had bid for the right to handle arrangements. They opposed Sprague's suggestion that a day of rest be allowed, arguing that their expenses "were from six to seven hundred dollars per day" and even one day's delay would mean "their hopes of making anything were gone." Sprague's Creek contingent was transported part of the way on "rotten, old, and unseaworthy boats" chartered by these contractors, on which "seven superficial square feet" were allocated to each passenger. Three hundred eleven members of a second convoy were drowned when their boat, proceeding at night up the wrong river channel, collided with another vessel and split in two.

Sprague was indignant at the contractors' reckless inhumanity, but also incensed by the behavior of Creeks in his charge. "If liquor could be found upon the road, or within four or six miles of it," he reported,

> men and women would congregate there, and indulge in the most brutal scenes of intoxication. If any white man broke in upon these bacchanals he did it at the imminent hazard of his life. Often in this state they would come reeling and singing into camp late at night, threatening the lives of all who came within their reach....They would taunt...sober Indians...as cowards and dare them to join them in some nefarious act.

It was an "absurdity to say," Sprague concluded, "that the Indians must take care of themselves; they are men it is true, but it is well known that they are totally incapable of it, and it's proverbial that they will never aid each other."[42]

The Creeks had seen their ancient sacral centers demolished, their homes seized, their leaders humiliated or slain. Force-marched to alien, uncultivated lands, the Creeks were inducted into their new western asylum in a desperate frame of mind. Other tribes were treated with equal harshness. This Native American Trail of Tears to the federal reservation, like the African American Middle Passage to slavery, was devastatingly disorienting. Coerced resettlement reduced many Native Americans to a level of helplessness that could then be used to justify pronouncing them inherently incompetent.

Andrew Jackson's methodical assault on tribes brutalized both tribes and the Constitution. Jackson's failure to cause even worse damage was due to resistance mounted by tribes in arms as well as by U.S. citizens and officials who scrutinized the Constitution in search of ways to defend the rights of tribes. The Supreme Court headed by Chief Justice John Marshall led this effort to affirm Constitutional protection for tribes.

Nine

Reinterpreting John Marshall's Tribal Opinions

UPON BECOMING CHIEF JUSTICE OF THE SUPREME COURT in 1801, John Marshall began trying to stabilize the legal status of tribes. At about the same time, Andrew Jackson began advocating radical change in federal treatment of tribes, and when Marshall administered the Presidential oath of office to Jackson in 1829, both knew they were likely to do battle over tribal rights.

In the decades preceding Jackson's capture of the Presidency, tribal land rights had been saved from obliteration in large part by the treaty framework established by President Washington. Although the Constitution said nothing about tribes beyond affirming the importance of commerce with them and the consequent imperative that the federal government must concern itself with them, Washington concluded that the best way to deal with tribes was by treaties negotiated according to ancient tribal traditions, and then ratified under the Constitution's brand-new procedure. By the end of his two precedent-setting terms as President, Washington had given substance to the Constitution's spare tribal language. Jefferson assisted this process as Washington's Secretary of State, and as President was reluctant to renounce it. In deciding to assail it, Jackson could not have expected easy success, yet he persisted for more than two decades before he was in a position to begin dismantling Washington's tribal treaty structure.

In 1803, Jackson had written President Jefferson advocating a more assertive stance toward tribes. In 1814, Jackson managed to get himself appointed a federal treaty commissioner, in which capacity he proceeded to demonstrate the kind of treatment he thought would work best with tribes. In 1817, at the beginning of James Monroe's Presidency, Jackson wrote him contending that tribes possessed only a hunting ground use right that lapsed *automatically* as soon as all animals worth hunting were gone. "The game being destroyed," reasoned Jackson, "...the right of possession granted to the Indians for the purpose of hunting ceases, and justice, sound policy and the Constitutional rights of the citizen, would require its being resigned to him." By extending this logic, Jackson could have pronounced poaching sound policy, because it helped eliminate an obstacle to settlement by U.S. citizens. Jackson did draw the conclusion that "the Legislature of the Union have the right to prescribe their bounds at pleasure...and enforce obedience to those just laws provided for their benefit." What about commitments made to tribes in federal treaties? Jackson labeled these "an absurdity not to be reconciled to the principles of our government," and therefore literally a "farce" or charade engaged in by President Washington and his successors out of "weakness":

> The Indians are the subjects of the United States, inhabiting its territory and acknowledging its sovereignty, then is it not absurd for the sovereign to negotiate by treaty with the subject....To this might be opposed the policy and practice of the government so long pursued towards them; to which I would answer, that this policy grew out of the weakness of the arm of government, and the circumstances under which the nations were placed, and not from rights acknowledged to be possessed by them, by the confederated government. The arm of government was not sufficiently strong to enforce its regulations amongst them, it was difficult to keep them at peace, and the policy of treating with them was adopted from necessity. Circumstances have entirely changed, and the time has arrived when a just course of policy can be exercised toward them. Their existence and happiness now depend upon a change in their habits and customs which can only be effected by a change of policy in the government. The game being destroyed, they can no longer exist by their bows and arrows and guns. They must lay them aside and produce by labor from the earth a subsistence; in short they must be civilized; to effect which their territorial boundary must be curtailed; as long as they are permitted to roam over vast limits in pursuit of game, so long will they retain their savage manners and customs....There can be no doubt but that in this way more justice will be extended to the nations than by the farce which has been introduced of holding treaties with them, for it is too true that avarice and fear are the predominant passions that govern an Indian.[1]

Washington had explicitly instanced "savages" when he expressed the view that all "human nature is such that it will adhere to the side from whence the best treatment is received."[2] Washington believed that *savage* life was a rational choice, and therefore being *civil* to *savages* made sense. Although Jefferson countenanced monetary pressure and even discreet bribery of tribal chiefs, he never questioned the formal right of tribes to exercise their free will as independent polities, or the underlying assumption that Native Americans, *savage* or not, were rational human beings with legal rights to the lands they occupied. "We will never be angry with others for exercising their own rights according to what they think their own interests," Jefferson informed chiefs of the Ohio region in 1808. "We find no fault with you for what you did not do, but thank you for what you did."[3] To Jackson, such Presidential assurances seemed worse than irresponsible, they sounded silly.

While Jackson advocated comprehensive structural changes as wise public policy, others interested only in personal gain were utilizing diverse legal gambits to acquire tracts of tribal land. Even before July 4, 1776, land claims based on incompatible definitions of "Indian title" abounded. Litigation, sometimes lasting for decades, resulted when U.S. citizens claimed to have bought the same tract from different tribes, or when more than one U.S. buyer claimed to have bought the same tribal tract. Still more troubling controversies resulted from speculation in tribal land futures: selling and buying land still occupied by tribes, in anticipation that they would soon leave.

During the pre-Constitutional years 1776-1789, states from Massachusetts to Georgia freely adopted whatever tribal land tenure theory they wished, and more than one state in need of cash recklessly sold tribal preemption rights to private buyers. Since they could realize no profit until tribes left, buyers of such rights were tempted to use threats or bribery to induce tribes to leave. The likely return on a preemption right to tribal land was speculative, it being unknown how many years investors might have to wait before realizing a profit. But there was no disagreement among U.S. officials that tribes when they did sell their "Indian title" would receive only a tiny fraction of what would be realized when these lands were resold to citizens. Speculation authorized by Georgia in such tribal land futures was at the base of the still notorious 1795 Yazoo land fraud, involving much of what is now the State of Mississippi. Similar speculation in western New York State, regarding which the Seneca chief Cornplanter appealed to Washington in 1790, dragged on for decades. On technical grounds, Washington declined to halt investor pressure on the Senecas during his two terms as President, and the consequences are still evident.[4]

Buying and selling tribal land futures was inherently corrupt. But it was legal, having been sanctioned by sovereign states prior to 1789, and therefore arguably beyond even Constitutional alteration. In 1810, the Supreme Court led by Marshall addressed this issue in *Fletcher vs. Peck*, a case involving Georgia's right to sell tribally-occupied lands stretching westward to the Mississippi River. The case obliged the Court to undertake an historical review of tribal land policy dating back to colonial days, and in particular to construe King George III's October 7, 1763 Proclamation, which established a watershed division between coastal colonial settlements and trans-Appalachian tribal hunting grounds. Both before and after the Revolution, dispute raged about whether this royal Proclamation had permanently detached western lands from seacoast colonies and provinces, and to this extent canceled the boundaries described for them by earlier royal charters. In 1776, states that could make western land claims quickly reasserted them. But states lacking such pretensions were attracted by the idea that the 1763 Proclamation had made all trans-Appalachian lands a royal preserve, allowing Congress to claim these lands for the central government of the United States by right of conquest. Since this issue was not touched by the 1783 Treaty of Paris, rivalry continued between states eager to revive pre-1763 claims and states that believed trans-Appalachian lands should go directly from the Crown to the central U.S. government. Marshall did not exaggerate when he stated in his Opinion for the Court that "The question, whether the vacant lands within the United States became a joint property, or belonged to the separate states...threatened to shake the American confederacy to its foundation." Marshall's legal euphemism "vacant" applied to tribally-occupied land suggests how difficult it was in 1810 to approach a definition of tribal land title.[5] "This important and dangerous contest has been compromised," Marshall concluded, "and the compromise is not now to be disturbed." Hammered out between 1780 and 1802, this "compromise" allowed states with trans-Appalachian claims to suppose them valid—but only if they agreed to cede them to the central U.S. government. This had the desired effect of saving the "American confederacy" from dissolution, and did ultimately work out more or less as hoped. But it took time and left enduring problems because states made numerous private land grants before ceding their jurisdictional claims, and insisted these grants must remain valid.

Acquiescing in state authority to grant land if exercised prior to formal cession of the region in question required that federal courts treat as legally binding anti-tribe state land grants. In *Fletcher vs. Peck* for example, the Court found itself contending with the Yazoo scandal, which pivoted on whether or not Georgia in 1795 could have legally granted to private individuals tribally-occupied lands that Georgia then ceded to the federal government in 1802. Rejecting the position that states had lost their western lands in 1763, Marshall's Court ruled that King George III's Proclamation was only a temporary interposition not intended to negate earlier charters granting western lands to colonies. The Court therefore held that Georgia in 1795 did indeed have the right to grant title to tribally occupied land in its as yet unceded trans-Appalachian regions.

After the messy political compromise of 1780-1802 in which one state after another ceded its inflated claims, but only on its own terms, had come countless lawsuits, and all too many rulings hostile to tribal interests. With his 1810 Opinion in *Fletcher vs. Peck,* Marshall sought to formulate a parallel theoretical synthesis which might salvage from this huge triumph of state interests some vestige of federal authority and tribal right. The key final words of Marshall's 1810 Opinion were

> The majority of the court is of opinion that the nature of the Indian title, which is certainly to be respected by all courts, until it be legitimately extinguished, is not such as to be absolutely repugnant to seizin in fee on the part of the state.

In other words, after 1776 states not tribes held fee title to intrastate "Indian title" lands, and even after 1789 could indeed traffic in tribal land futures. All the federal government could and therefore must do was to safeguard tribal tenancy on such lands until this was "legitimately extinguished."

Marshall's Opinion in *Fletcher vs. Peck* was a majority Opinion only. In a partially concurring, partially dissenting Opinion, Justice William Johnson expressed strong dissatisfaction with the Court's inability to distinguish the legal status of one group of Native Americans from another. Johnson contended that while some coastal tribes had "totally extinguished their national fire, and submitted themselves to the laws of the states...others retain a limited sovereignty, and the absolute proprietorship of their soil." While states could and did exercise full jurisdiction over the land rights of Native Americans groups that were no longer independent, Johnson questioned whether a state could hold any form of title to the lands of a truly self-governing tribe. Since the political condition of Native American groups was so "very various," it followed that the rights in land they could claim must also be "very various." The many treaties signed in the preceding decades with different tribes contained numerous specific terms and conditions, and Johnson felt these "very various" treaties rather than an arbitrary general rule were the best guides in determining what particular rights each tribe could claim.

It might have been better had the Court boldly done what Johnson preferred, and declared that a right of preemption to the lands occupied by an independent tribe could not legally pass into private hands. But for the Court to have followed Johnson's advice would have presupposed a determination on the part of the Court to overturn the history of tribal land rights of the preceding thirty years. The Marshall Court instead chose to compromise, combining validation of existing practice with an element of restraint represented by federal regulation.

Fletcher vs. Peck dealt with the nature of *state* title to tribal lands. Not until 1823, in *Johnson vs. McIntosh,* did the Court attempt to define *tribal* title. One party in this case based its claim to own a tract of Illinois land on the Jacksonian contention that tribes were mere tenants-at-will with no inheritable or alienable right to the land where they happened to dwell at any given moment. Lawyers for this side contended that even the largest tribes were not "independent communities, having a permanent property in the soil" but rather masses of hunters living "in a state of nature" who therefore possessed no "rights to land...in their national capacity; for the lands occupied by each tribe were not used by them in such a manner as to prevent their being appropriated by a people of cultivators." The other side, represented before the Court by Daniel Webster, argued that tribes had once been politically sovereign owners of their lands, and therefore free to sell to anyone they wished.

Versions of this *sovereign nation* theory had been advanced in the seventeenth century by Dutch colonists as well as by Rhode Island's Roger Williams, and in the mid-eighteenth century by land companies hostile to British restraints on the rights of tribes to sell land west of the Appalachians to these companies. Webster's clients traced their land claims back to such anti-imperial transactions.

Both the *roving hunter* and the *sovereign nation* theory of tribal land rights could claim lengthy North American histories. Each theory had prevailed at various times in one colony or another, and gained new champions in the Revolutionary era. Because nothing approaching a consensus on the issue of tribal land rights had yet been attained, both of these radically incompatible positions were still alive and well in 1823, advocated by U.S. citizens with land investments that would be worthless if their theory was not upheld. In an attempt to end these decades-old squabbles without rousing suspicion that the Court was making new law, Marshall began his Opinion by reproving proponents of both positions for letting selfish interests overwhelm their common sense, maintaining that he was "bestowing on this subject a degree of attention which was more required by the magnitude of the interest in litigation, and the able and elaborate arguments of the bar, than by its intrinsic difficulty."[6] Addressing proponents of the Jacksonian *roving hunter* school of thought, Marshall denied that the Court should or could decide a case involving tribal land rights on the basis of "whether agriculturalists, merchants, and manufacturers, have a right, on abstract principles, to expel hunters from the territory they possess, or to contract their limits"; the Court must also consider "those principles ...which our own government has adopted in the particular case, and given us as the rule for our decision." Daniel Webster's *sovereign nation* stance seemed no more sensible to Marshall, who contended that North American tribes were legally sovereign before Columbus but had by the seventeenth century been conquered by the Spanish, the French and the British. Nor did Marshall give credence to the idea that British-ruled tribes could have regained their lost sovereignty when abandoned by the British in 1783. Marshall preferred to suppose that, rather than lapsing, all Great Britain's rights vis-a-vis tribes passed by succession to the United States in 1776. He sidestepped the question of whether succession went to the thirteen states severally or collectively, sticking to his 1810 position that this issue was "compromised." In either case, having once been conquered, North American tribes could not expect to do with their lands as they chose. "The title by conquest is acquired and maintained by force," Marshall declared firmly, and did not need to be re-established by force when a new nation conquered the old conqueror. "Conquest gives a title which the courts of the conquerors cannot deny" and this title could pass to a conqueror's successor. The conqueror's title was finite however, because by conquest Marshall meant the triumph over one polity by another in a limited contest of strength, and a conquered tribe, although obliged to obey a conqueror's reasonable commands (and a conqueror's successor's reasonable commands) regarding such matters as land tenure, was presumed by Marshall to retain many inviolable rights.

The independent states after 1776 had chosen to uphold the validity of royal charters and land grants, insofar as these pertained to state land rights. To demarcate a route forward that would provide protection to tribes, Marshall argued that these same colonial charters and grants should be deemed a simultaneous guarantee of tribal title and therefore a limitation on the rights of Euro-American recipients of these royal charters and grants. Seeking a formula that would shield tribes from arbitrary expropriation, Marshall described as necessarily narrow the range of options available to any European or European-derived ruler of North America's tribes:

> To leave them in possession of their country, was to leave the country a wilderness; to govern them as a distinct people, was impossible, because they were as brave and as high spirited as they were fierce, and were ready to repel by arms every attempt on their independence.
>
> What was the inevitable consequence of this state of things? The Europeans were under the necessity either of abandoning the country, and relinquishing their pompous claims to it, or of enforcing those claims by the sword, and by the adoption of principles adapted to the condition of a people with whom it was impossible to mix, and who could not be governed as a distinct society, or of remaining in their neighborhood, and exposing themselves and their families to the perpetual hazard of being massacred....That law which regulates, and ought to regulate in general, the relations between the conqueror and conquered, was incapable of application to a people under such circum-

> stances. The resort to some new and different rule, better adapted to the actual state of things, was unavoidable....The peculiar situation of the Indians, necessarily considered, in some respects, as a dependent, and in some respects as a distinct people, occupying a country claimed by Great Britain, and yet too powerful and brave not to be dreaded as formidable enemies, required, that means should be adopted for the preservation of peace; and that their friendship should be secured by quieting their alarms for their property.

Marshall here portrayed tribal tradition in negative terms, as a constraint. Yet it is evident, even in Marshall's arms-length account, that the tribal system itself was what was really durable before and after 1776. North American continuity in tribal relations was not a result of the European legal theorizing Marshall distilled. Rather, North American continuity was insured by the tribes' alliance system, to which every European monarch, the thirteen sovereign states and then the President adjusted. Marshall was half-right—for the wrong reasons. Searching for logical comprehensiveness and historical continuity on the wrong side of the North American cultural encounter, Marshall nonetheless accurately sensed some legal significance in the fact that tribes themselves had limited the power of European monarchs, and then of the United States, to do with tribal land as they pleased.

In 1810, Marshall saw no political alternative to affirming the legality of state actions taken between 1776 and 1789. By 1823, Marshall wished to deny that many tribal policies pursued by states before 1789 were valid, and to affirm as definitive the tribal policies pursued by the federal government after 1789. To accomplish this goal, Marshall in 1823 chose to associate post-1789 federal tribal policy with pre-1776 British imperial tribal policy. Ignoring Revolutionary scorn for it, Marshall sought to refurbish Britain's tribal policy as not only admirable and coherent but binding on the Revolutionary United States. Marshall contended that "neither the Declaration of Independence, nor the treaty confirming it [the 1783 Treaty of Paris], could give us more than that which we before possessed, or to which Great Britain was before entitled." Selectively simplifying the colonial era—by for example leaving out the Dutch—Marshall implied that all European imperialists had asserted that "discovery gave a title to land still remaining in the possession of the Indians." He even noted with evident approval that "The charter granted to Sir Humphrey Gilbert, in 1578, authorizes him to discover and take possession of such remote, heathen, and barbarous lands, as were not actually possessed by any Christian prince or people." To invoke the archaically Eurocentric Doctrine of Discovery as the foundation of tribal title in the post-Revolutionary, secular United States was shocking in 1823, and is shocking today, especially since the silly and offensive Doctrine of Discovery has remained in effect.

Instead of drawing on such problematic precedents, the Court could have vindicated federal authority in a manner consonant with the nation's Revolutionary origins by adopting the argument made in 1790 by Secretary of State Jefferson. Discussing, with reference to the right of Georgia to regulate Creek land, many of the issues ultimately dealt with in Marshall's 1823 Opinion, Jefferson theorized that

> A society taking possession of a vacant country, and declaring they mean to occupy it, does thereby appropriate to themselves, as prime occupants, what was before common. A practice introduced since the discovery of America authorizes them to go farther, and to fix the limits which they assume to themselves; and it seems for the common good to admit this right to a moderate and reasonable extent. If the country, instead of being altogether vacant, is thinly occupied by another nation, the right of the natives forms an exception to that of the newcomers; that is to say, these will only have a right against all other nations except the natives: consequently they have the exclusive privilege of acquiring the native right by purchase or other just means. This is called the right of preemption; and is become a principle of the law of nations, fundamental with respect to America. There are but two means of acquiring the native title. 1. War; for even war may sometimes give a just title. 2. Contract, or treaty. The states of America, before their present union, possessed completely, each within its own limits, the exclusive right to use these two means of acquiring the native title: and by their act of union they have as completely ceded both to the general government. Article Two, Section Two. "The President shall have power, by and with the advice of the Senate, to make treaties, provided two thirds of the Senators present concur." Article One, Section Eight. "The Congress shall have power...to declare war...to raise and support armies." Section Ten. "No state shall, without the consent of Congress, keep troops or ships of war in time of peace, enter into any agreement or compact with another state, or with a foreign power, or engage in war, unless actually invaded, or in such imminent danger as will not admit of delay." These paragraphs of the Constitution, declaring that the general government shall have, and that the particular ones shall not have, the rights of war and treaty, are so explicit that no commentary can explain them further, nor can any explain them away. Consequently Georgia, possessing *the*

> *exclusive right to acquire the native title* but having relinquished the *means* of doing it to the general government, can only have put her grantees into her own condition. She could convey to them the exclusive right to acquire; but she could not convey, what she had not herself, that is, the means of acquiring. For these they must come to the general government, in whose hands they have been wisely deposited for the purposes both of peace and justice.[7]

Jefferson's closely-reasoned argument tied unique North American conditions to principles of universal law, without departing from the nation's secular commitments. Jefferson traced all necessary federal power to conscious political choices made during the Revolutionary era. Unlike Marshall, Jefferson saw no need base federal authority over tribes on rejected British imperial concepts.

Evidently believing that the deteriorating circumstances of tribes demanded an aggressive federal response, Marshall in 1823 had departed from the tortured caution of his 1810 Opinion and moved toward assertion of a neo-imperial federal protectorate over tribes. But the threat to tribal interests continued to strengthen, and on October 29, 1828, shortly before Andrew Jackson was elected President, in a letter to his Supreme Court colleague Joseph Story, Marshall confided an inclination to take yet bolder action. After thanking Story for a copy of his discourse delivered on the occasion of the bicentennial of Salem, Massachusetts, Marshall remarked that he had been "touched with your notice of the red man." Marshall was then led to reflect that

> The conduct of our forefathers in expelling the original occupants of the soil grew out of so many mixed motives that any censure which philanthropy may bestow upon it ought to be qualified. The Indians were a fierce and dangerous enemy whose love of war made them sometimes the aggressors, whose numbers and habits made them formidable, and whose cruel system of warfare seemed to justify every endeavor to remove them to a distance from civilized settlements. It was not until after the adoption of our present government that respect for our own safety permitted us to give full indulgence to those principles of humanity and justice which ought always to govern our conduct towards the aborigines when this course can be pursued without exposing ourselves to the most afflicting calamities. That time, however, is unquestionably arrived, and every oppression now exercised on a helpless people depending on our magnanimity and justice for the preservation of their existence impresses a deep stain on the American

> character. I often think with indignation on our disreputable conduct (as I think) in the affairs of the Creeks of Georgia; and I look with some alarm on the course now pursuing in the Northwest.[8]

Four months after writing to Story, Marshall administered the oath of office as President to Andrew Jackson. Just as Marshall resolved to bolster the federal government's commitment to protect tribes from states, the Presidency came into the possession of a man long opposed to this course. For years, Jackson had advocated state control of tribal affairs within state bounds, a position reaffirmed on December 8, 1829, in his first Annual Message to Congress.[9] Eleven days later, Georgia's Legislature passed "An Act to add the territory lying within the chartered limits of Georgia, and now in the occupancy of the Cherokee Indians, to the counties of Carroll, DeKalb, Gwinnett, Hall, and Habersham." Section Six declared "all the laws, both civil and criminal, of this State...extended over said portions of territory." Section Seven declared "all laws, ordinances, orders and regulations, of any kind whatever, made passed or enacted, by the Cherokee Indians... null and void, and of no effect, as if the same had never existed."

From an early date, the Cherokees had shown much more interest than their southern *brothers* (the Creeks, Chickasaws and Choctaws) in President Washington's plan of *civil*-ization. Lacking ready access to foreign markets and the freedom from U.S. domination such markets promised, many Cherokees chose to explore in earnest the route leading to their tribe's social and political transformation on a U.S. model. By the 1820s, Cherokees were literate practitioners of commercial, slave-based agriculture, along the lines advocated by their U.S. Agent. The tribe boasted written laws and even a written constitution incorporating phrases derived from U.S. sources.[10] To Georgia, these developments were altogether unacceptable, and after President Jackson signaled that states could with impunity exercise full control over tribes within their borders, Georgia promptly declared the Cherokee nation to be no more substantial than an encampment of nomads.

Faced by Georgia's assertion that their tribe did not legally exist and a federal executive that acquiesced in Georgia's initiative, the Cherokees asked the Supreme Court for an injunction to restrain Georgia. This led to Marshall's two climactic tribal Opinions, *Cherokee Nation vs. Georgia*

(1831) and *Worcester vs. Georgia* (1832). The first rejected the Cherokee request on technical grounds, but the second declared unconstitutional the actions hostile to the Cherokee claim to nation-state status taken by the State of Georgia.

To bring their case quickly to the Supreme Court, the Cherokees asserted in 1831 that they were a *foreign* nation with a Constitutional right to invoke the original jurisdiction of the Supreme Court. Article Three of the Constitution, which outlines the "judicial power of the United States," makes no mention of tribes, but "foreign nations" and "treaties" are covered. Because the Cherokees had signed treaties with the United States, the tribe contended that they must be considered a "foreign nation" in the sense intended by Article Three. A generation after the adoption of the Constitution and President Washington's decision to negotiate with tribes in accord with the Constitution's treaty procedure, the full legal import of this decision was finally considered.

A majority of the Court rejected the Cherokees' claim to be a *foreign* nation, but failed to provide a persuasive explanation. Marshall's majority Opinion ludicrously accounted for the absence of tribes in the Constitution's outline of "judicial power" by surmising that

> At the time the Constitution was framed, the idea of appealing to an American court of justice for an assertion of right or a redress of wrong, had perhaps never entered the mind of an Indian or of his tribe. Their appeal was to the tomahawk, or to the government. This was well understood by the statesmen who framed the Constitution of the United States, and might furnish some reason for omitting to enumerate them among the parties who might sue in the courts of the Union.

In fact both individual Native Americans and tribes were active litigants in North American courts long before the Revolution; Marshall himself had cited colonial cases such as *Mohegan Indians vs. Connecticut* (filed 1704, decided by the Royal Privy Council, 1773).[11] A better explanation than Marshall's tomahawk theory for the omission of tribes from the Constitution's Article Three is the lack of agreement in 1787 about where and how tribes and individual Native American litigants would fit in.[12] That the Constitution's drafters expected both tribes and individual Native Americans would utilize the federal court system in some fashion is corroborated by President Washington's assurance to the Seneca chief Cornplanter on December 29, 1790, that "the federal courts will be open to you for redress, as to all other persons."[13]

Marshall began his 1831 Opinion with a powerful affirmation of compassion for the Cherokees:

> If the courts were permitted to indulge their sympathies, a case better calculated to excite them can scarcely be imagined. A people once numerous, powerful, and truly independent, found by our ancestors in the quiet and uncontrolled possession of an ample domain, gradually sinking beneath our superior policy, our arts and our arms, have yielded their lands by successive treaties, each of which contains a solemn guarantee of the residue, until they retain no more than is deemed necessary to their comfortable subsistence. To preserve this remnant the present application is made.

Almost every element in Marshall's boldly phrased *Cherokee* Opinion was at least hinted at in his 1823 Opinion in *Johnson vs. McIntosh*. As he had in 1823 for example, Marshall in 1831 took note of the tribes' distinctiveness, even alluding to the tribes' use of the term *father:*

> The condition of the Indians in relation to the United States is perhaps unlike that of any other two people in existence [and]...is marked by peculiar and cardinal distinctions which exist nowhere else....They acknowledge themselves in their treaties to be under the protection of the United States...and address the President as their great father.[14]

This time however, as he indicated in his 1828 letter to Justice Story, Marshall was prepared to go further.

Constrained in 1831 by what he considered the Cherokees' mistake in seeking an injunction as a *foreign* nation, Marshall eagerly seized the opportunity presented the following year to elaborate an interpretation of a *dependent* tribal status intermediate between the categories *foreign* and *domestic.* From European international law, Marshall drew theories structuring unequal relations between nations. Concurrently, from U.S. domestic law, Marshall borrowed concepts regulating the unequal relations of individuals. He argued that

> the settled doctrine of the law of nations is that a weaker power does not surrender its independence—its right to self-government, by associating with a stronger and taking its protection. A weak state in order to provide for its safety, may place itself under the protection of one more powerful without stripping itself of the right of government and ceasing to be a state. Examples of this kind are not wanting in Europe. "Tributary and feudatory states," says Vattel, "do not thereby cease to be

> sovereign and independent states so long as self-government and sovereign independent authority are left in the administration of the state."[15]

The *sovereign feudatory state* theory of the eighteenth century Swiss authority on international law Emerich Vattel was then combined by Marshall with the domestic law idea that the Cherokees were "in a state of pupilage. Their relation to the United States resembles that of a ward to his guardian." Marshall in other words posited that tribes were both sovereign and yet in at least some respects dependent: *ward states.*

Already in 1831, in the context of dismissing the Cherokees' bid for *foreign* status, Marshall had characterized tribes as "domestic dependent nations." This was a reworking of his 1823 phrase "dependent...and distinct people" but with a crucial shift from "people" to nation-state. In the 1831 phrase, *domestic* emphasized U.S. jurisdiction over tribal lands; *nations* in contrast conceded the Cherokees' claim to be a nation-state; while *dependent* specified that a tribe though "capable of managing its own affairs and governing itself" was also justly subject to federal guidance. Marshall's provocative words "pupilage" and "ward" can be (and often have been) taken to imply childishness or incompetence but in context are best understood as referring instead to the kind of legally circumscribed unequal relationship existing between a master craftsman and apprentice, rather than that of a parent to a young child; to this extent, Marshall's Euro-American legal approach met part-way the tribes' special contractual understanding of the term *father.*

Marshall was emphatic that only the federal government could serve as guardian of a tribal ward state. In fact the entire fabric of Marshall's argument in both 1831 and 1832 can be seen as constructed to sustain this conclusion. Precisely because he viewed the Cherokees as "sinking," Marshall felt it best to *raise* them to the legal status of a nation-state, thereby enabling the federal government to monopolize relations with them. He maintained that states must not interfere in any way with federal-tribal relations. "The whole intercourse between the United States and this [Cherokee] nation is by our Constitution and laws," Marshall proclaimed in 1832, "vested in the government of the United States." In the face of open lawlessness by federal and state officials, Marshall attempted to move tribal policy away from the cautiously "compromised" language prominent in his own earlier tribal Opinions, and toward affirmation of an imperial-style federal protectorate over "Indian Country" where states, Marshall wrote in *Worcester vs. Georgia,* had no jurisdictional rights whatsoever: "The treaties and laws of the United States contemplate the Indian territory as completely separated from that of the states; and provide that all intercourse with them shall be carried on exclusively by the government of the Union." *Worcester vs. Georgia* applied in the first instance to the specific situation of the Cherokee tribe within Georgia as well as more generally to "the Indian territory" but the Opinion would in later decades be extended to state-regulated groups of Native Americans, which Marshall chose to ignore.

If Vattel's antique European concept of feudatory state relations combined oddly with U.S. federalism, Marshall's attempt to associate the federal government with imperial Britain's North American tribal policies was even more dubious. According to Marshall's 1832 Opinion, "While these states were colonies, this power [to regulate relations with tribes], in its utmost extent, was admitted to reside in the crown." Far from admitting this, rebel colonists vehemently rejected such a claimed power when the Crown attempted to assert it between 1763 and 1776. Indeed the Declaration of Independence singled out for particular denunciation Parliament's 1774 Quebec Act, the culmination of pre-Revolutionary royalist strategizing about how best to insure that development of the continent's interior would remain safely in aristocratic British control. Marshall sought to depict the aggrandizing imperial policy of the years 1763-1776 as the accepted pattern in pre-1776 British-tribal relations, thus selecting as normative that stance considered most objectionable by Revolutionaries. Colonies had been deeply involved in tribal policy before 1763, and resented Britain's belated efforts to expand royal control of relations with tribes.

The man who drafted the Declaration of Independence with its denunciation of the Crown's "arbitrary" and "absolute" plans for the interior of North America had in 1774 characterized Britain's tribal land policy as a latter-day attempt by corrupt monarchists to defraud colonists of their hard-won rights. In his "Summary View of the Rights of British America," Jefferson argued that rights to tribal land had been legitimately acquired by early English settlers acting on their own behalf, who either sacrificed their own lives in conquering tribes or expended their own funds in purchasing tribal land rights. In Jefferson's 1774 view, each colony had dealt separately with local tribes, and tribal land rights therefore were and always had been a matter to be settled between tribes and colonists, not by the King. This perspective allowed for the possible creation of a royal or federal authority restricting the autonomy of individual colonies or states to deal with tribal land right issues, but not without their explicit consent. The source of North American tribal land title lay with each colony, not in any supposed royal guarantee, and colonists were ready and willing to defend their autonomy in tribal relations by resort to arms. This theory was at the heart of the Revolutionary approach to tribal land rights, which Marshall some decades later tried to read out of legal existence.

Applying Jeffersonian land right principles, Revolutionary interests and jurisdictions made myriad claims to the western lands the British Crown had tried to restrict to tribal use, and before long opportunistic claims "overlapped the land like shingles on a roof."[16] Some persons eager to buy land from tribes pronounced them sovereign nations capable of selling land to anyone they chose. At the other end of the spectrum, North Carolina declared even powerful tribes such as the Cherokees and Choctaws "only tenants at will."[17] The Continental Congress considered claiming all land west of the Appalachians for the nation, as property conquered from the Crown. When this plan got nowhere because of state opposition, Congress did its best to mediate among state claims, attempting to insure that tribes ended up with at least some land. This was how matters stood in 1787 when the Constitution was drafted, and the Constitution's only real achievement in the area of tribal relations was to eliminate the explicitly pro-state language of the Articles of Confederation and the penultimate draft of the Constitution—quite a different thing from proscribing all state involvement. Washington's administration accepted fee title ownership of tribal lands by states, and the right of states to grant title to lands occupied by tribes, and attempted to persuade tribes to acquiesce voluntarily in the legal position taken by states. Subsequent administrations continued this approach, gradually increasing pressure on tribes to submit. Andrew Jackson in contrast reasoned that tribes would never willingly tolerate state aspirations, and that the Constitution should be reinterpreted, so as to permit states to abrogate unilaterally federal treaties that accorded tribes political rights. To counter this radical alteration in federal practice dating from Washington's administration, Marshall dusted off authoritarian British policies rejected by the Revolution.

Of Marshall's 1832 Opinion, Jackson is said to have muttered: "John Marshall has made his decision:—*now let him enforce it!*"[18] Jackson and his successors did however by and large accept Marshall's formulas, though only after completing the forcible removal of tribes. This acquiescence reflected the fact that Marshall's formulas turned out to be substantially compatible with the long-range objectives of his antagonist. Although Marshall is accurately thought of as a defender of tribal rights against President Jackson's assault on them, Marshall's defense was of a sort that prepared the way for tribal subjection to a protective tutelage that sought to separate tribes from their past, as well as from each other. Marshall's motive was to defend tribes, but the legal course he set resulted in damage to tribes almost as severe as that caused by Jackson's brutality, and much more lasting.

Dissatisfaction with Marshall's legal strategy was expressed not only by President Jackson (an interested party) but also by four Justices of the seven-member Supreme Court. Although *Worcester vs. Georgia* was decided unanimously, only two of Marshall's colleagues fully endorsed his 1831 *Cherokee* Opinion; two Justices dissented, while two wrote concurring Opinions. In a dissenting Opinion joined by Marshall's close friend Joseph Story, Smith Thompson argued that the Cherokees should in fact be designated a foreign rather than a domestic nation. While admitting this posed difficulties, Thompson noted that members of tribes were not U.S. citizens, and thus might have to be considered foreign nationals. At the other end of the spectrum, although he voted with Marshall against the Cherokee claim to be a foreign nation, Justice Henry Baldwin resisted Marshall's argument that the Cherokees were any sort of nation-state. Baldwin direly predicted that "countless tribes ...will rush to the federal courts in endless controversies" if not prevented by a strong Court decision denying them nation-state status.

The other Justice who voted with Marshall but had problems with his "domestic dependent nations" formula was William Johnson, who spoke in a more conciliatory voice, as he did throughout the thirty years during which he functioned on the Court as Marshall's loyal opposition. Marshall had been nominated Chief Justice in 1801 by the outgoing President John Adams, with a mandate to curb his radical successor Jefferson. To counter Marshall, Jefferson in 1804 chose Johnson as his first Supreme Court nominee. Once on the Court however, Johnson worked more cooperatively with Marshall than Jefferson entirely approved of, and in the process helped establish the important practice of filing concurring Opinions, as he did in 1810 in *Fletcher vs. Peck*. Twenty-one years later, in *Cherokee vs. Georgia*, Johnson revisited tribal policy in another partially concurring Opinion.

Johnson disliked calling tribes nation-states because he feared—notwithstanding Marshall's effort to distinguish them as domestic and dependent—that use of the term "nations" would rouse presumptions of comparability to other nation-states. Johnson felt that the Court would be well-advised to ignore their European treatises on international law and instead take note of the unique characteristics of U.S. tribes, which he aptly called "an anomaly unknown to the books that treat of states." Johnson also objected to the "domestic dependent nations" formula because it attempted to place in one legal category innumerable groups that were already diverse and in the future likely to become more so. Whereas some tribes such as the Cherokees were arguably viable as permanent nation-states, others were small roving bands that might stay intact for only a short time. Given such a spectrum,

> Where is the rule to stop? Must every petty *kraal* [a small autonomous village] of Indians, designating themselves a tribe or nation, and having a few hundred acres of land to hunt on exclusively, be recognized as a state? We should indeed force into the family of nations a very numerous and very heterogeneous progeny. The Catawbas, having indeed a few more acres than the republic of San Marino, but consisting only of eighty or an hundred polls, would then be admitted to the same dignity. They still claim independence, and actually execute their own penal laws, such as they are, even to the punishment of death; and have recently done so. We have many ancient treaties with them; and no

> nation has been more distinctly recognized, as far as such recognition can operate to communicate the character of a state.

The Catawbas posed certain questions, the Cherokees with their U.S.-style Constitution posed others. The Cherokees' "present form of government," wrote Johnson, "certainly must be classed among the most approved forms of civil government. Whether it can be yet said to have received the consistency which entitles that people to admission into the family of nations is, I conceive, yet to be determined." Once wholly sovereign, the Cherokees might some day regain this status. But Johnson could not see in the Cherokees' present situation the requisites of sovereignty:

> They have in Europe sovereign and demi-sovereign states and states of doubtful sovereignty. But this state, if it be state, is still a grade below them all; for not to be able to alienate without permission of the remainderman or lord, places them in a state of feudal dependence.

The Cherokees' "right of soil," Johnson noted, "is held by the feeble tenure of hunting grounds, and acknowledged on all hands subject to a restriction to sell to no one but the United States, and for no use but that of Georgia."

Johnson considered the Cherokees' legal situation peculiar and undesirable, and not likely to last. On the other hand, how the Cherokees came to be in such a predicament was a tale with legal implications that could not be simply wished away. Johnson reminded the Court that Revolutionary policy-makers had assigned tribes only the rights of hunters to use hunting grounds, and pointed out that officials viewing tribes in this way could not have intended that tribes would become nation-states-within-states. This presumption against tribal nation-state status had moreover been made incumbent on the federal republic through the conditions established by the states' cession of their western land claims, a process begun by New York State in 1780 but not completed until Georgia's 1802 cession, long after the Constitution was drafted and approved. Therefore

> the project of ultimately organizing...[tribes] into states within the limits of those states which had not ceded or should not cede to the United States the jurisdiction over the Indian territory within their bounds, could not possibly have entered into the contemplation of our government. Nothing but express authority from the states could have

justified such a policy, pursued with such a view.

Johnson saw in the circumstances surrounding the adoption of the Constitution no justification for an "unshackled" federal-tribal relationship insulated from state interference. Nor could Johnson find in the Constitution itself any obscurely lodged intent to insulate tribes from states. The Constitution, he believed, was entirely silent about the land rights of independent tribes within states. These tribes occupied no firm place in the federal Union other than that they secured for themselves through the negotiation of treaties. But, in Johnson's view, such treaties had to be respected, even when they contained disputed concessions extracted by tribal chiefs. Johnson stood with Marshall in repudiating Jackson's contempt for treaty obligations. Unlike Great Britain's treaty "assurances" to tribes, understood as always revocable at the monarch's royal "pleasure," U.S. treaties were binding guarantees with the full status of federal law. Wherever there was a treaty securing tribal rights, Johnson considered its terms enforceable.

Johnson was no closer than Marshall to an understanding of how tribes themselves thought or functioned. But Johnson's emphasis on the importance of treaties, the one product of the tribal familial system that made sense in Euro-American legal reckoning, rendered his approach more compatible than Marshall's with the tribal viewpoint. Johnson's approach was also better designed to comprehend present diversity and future evolution in the condition of tribes. Marshall suggested that all tribes should be "denominated domestic dependent nations" because he thought of them as identical in their dependence on the federal government and insular in their internal functioning. Assuming that tribes would stagnate quietly in separate nation-state boxes, Marshall rejected Johnson's plea for a flexible legal approach. Johnson saw in the early federal treaties incorporating tribal legal presuppositions the basis for an adaptable and therefore enduring structure of U.S.-tribal relations embracing Native American traditions which had made an art of assimilating change, and of relating large to small tribes as well as collaboratively relating all tribes to a *father* nation.

It is difficult today to take seriously either the Cherokees' claim to be a foreign nation or the Georgia-Jackson position that no political status could be asserted by a tribe within the bounds of a state. But nothing in the Constitution precluded these positions. More than a generation after the Constitution was drafted, Marshall fashioned a definition of tribal status arrived at by abstract legal reasoning and misleading use of colonial precedents. In response to a clearly unconstitutional attempt by one state to monopolize relations with tribes within that state's boundaries, Marshall sought to require a reluctant federal government to impose its own monopoly on tribal relations. In doing so, Marshall ignored the substantial body of federal treaties in which tribes and federal (and sometimes state) treaty commissioners had collaboratively pieced together a structure of federal-state-tribal relations. Had the Court resisted the temptation to construe—and then to misrepresent—colonial precedents and instead boldly defined a post-Revolutionary status for tribes based broadly on the Constitution and concretely on the texts of these treaties embodying tribal perspectives, this might over time have allowed the tribes' own legal concepts to come into increasing play in Court decisions.

A century and a half after Marshall's Supreme Court articulated the doctrine that the Constitution obligated the federal government to protect tribes in "Indian Country" as wards, this concept is still federal law. The very rigidity of Marshall's stance remains attractive to many who view tribes as still vulnerable. But now that tribes are clearly rebounding, the time may have finally come to recognize that the Constitution did not decree that tribes must be wards of the federal government, and that the pattern of treaty relations initiated by President Washington was quite unlike that described by Marshall as Constitutionally mandated. By returning to the treaty era of the early republic, we can then perhaps move forward to a paradigm of tribal relations based on a presumption of parity and stability. Meanwhile, tribal-state-federal controversies overlap more than ever, especially since numerous Native American groups once under "ordinary state jurisdiction" now desire federal tribal status with its "sovereign nation" presumption. In the early years under the Constitution, the issue was not whether but how states and tribes would resolve matters of common concern. Aspects of the thinking of those times can be usefully invoked by modern reformers, as can the authority of the Constitution.

Ten

Past as Prologue

NORTH AMERICA IN 1775 WAS A COMPLEX PLACE, and an array of peoples kept separate from one another by British policy joined in the Revolution's effort to define a new future for the continent. These diverse groups had trouble cooperating or agreeing about anything, but quite a lot was achieved: the Revolutionary War was won, the Constitution was drafted, adopted and implemented—and treaties negotiated according to tribal custom brought many tribes into the U.S. political system. In the Revolutionary era, North American tribes suffered population losses and property destruction, at the hands of British subjects as well as citizens of the new United States. Somewhat counterbalancing these reverses is the fact that tribes secured standing in the Constitution and in due course recognition of the validity of their cultural distinctiveness in treaties negotiated pursuant to the Constitution. The American Revolution truly did, as claimed by the Great Seal of the United States approved in 1782, institute a "novus ordo seclorum"—a political system such as the world had never seen. The Constitution insured its survival, just as the Constitution's incorporation of tribes contributed its uniqueness.

In the years following the outbreak of the American Revolution, four quite different outcomes in U.S.-tribal relations were imaginable. The most severe of these possibilities was the driving of tribes by force beyond U.S. borders, to the north, south and west. On August 5, 1776, a month after describing hostile Native Americans as "merciless Indian Savages" in the Declaration of Independence, Thomas Jefferson for example sternly insisted that "Nothing will reduce those wretches so soon as pushing the war into the heart of their country. But I would not stop there. I would never cease pursuing them while one of them remained on this side the Mississippi."[1] Ironically, Jefferson himself ended the fantasy that driving "savages" across the Mississippi River could be a real solution, when as President in 1803 he purchased

Louisiana, giving the United States continent-spanning scope—and responsibility for "savages" west of the Mississippi. But even after 1803, the United States possessed northern and southern borders across which "savages" could be thrust, and in 1808 President Jefferson echoed his 1776 threat, bluntly warning any tribe that

> shall prefer our enmity to our friendship, and engage in war against us, that nation must abandon forever the land of their fathers. No nation rejecting our friendship, and commencing wanton and unprovoked war against us, shall ever after remain within our reach; it shall never be in their power to strike us a second time. These words, my *children*, may appear harsh; but they are spoken in kindness; they are intended to warn you beforehand of the ruin into which those will rush, who shall once break the chain of friendship with us.[2]

Jefferson here employed the ancient Native American image of a chain in threatening tribes with eternal banishment. Those who were driven into Spanish Florida and British Canada continued from there, as General Washington predicted, to harass the United States.

A second tribal fate, imaginable until the end of the War of 1812, was that tribes allied with Great Britain and Spain might defeat U.S. claims to ownership of large regions west of the Appalachians and establish a powerful nation trading with Europe via the Mississippi River and/or the Great Lakes and the Saint Lawrence River. Authorities in British Canada and Spanish Florida actively encouraged this outcome, and had he lived longer the Creek leader Alexander McGillivray might have made it a reality. This idea also informed Tecumseh's effort to forge a pan-tribal alliance prior to the War of 1812.

Thirdly, while remaining within the United States, tribes might have been destroyed as political entities, their members merging with the general U.S. population. This was the alternative to flight offered tribes by Jefferson who conceptualized it, modifying another Native American metaphor, as becoming "our *brothers* instead of our *children*. My *children*," he told the Upper Cherokees in 1808, "I shall rejoice to see the day when the red men, our neighbors, become truly one people with us, enjoying all the rights and privileges we do."[3] While Jefferson's attempts to destroy tribes as polities and assimilate individual Native Americans into U.S. society achieved little, he did—along with Tecumseh —undermine what success Washington attained in establishing a

Constitutional basis for collaborative tribal relations.

This fourth outcome involved acknowledgment by tribes that they now lived under U.S. jurisdiction, with the United States in turn conceding that tribes could if they desired remain intact as distinctive political entities. This outcome was the only one of the four that could have been reached peaceably, and was the only one actively fostered by both U.S. and tribal leaders, though by no means all.

More than any other individual during the Revolution's first two decades, George Washington made tribal complementarity viable, and difficult for his successors to destroy altogether. Washington described "the friendly tribes" as "neighbors" capable of living in "harmony" with the United States, and hoped to "render tranquillity with the savages permanent, by creating ties of interest."[4] Though himself a western land speculator, Washington recognized the tribes' rightful possession of interior sections of North America, and believed tribal control would limit the advance of U.S. settlement, with beneficial consequences for political stability. As President, Washington worked hard to establish a pattern of mutually respectful relations with "savage" tribes, an accomplishment that is noteworthy even today as a reference point and standard.

Washington is often attacked as a hypocrite because he moved slowly. But hypocrites retard progress, whereas Washington steadily drew all parties toward agreement. Moreover, by his example Washington inspired other Revolutionary leaders. Notably, Colonel Benjamin Hawkins devoted decades of his life to implementing Washington's vision of constructive collaboration between the United States and tribes. Hawkins' career as Agent to the Creeks is peculiarly emblematic, because of the way Hawkins continued trying until his death in 1816 to implement Washington's policy despite polite challenges from Jefferson and hostile challenges from Jackson.

Tribal chiefs were equally instrumental in furthering political consensus. Notably, Colonel Louis Atayataghronghta articulately expressed a pro-Revolutionary tribal viewpoint. Though considered more a junior ally than a fellow-Revolutionary by General Washington, Colonel Atayataghronghta and other tribal warriors contributed to U.S. military victory, and demanded a rightful share of the spoils for tribes.

Ironically, latter-day chroniclers of the Revolution have ignored the highest-ranking of Native American Revolutionary War heroes, and instead focused on tribal leaders opposed to the Revolution, such as British Captain Joseph Brant. As a result, many people today assume the Revolution was wholly incompatible with tribal aspirations. But the real enemy of tribes was the later nineteenth century racism, which ravaged the Constitution just as surely as it did tribes. Tribes were effective participants in the original founding and shaping of the United States, and this needs to be recalled in pondering future prospects.

Through a process that began in 1775 and continued well past the inception of the Constitution in 1789, tribes obtained a foothold within the federal system. The Revolutionaries' confusions and inexperience, as well as conflicts between state and central U.S. governments, made it possible for skillful and persistent tribal leaders to bargain their way into the federal system on terms that safeguarded tribal institutions, not only from President Jefferson's surgical probings but even from President Jackson's uncompromising assault. Although not directly represented in Congress or at the Constitutional Convention, tribes successfully pressured those who drafted and initially interpreted the Constitution, and secured by treaties entered into pursuant to the Constitution a recognized legal status within the United States. This achievement was nonetheless vulnerable because it was not reinforced by formal repre-sentation. Indeed the position of tribes after 1789 was somewhat comparable to that of the thirteen colonies within the British Empire prior to 1776, when the Crown assured colonists that they enjoyed virtual, indirect representation in Parliament, and that their interests were safeguarded by a benevolent sovereign. Numerous tribes willingly accepted a similarly subordinate status within the United States, because tribes were accustomed to hierarchical relationships of deference and dependence in their dealings with each other as well as with several European monarchs. But self-governing tribes were also accustomed to enjoying substantial autonomy, and assumed this would continue in "Indian Country" under U.S. protection. After 1800, when tribal autonomy was undercut and virtual representation began to seem no longer a sufficient guarantee of their traditional freedoms, tribes responded much as had colonists to their British rulers, with a variety of tactics ranging from polite lobbying pressure to violent harassment. Eventually, Tecumseh of the Shawnees and the Tallassee Mico of the Creeks launched a war intended to restore meaningful tribal independence. But the result was not, as in 1775-1783, victory for the resisters. Tribal revolt was crushed and Tecumseh and the Tallassee Mico were slain, along with thousands of their followers. The lot of tribes became reservation confinement—and the courts.

In white racist imagining, tribes were rescued from their own self-destructive impulses by a charitable federal government. In fact tribes saved themselves, not only by acts of desperate defiance but with their pragmatic skills as lobbyists and litigators determined to build for tribes a solid legal and economic foundation. To this end, when tribes sold land they wanted a fair price. But in 1783 the U.S. government committed itself to the view that tribal compensation for land rights in "Indian Country" should be based on a calculation of the commercial value of the game remaining, and this rationale persisted as federal policy for many decades. President Washington's commitment to "fair" tribal land sales had to do with candor, not with market value. Similarly, Chief Justice Marshall's tribal Opinions pertained to security of tenure for tribal land rights, and implied nothing about their market value. Taking up the hatchet could not shatter the self-serving delusions of whites, so tribes tried persuasion. At a federal treaty session held in Albany in 1802, the Seneca Red Jacket proposed selling tribal land rights fronting the Niagara River on these terms:

> For the whole tract we ask $7500. We think this reasonable, and that in a few years it will refund you much more than this sum. *Brothers*: With respect to this price, you may perhaps think it high, and much more than you have heretofore given for any lands, but you must also acknowledge that this land, from its situation and other circumstances, is more valuable than any other land you have purchased. *Brothers*: Let us reflect a few years back. When the white people first came to our country, we considered them poor and sold them large tracts of land, by which they became rich, and our land being diminished, it is reasonable that we should now value it higher than formerly.[5]

Red Jacket's offer and the reasoning behind it were both rejected. Indeed, twenty-four years later General Lewis Cass informed an assemblage of Miamis and Pattawatomies,

> My *children*, there are a great many of the white children of your *father* who would be glad to live upon this land. They would build houses, and raise corn, and cattle, and hogs....Your great *father* is willing to give for this land much more than it is worth to you. He is willing to give more than all the game upon it would sell for.[6]

Only after additional decades of frustration did tribes finally succeed in persuading the federal government to accept responsibility for insuring that tribes received full market value when their lands were sold. "Conscionable consideration" was advocated by tribes from the outset, but not accepted as reasonable by the federal government until the twentieth century.

That any tribes survived the chaos of the Revolutionary decades and then the militarism and racism of the nineteenth century is an amazing accomplishment. But tribes did survive. From a low point in the late nineteenth century when the number of enrolled members of tribes dwindled to less than three hundred thousand, the total has risen to around two million, in part because of voluntary re-affiliation. In recent decades tribes have successfully built a modernized social and economic basis for political autonomy. Tribes will thus certainly be part of the future U.S. federal system. But with what legal status?

Congress and the Supreme Court have scarcely begun the process of overturning more than a century of racist laws and decisions. Impatient tribal advocates meanwhile denounce the record of the U.S. government from end to beginning, often reading the racism of the nineteenth century back into the nation's eighteenth century origins. Reacting against this, critics of tribes sometimes label them an embarrassment in a democratic republic with universalistic pretensions, and view recent indications of tribal vitality as proof that the time has come to terminate tribal status once and for all. The result has been intellectual polarization and a tense political impasse.

Though not yet in sight, a middle ground must be sought because the current legal status of U.S. tribes isn't just anomalous and hard to understand, it is genuinely bad, for members of tribes as well as for those who are not. Every U.S. citizen, tribal or not, has reason to feel frustrated by nonsensical legal distinctions between Native Americans and others, as well as among Native Americans. Great changes are now occurring in the circumstances of Native Americans on and off reservations but, despite a rapid increase in interaction and therefore in the potential for conflict between tribes and the rest of U.S. society, the legal status of tribes has not been updated. Marshall's concept of tribal "wardship" remains the basic premise of federal tribal law, as can be seen for example in the rule that in construing any written agreement "weak and defenseless" tribes must always be given the benefit of the doubt. As expounded in a 1930 Supreme Court Opinion, this means that

> Doubtful expressions are to be resolved in favor of the weak and defenseless people who are the wards of the nation, dependent upon its protection and good faith. Hence, in the words of Chief Justice Marshall [in *Worcester vs. Georgia*], "The language used in treaties with the Indians should never be construed to their prejudice. If words be made use of, which are susceptible of a more extended meaning than their plain import, as connected with the tenor of the treaty, they should be considered as used only in the latter sense."[7]

This 1930 Opinion citing Marshall's 1832 Opinion illustrates how distorted assumptions arise when the original context is lost; "weak and defenseless" are not Marshall's words. Marshall never spoke of tribes as incompetent, but as recently as 1985 Marshall's wardship concept was once again cited by four justices of the Supreme Court as implying a childlike incapacity. In *County of Oneida vs. Oneida Indian Nation*, a dissent by Justice Stevens, signed as well by Chief Justice Burger and Justices Rehnquist and White, argued that wardship "would require flexible consideration of the development of the particular tribe's capacity to govern its own affairs." Considered relevant to this tribal capacity was the fact that the Oneidas had "received formal schooling at least since 1796 in New York, and have gradually become literate in the English language." This argument misses the point that Marshall could not have considered tribes to be nations in any sense had he thought of them as mentally frail or undeveloped. Also ignored was the fact that the Oneidas possessed powerful governmental institutions long before they began learning English, and that 1796 was a low point in Oneida history.[8]

The deleteriousness of current tribal policy has been aggravated by a pious misreading of the Constitution and the early Trade and Intercourse Acts, which projects back to the nation's founding a number of commitments not in fact made until much later. This has resulted in a flood of lawsuits accurately alleging that modern-day "trusteeship" standards were not followed in transactions of the eighteenth and nineteenth centuries. Adding to the confusion is the belief that the early Trade and Intercourse Acts extended fiduciary protection to the lands of *all tribes*, including many that had held land under ordinary colonial and then state jurisdiction since the seventeenth century. The failure to see that states and the federal government shared tribal responsibilities under the Constitution and that this was taken as a given in the early federal Trade and Intercourse Acts has resulted in chaotic situations in many states which stand accused of having for centuries improperly exercised jurisdiction over tribes.

With the emergence of a more accurate understanding of the evolving historical relationship of tribes and the American Constitution, it may be possible to resume the early republic's dialogue, which was broken off in the nineteenth century and all but forgotten in the twentieth. Given the current political deadlock in Congress and the pace of federal court rulings, revision of the tribes' standing in federal law can only be accomplished gradually. But even in the absence of new Congressional legislation, much may be achieved through established Court procedures. Future Supreme Court decisions could draw on Justice Johnson's Opinions, as well as the treaties on which he relied, to define a new status for tribes. President Jefferson, who appointed Johnson to the Supreme Court, outlined succinctly what could become the basis of such a new understanding. On January 31, 1809, in the closing days of his Presidency, Jefferson advised a delegation of tribal chiefs that "we do not consider you as another nation, but as a part of us, living indeed under your own laws, but having the same interests with us."[9] Not hapless "domestic dependent nations" but *domestic autonomous tribes*: unique self-governing entities within the United States, whose particular rights were spelled out in U.S. treaties. Neither Jefferson nor Johnson understood tribes very well, but they did understand treaties, and acknowledged the binding legal validity of the tribal treaty process through which tribes had bargained their way into the U.S. federal system.

A more fundamental structural change would be the gathering of dispersed tribal territories into a Native American state government. This would need approval by tribes as well as by Congress and the state governments within which tribal territories are located, but might gain acceptance as the fulfillment of aspirations dating from the Revolutionary era. The idea of forming a Native American state within the Union stretches back to 1778, to the mid-Revolutionary War proposal that the Delaware tribe organize pro-U.S., anti-British tribes into an alliance that might evolve into a state along-side the original thirteen. After the War, in 1785, Benjamin Hawkins discussed a similar proposal with the Cherokees. A century later, interest was expressed by both Congress and the federal executive in making the Oklahoma Territory into "a state, exclusively Indian, that should be a *bona fide* member of the American Union."[10] As with the Delaware and Cherokee proposals, tribal opposition was a factor conducing to the failure of the Oklahoma plan. Opposition from U.S. citizens was also strong, because homesteaders disliked being excluded from the extensive lands to be set aside for the Native American State of Oklahoma.[11] Today the most sensible place to locate a Native American state is probably on an "archipelago" consisting of many if not all of the several hundred tribal reservations now located within the bounds of the contiguous forty-eight states.[12] Odd as a plan for such a state may seem, it would actually be preferable in some respects to the Delaware and Oklahoma proposals, because it would symbolize the continent-wide pervasiveness of Native American culture, and encourage interaction among far-flung tribes and between tribes and surrounding states.

In the early republic, most federally supervised tribes resided in "Indian Country," a continuous territory within the claimed bounds of the United States where tribes enjoyed substantial freedom from federal interference as well as almost complete independence in relations with one another. In distinct ways, the imperial British and the Revolutionary Americans both came to terms with "Indian Country" and the tribal mores that governed it. But beginning with Jackson's coercive Presidency, tribes were force-marched to unfamiliar locations and "Indian Country" was chopped up into scattered segments, hindering intertribal contacts. Once a vast area, "Indian Country" by the early twentieth century had disappeared from U.S. maps, swallowed up by the several states of the Union when Oklahoma became the forty-sixth state in 1907, and New Mexico and Arizona the forty-seventh and forty-eighth states in 1912.[13] The fourteen-million-acre Navajo reservation, which is almost twenty times larger than the State of Rhode Island and spreads across areas of four states, is not even delineated on most U.S. maps, which typically show the superimposed outlines of Arizona, Utah, Colorado and New Mexico criss-crossing the Navajo reservation in a manner reminiscent of the way nineteenth century Africa was portioned out by Europe's imperial powers. "Indian Country" survives today only as a legal fiction applying in hopscotch fashion and with often bizarre consequences. The federal courts are disposed to find "Indian Country" wherever tribal law pertains, on and off tribal reservations, and thus potentially in conflict with the policies of almost forty states and the rights of countless non-tribal citizens.[14] Although the territorial setting of tribal life in the early republic has been destroyed, and the confusing concept of "Indian Country" may well be best dispensed with, systematic tribal interaction can yet be revived if a new structural basis for it is found, such as might be afforded by a Native American state government consolidating tribal reservations in a single administrative unit.

With a state of their own, Native Americans would literally re-emerge on the map of the United States. Including tribal lands within state boundaries was an arrangement anticipating that tribal territories would shrink or disappear, thereby allowing states to absorb them. Intrastate tribal territory is guaranteed to tribes by the federal government, but states have always looked forward to reducing or eliminating these exceptions to ordinary state jurisdiction, and this has encouraged a beleaguered mentality on reservations. The assignment of tribal lands to a Native American state government would ease such anxiety, and counter the still-widespread presumption that reservations will someday vanish. State boundaries on U.S. maps would look somewhat different if tribal lands were shown as part of a newly-created Native American state. More importantly, this would be a symbolic as well as legal affirmation of a durable Native American presence within the federal system. The treaties signed by tribes with the federal government made them part of the United States, but not parts of the federal Union, as are states. A Native American state would complete the process begun by President Washington's treaties, and be more meaningfully sovereign than today's "sovereign" tribal nations.[15]

Such a state could coordinate contact between tribes and the federal government, deal as an equal with other states of the Union, and renew and consolidate Native American legal traditions. Members of tribes resent meddling by state governments, which are presumed (thanks to Marshall) to have no Constitutional justification for involving themselves in tribal matters. Federal encouragement of gambling casinos located on tribal reservations but catering to non-tribal customers and thereby generating social ills that states must cope with has for example led to protests by state governments, answered scornfully by some tribal advocates claiming this is "not our problem." With their own state government, tribes would "join the club" and gain incentives to address common problems in concert with the governors and attorneys general of neighboring states.

Tribal tax and citizenship dilemmas would also be resolved. Ever since U.S. citizenship was extended to U.S.-born tribal members in 1924, they have exercised citizenship within the states where their reservations are located, while remaining exempt from many state taxes. States have predictably made it difficult for tribal members to vote, and resented their tax-exempt privileges. In their own state, tribal citizens would vote—and pay taxes.

The federal government is scarcely better liked by tribes than are state governments. The federal Bureau of Indian Affairs, in theory the tribes' protector, is seen as an enemy with a neo-colonial if no longer assimilationist agenda, and the appointment of Native Americans to Bureau positions has done little to modify this perception. As then-Congressman Bill Richardson of New Mexico, chairman of the House Subcommittee on Native American Affairs, contended in 1993, "It is time to junk or radically transform the...wasteful and patriarchal Bureau of Indian Affairs, which in large measure has held back tribes from helping themselves."[16] The current neo-imperial system, in which a federal bureaucracy presides as arbiter over hundreds of separate tribes, has fostered a defensive, self-protective mentality. Recent federal efforts to promote internal tribal autonomy have not addressed the need for institutions that will facilitate cooperation and coalition-building among separated tribes. Hundreds of self-governing tribes is an improvement over hundreds of enclaves deemed incompetent, but not a solution. If anything, encouragement of "self-government" within the current structure seems likely to stimulate greater intertribal and intratribal divisiveness and factionalism.

As a new structure, a Native American state government would shake up entrenched rivalries by defining new goals. It would also stimulate thinking about how to articulate general Native American norms, and thus provide a coherent way of addressing and resolving, subject to review by the U.S. Congress and U.S. Supreme Court, tribal policy issues that Congress and the Supreme Court have not been zealous to take up. Indeed when they have taken them up, Congress and the Court have raised more questions than they answered. Much was expected when Congress created a broad-gauge American Indian Policy Review Commission, which was inundated with complaints and suggestions. But its 1977 *Final Report* was riven by contradictions—and wholly ignored. Scarcely more conclusive was the Supreme Court's 1978 decision in *Martinez vs. Santa Clara Pueblo* upholding the right of a tribe using its own criteria to exclude persons from membership. This was hailed by many as a landmark recognition of tribal autonomy but has also sparked much controversy because tribal members now complain of being deprived by *Martinez* of rights within their tribes otherwise guaranteed them as U.S. citizens.

Full tribal status is meanwhile sought by scores of federally unrecognized groups. In 1971 Tom Tureen, a young lawyer employed by Pine Tree Legal Assistance in Calais, Maine, drew attention to the "approximately 120,000...tribal Indians, mostly residing in the eastern United States, who...have been ignored by the federal government. As a result," concluded Tureen, "these Indians are denied services which the federal government provides for Indians, and are prevented from invoking the protections provided by federal law." Benefits available to federally recognized tribes dwelling in "Indian Country" had greatly expanded since the early nineteenth century. Simultaneously, the distinctions in the ways of living of federally recognized tribes and state tribes had greatly diminished. Instead of being perceived as comparatively privileged, state tribes seemed discriminated against. Tureen and a few colleagues set out to rectify this inequity by eliminating what he called "the dichotomy between federal and state Indians."[17] Tureen's well-intended efforts garnered much sympathy and achieved some remarkable successes. A number of erstwhile state tribes have attained federal recognition, become "sovereign nations"—and launched casinos and other tax-exempt enterprises. Understandably, other Native American-descended groups are pressing for like privileges. Tureen was right to advocate abolishing the distinction between state and federal tribes. But attempting to do so by history-distorting litigation has worsened a bad situation, generating bitterness and backlash—as well as many new inequities. Restructuring the status of federal tribes should logically have preceded efforts to expand the number of such tribes.

There is an obvious need for a central place where the everyday dilemmas of tribal life can be considered methodically and not just in unpredictable *ad hoc* contexts at twenty-year intervals by the Supreme Court. As an overtly hybrid entity, a Native American state government would not find it difficult to recognize that real solutions must be compromises, which will work only if their ramifications are thoroughly assessed. Tribal traditions could then be updated within a coherent framework.

If the idea of a Native American state government fails to gain adequate support, other measures can still be taken to restore more consensual relations among and between tribes and federal and state governments. A federally-authorized all-tribe assembly would be easier to establish than a state government, and could serve as a test of the feasibility of a Native American state, while coordinating and focusing diffuse tribal energies and encouraging a more collaborative relationship between tribes and federal and state governments.

An increasing tribal role in the nation's future is assured, even though no consensus presently exists about what this role should be. Many unforeseen proposals will no doubt be made. As a paradigm for the discussions sure to come, Robert A. Williams, Jr. recently suggested the Iroquois "Two Row Wampum," a belt with two parallel lines. "At the core of this Americanized vision of law," Williams explains, "is the idea that freedom requires different peoples to respect each other's vision of how their respective vessels should be steered."[18] Two lines that never touch is however not adequately reflective of the protean tribal tradition. A more pertinent wampum belt was expounded in 1798 by Creek chief Efau Hadjo, a belt

> of six strands, with two white ends, two rows of blue wampums on each edge, and two rows of white wampums through the middle....The two rows of white are the path of perpetual peace, leading from one white end to the other, and the two white ends are...one of them...General Washington and his children...and the other, the Creeks and Seminoles. It is with a view to join the hands of the people of the United States and the people of my land that I offer this belt, that they may never again be separated or at enmity....If anything interposes to cause uneasiness let both sides strive to remove it earnestly. It is a great talk I now give and I hope that I may live to see the good effects from it, and when we are dead and gone, that the young people will see and remember it and the good effects produced by it.[19]

Efau Hadjo thought of himself as an educator explicating tribal ways to "General Washington and his children." As tribes regain strength, they may well be inclined to revive this beneficial tribal practice. Tribes will however have little incentive to do so unless non-Native Americans respond by acknowledging that living tribal traditions are part of this North American nation's heritage.

Notes

Abbreviations in Notes:
AA: *American Archives.*
ASPIA: *American State Papers, Documents Legislature and Executive of the Congress of the United States, Indian Affairs* (Washington, 1832-34).
Fitzpatrick: John C. Fitzpatrick, ed., *The Writings of George Washington* (Washington).
Hough Proceedings: Franklin B. Hough, *Proceedings of the Commissioners of Indian Affairs Appointed by Law for the Extinguishment of Indian Titles in the State of New York* (Albany, 1861).
Kappler: Charles J. Kappler, ed., *Indian Affairs, Laws and Treaties* (Washington, 1904).
Lipscomb & Bergh: Andrew A. Lipscomb and Albert E. Bergh, eds., *The Writings of Thomas Jefferson* (Washington, 1903).
JCC: *Journals of the Continental Congress* (Washington, 1905).
PCC: *Papers of the Continental Congress, 1774-1789* (National Archives, Washington, D.C.).

N.B. In many quotations, spelling and punctuation have been modernized.

Chapter One

1. James H. Merrell suggests "there were perhaps 200,000 Indians living east of the Mississippi River, made up of 85 different nations" in 1775. See his "Indians and the New Republic," in Jack P. Greene and J.R. Pole, eds., *The Blackwell Encyclopedia of the American Revolution* (Cambridge, 1991) 392.

2. Carl Van Doren has called the treaty session transcripts Franklin published "for both matter and manner...the most original and engaging documents of their century in America....Nothing quite like the Indian treaties exists anywhere in the literature of the world." See his "Introduction" in Julian P. Boyd, ed., *Indian Treaties Printed by Benjamin Franklin, 1736-1762* (Philadelphia, 1938) viii, xviii; also William Fenton, "The Indian Treaty: A Native Literary Form," in Francis Jennings, ed., *The History and Culture of Iroquois Diplomacy* (Syracuse, 1985) 5-7; and Lawrence C. Wroth, "The Indian Treaty as Literature," *Yale Review*, New Series, 17(1928):49-66. See also Francis Jennings, *Benjamin Franklin, Politician* (New York, 1996).

3. Regarding the Albany Plan, see Leonard W. Labaree, ed., *The Papers of Benjamin Franklin* (New Haven, 1962) 5:335-417.

4. Franklin on March 20, 1751, in Labaree 4:118-19, quoted in Jennings *Franklin* 86.

5. JCC 2:195-99.

6. AA 4:1:1347.

7. Patrick Frazier, *The Mohicans of Stockbridge* (Lincoln, 1992) 197-98.

8. Bernard Romans, *A Concise Natural History of East and West Florida* (New Orleans, 1961; originally published New York, 1775), 28.

9. Ethan Allen to the Caghnawagas. Crown Point, May 24, 1775 in K.G. Davies, ed., *Documents of the American Revolution* (Dublin) 9:142-43.

10. George Washington to Philip Schuyler. New York, April 19, 1776, AA 4:5:988-89.

11. JCC 4:191.

12. Regarding revision of the Declaration, see Pauline Maier, *American Scripture: Making the Declaration of Independence* (New York, 1997).

13. Washington to Schuyler. New York, April 19, 1776. AA 4:5:988-89.

14. PCC M. 247, reel 56, v. 8, p. 83. Though undated, this document may be from around January 4, 1776, when Atayataghronghta visited General Schuyler in Albany because General Montgomery, killed at Quebec on December 31, 1775, was evidently believed to be still alive.

15. For Washington's account of this meeting, see his letter to President of Congress, August 4-5, 1775. PCC M-247, reel 166, p.51. See also Franklin B. Hough, *A History of St. Lawrence and Franklin Counties* (Albany, 1853) 184-85.

16. PCC M. 247, reel 56, v. 8, p. 83.

17. Hough Proceedings 39-40. Another hero of the Revolution, Crispus Attucks, is also believed to have been half African American, half Native American.

18. AA 4:3:442.

19. See for example details of a conference between General Richard Montgomery and Caghnawagha representatives at St. John's on September 24, 1775, AA 4:3:798; PCC M. 247, reel 56, 8:83.

20. For more concerning this painting, see pp. 19-20.

21. Schuyler to Washington. Albany, January 5, 1776.AA 4:4:581; Jonathan Trumbull to Washington. Lebanon, January 15, 1776. AA 4:4:684.

22. Washington to Schuyler. Cambridge, January 27, 1776. PCC M.247, reel 166, p.455.

23. AA 4:4:893.

24. Washington to Schuyler. Cambridge, February 1, 1776. AA 4:4:908.

25. Hough *History*, 187-88.

26. Barbara Graymont, "The Oneidas and the American Revolution," in Jack Campisi and Laurence M. Hauptman, eds., *The Oneida Indian Experience* (Syracuse, 1988) 37.

27. Schuyler to H. Laurens. Albany, March 15, 1778. PCC M.247, reel 173, pp. 286-90. Saint Johns was a fort on the Richelieu River, which flows from Lake Champlain to the Saint Lawrence.

28. James Deane to Schuyler. Fort Schuyler, March 29, 1779. PCC M.247, r.173, p.493

29. PCC M.247, reel 166, pp.435-38.

30. Schuyler to H. Laurens. Albany, March 15, 1778. PCC M.247, reel 173, pp.286-90.

31. Request signed by Timothy Pickering, June 5, 1779. PCC M.247, reel 158, p.391.

32. Washington to Sullivan, May 31, 1779, from *Letters and Papers of Major-General John Sullivan* (Concord, 1939) 3:49.

33. Sullivan to Washington, August 15, 1779; *Sullivan Letters* 3: 100, 112, 134.

34. *Sullivan Letters*, 117, 137. For a direct reference to Atayataghronghta during the 1779 campaign, see PCC M.247, reel 170, p.149.

35. Washington, *Writings* (New York, 1997) 365.

36. Durand Echeverria, "The Iroquois Visit Rochambeau at Newport in 1780," *Rhode Island*

History, 11(1952):73-81. Hough *History* 190.

37. PCC M.247, r.98, p.489.

38. Graymont, "The Oneidas..." 40.

39. Lincoln to President of Congress. PCC M.247, r.162, p.473.

40. See Oliver E. Allen, *The Tiger, the Rise and Fall of Tammany Hall,* Reading, 1993, 2-3.

41. Quoted in Richard White, *The Middle Ground* (New York, 1991) 370. Spelling and punctuation altered. For admiration of Revolutionaries for tribal foes, see White 388.

42. Lipscomb & Bergh, 16:371-73. As promised, Jefferson displayed these decorated skins at Monticello. See Anthony F.C. Wallace, *Jefferson and the Indians* (Cambridge, 1999) 73. About Native Americans as cultural referents for white American Revolutionaries, see Philip J. Deloria, *Playing Indian* (New Haven, 1998).

43. Thomas Jefferson, *Notes on the State of Virginia* (New York, 1982) 92-93. In Paris representing the United States from 1784 to 1789, Jefferson fell under the influence of French *philosophes.* He completed and published in Paris his *Notes on the State of Virginia,* inviting French intellectuals to turn their speculative attention to North America. Decades later, Jefferson again contended that among tribes "Every man...is perfectly free to follow his own inclinations" and was therefore not constrained by any law from violating "the rights of another." Thomas Jefferson to Francis W. Gilmer, June 7, 1816, in Lipscomb & Bergh 15:25-26. Concerning the possible influence of Rousseau on Jefferson, consider these lines from Rousseau's 1754 "Discourse on the Origin of Inequality": "The savage and the civilized man differ so much in the bottom of their hearts and in their inclinations, that what constitutes the supreme happiness of one would reduce the other to despair. The former breathes only peace and liberty....Civilized man, on the other hand...pays his court to men in power, whom he hates, and to the wealthy, whom he despises....What a sight would the perplexing and envied labours of a European minister of State present to the eyes of a Caribbean! How many cruel deaths would not this indolent savage prefer to the horrors of such a life." *The Social Contract and Discourses*, trans. G.D.H. Cole (New York, 1950) 270. For Jefferson's Enlightenment preoccupations as related to Native Americans, see Wallace; and Bernard W. Sheehan, *Seeds of Extinction, Jeffersonian Philanthropy and the American Indian* (New York, 1974).

44. Jefferson, *Notes*, 92-3.

45. Francois, Marquis de Barbe-Marbois, *Our Revolutionary Forefathers*, trans. Eugene Parker Chase (New York, 1929) 211-12.

46. John Heckewelder, *History, Manners, and Customs of the Indian Nations Who Once Inhabited Pennsylvania and the Neighboring States* (New York, 1971; originally published 1817) 189.

47. Article Six of the September 17, 1778 Treaty of Fort Pitt suggested that the Delawares might "form a state where the Delaware nation shall be the head, and have representation in Congress." Comparably, Article Twelve of the November 28, 1785 Treaty of Hopewell, negotiated by Benjamin Hawkins, promised the Cherokees "the right to send a deputy of their choice, whenever they think fit, to Congress." Kappler 2:5, 10.

48. Trumbull probably met Atayataghronghta on August 1, 1775, when the Caghnawagha

receive company." John Trumbull, *Autobiography* (New Haven, 1953) 23. See John Hill Morgan, *Paintings by John Trumbull at Yale University*, (New Haven, 1926) 33; and Irma Jaffe, *John Trumbull: Five Paintings of the Revolution* (Hartford, 1975) 16-19. Benjamin West's "Death of General Wolfe" is in the National Gallery, Ottawa.

49. The Iroquois "Covenant Chain" is the best-known adaptation of the tribal system to include Europeans. See Francis Jennings, *The Ambiguous Iroquois Empire* (New York, 1984).

50. Robert A. Williams, Jr., *Linking Arms Together American Indian Treaty Visions of Law and Peace, 1600-1800* (New York, 1997) provides an overview of Native American kinship diplomacy. For more detailed exposition, see Francis Jennings, ed., *The History and Culture of Iroquois Diplomacy* (Syracuse, 1985), especially pp. 119-20, where the point is made that the term "woman" though sometimes encountered was not used in a stable, reciprocal tribal alliance. A tribe was labeled a "woman" only in controversial circumstances. The word translated as "woman" in fact referred to a (metaphorically) castrated man; such symbolic castration was of course reversible. Individual women did on the other hand play prominent roles in tribal decision-making and even in warfare. Regarding the Delaware-Wyandot relationship, see *North American Review* 22(1826):69. The flexibility of tribal kinship diplomacy is emphasized in William Fenton, *The Great Law and the Longhouse* (Norman, 1998). See also Mary A. Druke, "Linking Arms, The Structure of Iroquois Intertribal Diplomacy," in Daniel K. Richter and James H. Merrell, eds., *Beyond the Covenant Chain* (Syracuse, 1987) 29-29, and James H. Merrell, *Into the American Woods* (New York, 1999).

51. Edmund B. O'Callaghan, ed., *Documents Relative to the Colonial History of the State of New York* (Albany, 1853-1887) 4:902-03.

52. See John G. Garratt, *The Four Indian Kings* (Ottawa, 1985).

Chapter Two

1. JCC 5:763.

2. Edmund Burke, Letter to the New York General Assembly, August 2, 1774, in *Report of the Regents of the University on the Boundaries of the State of New York* (Albany, 1874) 92-100.

3. For background, see Peter S. Onuf, *The Origins of the Federal Republic* (Philadelphia, 1983) Ch. 5; and Julius Goebel, Jr., ed., *The Law Practice of Alexander Hamilton, Documents and Commentary* (New York, 1964) Vol.1, Chapter 4.

4. *Laws of New York* 3rd Sess., Chapter 29.

5. *Report of Regents* 137-141.

6. On March 20, 1781 the New York Legislature passed "An Act for raising two regiments for the defence of this State." The act declared all Iroquois land within the State's claimed boundaries available for State award to soldiers except "lands belonging to the [pro-Revolutionary] Oneida and Tuscarora Indians." On July 25, 1782, the Legislature designated a portion of the homelands of the Cayugas and Onondagas the State's Military Tract. *(Laws of New York*, 4th Sess., Chapter 32; 6th Sess., Chapter11.)

7. Schuyler to Thomas Mifflin, President of Congress, July 29, 1783, in PCC.

8. Washington to James Duane, September 7, 1783, Fitzpatrick 27:136-40.

9. Fitzpatrick 27:134-35. Washington's emphasis.

10. June 17, 1783, Fitzpatrick 27:17.

11. Regarding Cooperstown, see Alan Taylor, *William Cooper's Town* (New York, 1995).

12. E. Wilder Spaulding, *His Excellency George Clinton* (New York, 1938) 232-3.

13. Fitzpatrick 27:136-40.

14. Fitzpatrick 27:53.

15. JCC 25:680-95. See also the variant in New York Public Library, *Philip Schuyler Papers.*

16. By terms of the draft report, Congress's Commissioners could have negotiated a land swap with the Oneidas and Tuscaroras, allowing them to move to western New York State. This disappeared from the report approved by Congress; JCC 25:680-95.

17. *Schuyler Papers* 14. Another copy is in Colonial Office Records, Public Archives of Canada, Ottawa, "Q" Series, M.G. 11, Volume 23, pp. 128-44.

18. JCC 26:135. See also Schuyler Papers, for the undated draft resolution of protest Schuyler prepared for consideration of the New York Legislature in the spring of 1784.

19. *Report of Regents* 182-83.

20. Hough Proceedings 21n-24n. Emphasis in original. The letter's date is uncertain.

21. The phrase "dependent nations" anticipates Chief Justice John Marshall's 1831 formula in *Cherokee Nation vs. Georgia* that tribes are "domestic dependent nations." Marshall cited New York State's pre-Constitutional usage as one basis for his formula. See Chapter Nine, page 232.

22. Henry S. Manley, *The Treaty of Fort Stanwix, 1784* (Rome, 1932) 54-55. See also William N. Fenton, *The Great Law and the Longhouse,* (Norman, 1998), Chapter 38.

23. Manley 55-56.

24. Neville B. Craig, *The Olden Time* (Pittsburgh, 1848) 2:409.

25. This controversy was resolved when a new Fort Schuyler was built in Utica. All parties then agreed to call the old British fort by its old British name. Fort Stanwix (in modern-day Rome, New York) has recently been handsomely rebuilt.

26. Hough Proceedings 49-62.

27. Hough Proceedings 64-66.

28. Barbara Graymont, *The Iroquois in the American Revolution* (Syracuse, 1972) 267. The Commissioners were Richard Butler of Pennsylvania, Arthur Lee of Virginia and Oliver Wolcott of Connecticut

29. Craig 2:406-07.

30. Craig 2:429. Stanley J. Idzerda and Robert Rhodes Crout, eds., *Lafayette in the Age of the American Revolution* (Ithaca, 1983) 5:245-74.

31. Craig 2:412, 415.

32. Craig 2:408.

33. Craig 2:412.

34. Craig 2:415

35. Francois de Barbe-Marbois, "Journal," in Idzerda and Crout, 5:250.

36. Barbe-Marbois, 251.

37. Craig 2:424. For examples of mutual adaptation in pre-Revolutionary treaty sessions,

see James H. Merrell, *Into the American Woods* (New York, 1999), chapter 5.

38.Craig 2:414-9; Timothy Pickering to Henry Knox, December 26, 1794, *Pickering Papers,* Massachusetts Historical Society, 62:192-97.

39. *Laws of New York,* 9th Sess., Chapter 67.

40. The Hartford Compact is in *Report of Special Committee to Investigate the Indian Problem of the State of New York* (Albany, 1889) 105-111. See also Harold C. Syrett, ed., *The Papers of Alexander Hamilton* (New York, 1962) 3:702-03.

41. JCC 33: 617–29, October 8, 1787.

42. Fort Stanwix Commissioners Richard Butler and Arthur Lee were joined by George Rogers Clark. See Francis Paul Prucha, *American Indian Treaties* (Berkeley, 1994) 50-53.

43. ASPIA 1:51, 41, 38.

44. ASPIA 1:42.

45. ASPIA 1:43, 39.

46. ASPIA 1:44.

47. ASPIA 1:39.

48. Merritt B. Pound, *Benjamin Hawkins, Indian Agent* (Athens, 1951) 49.

49. ASPIA 1:17.

50. Letter, Benjamin Hawkins to Thomas Jefferson, June 14, 1786, in Julian P. Boyd, ed., *The Papers of Thomas Jefferson* (Princeton, 1954) 9:640-42.

51. JCC 31:488-493, August 7, 1786.

Chapter Three

1. *Worcester vs. Georgia* (1832).

2. JCC 2:198.

3. *Fletcher vs. Peck.*

4. Article 9, Clause 4.

5. Monroe to Madison, November 15, 1784; Madison to Monroe, November 27, 1784, in Robert Rutland, ed., *Papers of James Madison* (Chicago, 1984) 8:140-3, 156-58.

6. *Worcester vs Georgia* (1832).

7. ASPIA 1:17.

8. William Few, "Autobiography," *Magazine of American History,* 7(1881): 352-53.

9. See for example Staughton Lynd, *Class Conflict, Slavery, and the United States Constitution*, Indianapolis, 1967, Chapter 8.

10. JCC 33:454.

11. JCC 33:455-62.

12. Max Farrand, ed., *Records of the Federal Convention of 1787* (New Haven, 1911) 2:324.

13. William Masterson, *William Blount,* (New York, 1969) 132.

14. Farrand 2:367.

15. Letter, Benjamin Hawkins to Thomas Jefferson, June 14, 1786, Boyd 9:640-42.

16. *Worcester vs. Georgia* (1832).

17. "The true import of this provision [Article 9.4 of the Articles of Confederation],"

wrote Thompson, "is certainly not very obvious, see *Federalist 42*. What were the legislative rights intended to be embraced within the provision, is left in great uncertainty. But whatever difficulty on that subject might have arisen under the confederation it is entirely removed by the omission of the provision in the present Constitution, thereby leaving this power entirely with Congress, without regard to any state right on the subject, and showing that the Indian tribes were considered as distinct communities although within the limits of a State."

Chapter Four

1. These included financial and foreign policy questions. See Jack N. Rakove, *The Beginnings of National Politics* (New York, 1979).

2. JCC 33: 478-80.

3. JCC 34:124-26. Knox's recommendations were accepted July 2, 1788; JCC 34:285.

4. Fitzpatrick 27:136-40.

5. Linda Grant De Pauw, ed., *Documentary History of the First Federal Congress* (Baltimore, 1974) 2:4-6.

6. Knox to Washington, July 7, 1789, ASPIA 1:53. For exchanges between Senate and President, see DePauw.

7. De Pauw 2:40-1.

8. Ralston Hayden, *The Senate and Treaties, 1789-1817* (New York, 1920) 23n. See Francis P. Prucha, *American Indian Treaties* (Berkeley, 1994) 70-79.

9. ASPIA 1:31.

10. Edward J. Cashin, *Lachlan McGillivray, Indian Trader* (Athens, 1992).

11. John Pope, *A Tour through the Southern and Western Territories of the United States...* (Richmond, 1792) 47-49; Benjamin Hawkins, *A Sketch of the Creek Country, in the Years 1798 and 1799* (Spartanburg, 1982) 39.

12. Helen H. Tanner, *Zespedes in East Florida, 1784-1790* (Coral Gables, 1963) 86; "A Short Account of Mr. McGillivray," *American Museum*, 8(1790):171-72; Michael D. Green, "Alexander McGillivray," in R. David Edmunds, ed., *American Indian Leaders* (Lincoln, 1980) 41-63.

13. Joel W. Martin, *Sacred Revolt* (Boston, 1991) 87.

14. John Caughey, *McGillivray of the Creeks* (Norman, 1938) 64, 78.

15. David Corkran, *The Creek Frontier, 1540-1783* (Norman, 1967) 239, 281.

16. Tanner 58.

17. Caughey 74.

18. William Few, "Autobiography," *Magazine of American History*, 7(1881):354.

19. Francis Humphreys, *Life and Times of David Humphreys* (New York, 1917) 2:4, 6.

20. Humphreys 2:8, 6.

21. Caughey 254; Helen G. Cruickshank, *John and William Bartram's America* (New York, 1957) 289.

22. Angie Debo, *The Road to Disappearance* (Norman, 1941)22-3; John H. Goff, "Of

Warriors and Chiefs," *Emory University Quarterly* 9:(June 1953)103; Humphreys 2:7; Charles H. Fairbanks, "The Function of Black Drink among the Creeks," in Charles M. Hudson, ed., *Black Drink, A Native American Tea* (Athens, 1979).

23. ASPIA 1:73.

24. Few 354.

25. Caughey 260, Humphreys 2:10.

26. Caughey 253-54; ASPIA 1:73, 78.

27. Caughey 256.

28. ASPIA 1:77-78, 60, 63.

29. Pound, "Benjamin Hawkins, Indian Agent," *Georgia Historical Quarterly*, 13:398; Caughey 258.

30. *Henry Knox Papers*, Morgan Library, New York, New York, 26:120.

31. Caughey 43.

32. Abigail Adams to Mary Cranch, August 8, 1790, in Stewart Mitchell, ed., "New Letters of Abigail Adams," *Proceedings of the American Antiquarian Society*, 55:(1945)168-69. See John Trumbull, *Autobiography* (New York, 1841) 164-65. Also Gary Roberts, "The Chief of State and the Chief," *American Heritage* 26(1975).

33. *Pennsylvania Packet and Daily Advertiser*, August 18, 1790, in Caughey 278.

34. For treaty texts, see De Pauw, 2:241-50, 165-9, 180-3).

35. Tanner, "Pipesmoke and Muskets," in Samuel Proctor, ed., *Eighteenth Century Florida and its Borderlands* (Gainesville, 1975) 38.

36. Caughey 293; Pope 51.

37. Caughey 332, 347.

38. William Panton to Lachlan McGillivray, April 10, 1794, in Marie T. Greenslade, "William Panton, c. 1745-1801," *Florida Historical Quarterly*, 14:(1935)115. See also William S. Coker and Thomas D. Watson, *Indian Traders of the Southeastern Spanish Borderlands* (Pensacola, 1986).

39. Letter, Washington to Senate, August 7, 1790, in Fitzpatrick 31:76-77.

40. Joseph Blunt, *Historical Sketch of the Formation of the Confederacy* (New York, 1825) 97.

41. ASPIA 1:17.

42. De Pauw 6:1544-1551.

43. De Pauw 2:185-88, 199-201.

44. *American State Papers, Public Lands*, 1:22-25.

45. For background, see Richard White, *The Middle Ground* (New York, 1991) Ch. 11.

46. ASPIA 1:564-581. Vermont and Kentucky were the two additional "fires."

47. Address to chiefs, January 31, 1809, in Lipscomb & Bergh, 16:470-71.

48. Federal relations were subsequently renewed by the 1796 U.S.-Creek Treaty of Colerain. See Kappler 2:46-50.

49. ASPIA 1:140, 7 64. See also White *Middle Ground* 84-85.

50. In the mid-eighteenth century, the word Civilization referred to transferring an offense from criminal to civil legal status. In Samuel Johnson's *Dictionary*, first published

in 1755, "civilisation" was defined as "A law, act of justice, or judgment, which renders a criminal process civil...." It was thus distinct from the word "civility" in the sense of politeness, or as opposed to "savagery" or "barbarity." In 1772, while Johnson was preparing a new edition of the *Dictionary*, his friend James Boswell proposed that Johnson include a second meaning for "civilisation." Boswell would have left unchanged Civility in the sense of politeness, but substituted "civilisation" for Johnson's use of Civility in the sense of "Freedom from barbarity; the state of being civilized...." Johnson had also defined "to civilize" as "To reclaim from savageness and brutality; to instruct in the arts of regular life"; Boswell urged Johnson to describe the highest form of "regular life" as "civilisation" rather than as Civility. Boswell recorded his reply as follows:

> He would not admit *civilisation* [in the sense of "freedom from barbarity"], but only *civility*. With great deference to him I thought *civilisation*, from *to civilise*, better in the sense opposed to *barbarity* than *civility*; as it is better to have a distinct word for each sense, than one word with two senses, which *civility* is, in his way of using it. (James Boswell, *The Life of Samuel Johnson.*)

Regarding seventeenth and eighteenth century usage, see Bernard Sheehan, Savagism and Civility (Cambridge, 1980).

51. Francis P. Prucha, *The Great Father* (Lincoln, 1984) 1:xxvii.

Chapter Five:

1. ASPIA 1:53. On the limitation of the 1790 Act to "Indian Country," see John M.R. Paterson and David Roseman, "A Reexamination of *Passamaquoddy vs. Morton*," *Maine Law Review* 31(1979):1.

2. John Catanzariti, ed., *The Papers of Thomas Jefferson* (Princeton 1992) 25:258, 272 (February 25-26, 1793). When the United States purchased Louisiana in 1803, President Jefferson drafted a Constitutional amendment in which he laid out the basic concepts governing tribal rights with even greater care and precision. In Louisiana, tribes would continue to enjoy "rights of occupancy in the soil, and of self-government...as they now exist." The federal government was to hold only a preemption right until occupancy by self-governing tribes was terminated, at which time the federal government would claim "the full rights of possession as well as of property and sovereignty," rights that Jefferson believed self-governing tribes occupying hunting grounds could by definition never possess. For text of Jefferson's amendment, see Anthony F.C. Wallace, *Jefferson and the Indians* (Cambridge 1999) 255.

3. Hough Proceedings 243-44. In *Cherokee Nation vs. Georgia* (1831), Marshall wrote, "Treaties were made with some tribes by the State of New York under a then unsettled construction of the confederation, by which they ceded all their lands to the State, taking back a limited grant to themselves, in which they admit their dependence."

4. Knox to Clinton, August 17, 1791, ASPIA 1:169.

5. Massachusetts Historical Society, *Pickering Papers,* 60:115.

6. *Pickering Papers* 60:223-8. Pickering proposed that the Oneidas petition the President

instead of going to court because he was unsure whether they could do so. Among Pickering's concerns at Canandaigua was whether a new law would be required to give effect to President Washington's assurances that U.S. courts would be open to tribal litigants. See *Pickering Papers* 62:97-98.

7. *Pickering Papers* 62:99-105.

8. Secretary of War Pickering to Governor Clinton, January 30, 1795. *Philip Schuyler Papers,* New York Public Library.

9. Letter, Pickering to Chapin, Jr., April 6, 1795, New York Historical Society, *O'Reilly Papers*, vol. 11.

10. In the *Philip Schuyler Papers* is a letter from Schuyler to "Brothers, Sachems and Warriors of the Oneida Nation," dated February 15, 1795, responding to their request for his advice.

11. New York Historical Society, *Henry O'Reilly Papers,* 11:26.

12. *O'Reilly Papers* 11: 27.

13. The 1793 Act contained language acknowledging the existence of "Indians" under "ordinary" state jurisdiction. Whether this referred to tribes or to individuals is disputed, as is whether this section of the Trade and Intercourse Act referred to land sales.

14. *O'Reilly Papers* 11:29.

15. Text in 36 Indian Claims Commission 75, 88.

16. Text in 36 Indian Claims Commission 75, 88-89.

17. Text in 36 Indian Claims Commission 75, 89.

18. 36 Indian Claims Commission 75, 90.

19. Pickering to Washington, July 21, 1795. Massachusetts Historical Society, *Pickering Papers* 35:209

20. Fitzpatrick 34:250-51. Less than a month later came Pickering's most famous act of imprudence, when he charged Secretary of State Edmund Randolph with a "detestable and nefarious conspiracy" with France, precipitating Randolph's resignation in protest. For background, see Gerard H. Clarfield, *Timothy Pickering and the American Republic* (Pittsburgh, 1980) 158-162. Elias Boudinot served for some years as Director of the U.S. Mint, and was father-in-law of Attorney General Bradford.

21. New York Public Library, *Philip Schuyler Papers.*

22. Text of agreement in *Report of Special Committee* 224-28.

23. Text of agreement in *Report of Special Committee* 199-204. The agreement also covered small additional land relinquishments, further increasing the annuity.

24. *O'Reilly Papers* 11:33.

25. *O'Reilly Papers* 11:37.

26. *O'Reilly Papers* 11.

27. New York Public Library, *Philip Schuyler Papers,* box 15.

28. Text of agreement in *Report of Special Committee* 244-49. Dated September 15, 1795, it was called an "Indenture" rather than a treaty. The land leased to Peter Smith for twenty-one years was included in the sale to New York State, which took over the lease.

29. *Laws of New York*, 19th Sess., Ch. 39. For approval by the Governor's Council of Revision, see *Journal of the Senate of the State of New York, Nineteenth Session* (New York, 1796) 97-8. On March 26, 1796, Captain Chapin witnessed the Cayuga treaty when it was officially recorded and in June of that and subsequent years he implemented it by distributing the annuity payments it provided for. Chapin, Jr. also received from the New York State Legislature the requested grant of a square mile of the land relinquished by the Cayugas with his help. Record of witnessing the treaty in *Philip Schuyler Papers*, New York Public Library. Instructions to Captain Chapin for distributing the annuity to the Cayugas in *O'Reilly Papers* 11. The Legislature authorized Chapin's grant April 1, 1796.

30. ASPIA 1:642.

31. ASPIA 1:641.

32. Washington to Edmund Pendleton, January 22, 1795; Washington's emphasis. Washington, *Writings*, (New York, 1997) 904.

33. *Pickering Papers*, Massachusetts Historical Society 61:79.

34. Hough Proceedings 166n-67n.

35. *Journal of the Assembly of the State of New-York, Eighteenth Session* (New York, 1795) 180-81. Emphasis in original. For the Legislature's February 13, 1794, Resolution, see *Journal of the Assembly of the State of New-York, Seventeenth Session* (Albany, 1794), 77. See also Barbara Graymont, "New York State Indian Policy after the Revolution," *New York History* 58(October 1976):464-65.

36. The two Supreme Court decisions are *Oneida Indian Nation vs. County of Oneida*, January 21, 1974, and *County of Oneida vs. Oneida Indian Nation*, March 4, 1985.

37. Stevens' Dissent focused on the legal concept of Laches, which holds that a victim's right to obtain legal redress may lapse after a period of time.

Chapter Six:

1. Jefferson's draft amendment is discussed in Annie Heloise Abel, *History of Events Resulting in Indian Consolidation West of the Mississippi River*, American Historical Association, *Annual Report*, 1906.

2. ASPIA 1:562-63.

3. Hough Proceedings 229-31.

4. ASPIA 1:618. This May 23, 1796 speech is attributed to three Mohawk chiefs, of whom one was Colonel Atayataghronghta.

5. ASPIA 1:681.

6. *Sporting Magazine* 19(1802):130. The name Efau Hadjo is often translated "Mad Dog." The word *efau* does mean dog, but while *hadjo* can be translated "mad," in Muscogee *hadjo* has connotations of admirably reckless daring, not of mental or physical impairment.

7. Hawkins to Washington, February 10, 1792, in Elizabeth G. McPherson, "Unpublished Letters from North Carolinians to Washington," *North Carolina Historical Review*, 12:2 (April, 1935), 162-65.

8. Fitzpatrick 31:491.

9. Fitzpatrick 27:133, 136; ASPIA 1:615. Figures are based on population statistics in U.S. Bureau of the Census, *Historical Statistics of the United States* (Washington, 1975) 1:26, and areas in S.G. McLendon, *History of the Public Domain in Georgia*, 57. ASPIA 1:611. For Hawkins' 1783 views, see JCC 25:694, report of Committee of which he was a member: "feeble, disorderly and dispersed settlements" encouraged "depravity of manners" as well as "frequent and destructive wars with the Indians."

10. George Washington, *Writings* (New York, 1997), 1978, December 7, 1796.

11. Washington to Edmund Pendleton, January 22, 1795, in Washington *Writings*, 904.

12. Washington's Seventh Annual Message to Congress, December 8, 1795, in Washington *Writings*, 923.

13. Washington to Edmund Pendleton, January 22, 1795, Washington *Writings*, 905.

14. Fitzpatrick 27:137.

15. Washington, *Writings*, 958.

16. Benjamin Hawkins, *A Sketch of the Creek Country, in the Years 1798 and 1799* (Spartanburg, 1982) 27; John Hambly, "Diary," *Florida Historical Quarterly* 55(1976):67.

17. Caleb Swan, "Position and State of Manners and Arts in the Creek, or Muscogee Nation in 1791," in Henry R. Schoolcraft, ed., *Information Respecting the History, Condition and Prospects of the Indian Tribes of the United States* (Philadelphia, 1855) 6:264.

18. ASPIA 1:647.

19. George Stiggins, "A Historical Narration of the Genealogy, Traditions and Downfall of the Ispocaga or Creek Tribe of Indians," in Theron A. Nunez, Jr., "Creek Nativism and the Creek War of 1813-14," Ethnohistory 5(1958). Hawkins *Letters* 222; ASPIA 1:647.

20. Washington *Writings* 959.

21. Hawkins *Letters* 316.

22. Hawkins *Letters* 241, 316; ASPIA 1:647; Hawkins *Sketch* 51, 67.

23. Carl Mauelshagen and Gerald H. Davis, eds., *Partners in the Lord's Work: The Diary of Two Moravian Missionaries in the Creek Indian Country 1807-1813* (Atlanta, 1969) 51-52. The boys' father was Alex Cornells.

24. Hawkins *Sketch* 74; John Pope, *A Tour through the Southern and Western Territories of the United States...* (Richmond, 1792) 56.

25. Hawkins *Sketch* 74, 78.

26. Hawkins *Sketch* 81.

27. Hawkins *Sketch* 50.

28. Andrew Ellicott, *Journal* (Chicago, 1962) 220-23.

29. Merritt B. Pound, *Benjamin Hawkins, Indian Agent* (Athens, 1951) 136-37; J. Leitch Wright, Jr., *Creeks & Seminoles* (Lincoln, 1986) 151.

30. Hawkins *Letters* 424-25.

31. Hawkins *Letters, Journals* 508.

32. Hawkins *Letters, Journals* 508.

33. Hawkins *Letters, Journals* 504.
34. ASPIA 1:265.
35. ASPIA 1:674-5.
36. Washington to Jefferson, July 1, 1796, in Fitzpatrick, 35:112; Washington to Richard Henry Lee, December 14, 1784, in Fitzpatrick 28:12; ASPIA 1:658, 53, 544.
37. Hawkins to Washington, February 10, 1792, in McPherson.
38. ASPIA 1:587.
39. Hawkins to Edward Wright, December 12, 1799, "Correspondence, 1795-1814," Creek Factory, Records of the Office of Indian Trade, Record Group 75, National Archives, Washington, D.C.
40. Price to Hawkins, August 22, 1798, "Creek Letter Book," 157, in Creek Factory, Records of the Office of Indian Trade, Record Group 75, National Archives, Washington, D.C.; Price to Secretary of War James McHenry, October 1, 1798, 162-63.
41. "Creek Letter Book," 172-3.
42. Price to Hawkins, October 15, 1798, "Creek Letter Book," 167-69.
43. Charles Magnan to General John Mason, April 11, 1816, "Creek Letter Book," 360.
44. Price to Freeman, September 4, 1798.
45. ASPIA 1:674.
46. "Creek Letter Book," 157-58; 1799 muster, "Records of the Fort Wilkinson Garrison, 1795-1801," Entry 53, Creek Factory, Records of the Office of Indian Trade, Record Group 75, National Archives, Washington, D.C.
47. Benjamin Hawkins, *Letters, Journals and Writings*, ed. C.L. Grant (Savannah, 1980) 468.

Chapter Seven:

1. Lipscomb & Bergh 5:390.
2. Hawkins to Jefferson June 9, 1787, Julian P. Boyd, ed., *The Papers of Thomas Jefferson* (Princeton, 1955) 11:413-14.
3. Bernard W. Sheehan in *Seeds of Extinction, Jeffersonian Philanthropy and the American Indian* (Chapel Hill, 1973) discusses Buffon and the eighteenth century intellectual background of Jefferson's thought. On December 28, 1783, five days after General Washington's resignation, Jefferson had written Hawkins seeking, according to Jefferson's files, comment on "Buffon's character of Indians." The letter itself has not been found. See Julian P. Boyd, ed., *The Papers of Thomas Jefferson*, Princeton, 6:427. Also *Notes on the State of Virginia* in Jefferson, *Basic Writings*, ed. Philip Foner (New York, 1944) 88-90.
4. Hawkins to Jefferson, June 14, 1786, Boyd 9:641; Hawkins to Jefferson, March 8, 1787, Boyd 11:201-03.
5. July 12, 1800. Hawkins *Letters* 340.
6. Hawkins *Letters* 351.
7. October 25, 1801. Hawkins *Letters* 385. On President Jefferson's tribal policy, see Anthony F. C. Wallace, *Jefferson and the Indians* (Cambridge, 1999), chapter 7.

8. Jefferson to Jackson, February 16, 1803, Lipscomb & Bergh, 10:358-9.

9. Jefferson to Hawkins, February 18, 1803, Lipscomb & Bergh 10:360-5.

10. Benjamin Hawkins, *Letters, Journals and Writings*, ed. C.L. Grant (Savannah, 1980) 455-56.

11. John Caughey, *McGillivray of the Creeks* (Norman, 1938) 101-102.

12. Hawkins *Letters, Journals* 163-4.

13. Hawkins *Letters, Journals* 85; Hawkins *Sketch* 74.

14. Hawkins *Letters, Journals* 239, 243.

15. Hawkins *Letters, Journals* 455-6.

16. Hawkins *Letters, Journals* 454-6. See Annie Heloise Abel, *The History of Events Resulting in Indian Consolidation West of the Mississippi* (Washington, 1908). Also Jefferson's letter to W.C.C. Claiborne, May 24, 1803, in Lipscomb & Bergh 10:394. Also Wallace 273-75.

17. Hawkins to Charles G. Reichel, Lewis Benzien and Simon Peter, July 25, 1807, in "Letters, Papers, Reports and Diaries of the Undertaking of a Mission Among the Creeks," Moravian Archives, Salem, North Carolina.

18. The plan is reproduced in J. Leitch Wright, Jr., *Creeks & Seminoles* (Lincoln, 1986) 144, and in Florette Henri, *The Southern Indians and Benjamin Hawkins, 1796-1816* (Norman, 1986) 158-9. See also Hawkins, *Sketch*, 56. ASPIA 1:647; Merritt B. Pound, *Benjamin Hawkins, Indian Agent* (Athens, 1951) 147, 247-8; Absalom Chappell, *Miscellanies of Georgia* (Columbus, 1874) 68.

19. Hawkins, *Letters, Journals* 231, 236, 240, 242. "Muscogee" was what Creeks called themselves, and the language they spoke.

20. Hawkins, *Letters, Journals* 457; ASPIA 1:837.

21. Hawki ns, *Letters, Journals* 386-7.

22. Hawkins, *Letters, Journals* 231.

23. C.L. Grant and Gerald H. Davis, "The Wedding of Col. Benjamin Hawkins," *North Carolina Historical Review* 54(1977):315.

24. Pound 248; Hawkins to Madison, March 11, 1811, *James Madison Papers*, Library of Congress, Washington, D.C.

25. Hawkins, *Letters, Journals* 341. The "Yuchis" were Native Americans intermingled with the Muskogee-speaking Creeks, but who had their own language.

26. Hawkins, *Letters, Journals* 458-59.

27. Carl Mauelshagen and Gerald H. Davis, eds., *Partners in the Lord's Work: The Diary of Two Moravian Missionaries in the Creek Indian Country 1807-1813* (Atlanta, 1969) 53, 58-59.

28. Hawkins *Letters, Journals* 24. Hawkins, *Sketch* 26. Discussions of blacks among the Creeks are in Wright 73-99; and Daniel F. Littlefield, Jr., *Africans and Creeks* (Westport, 1979).

29. Hawkins *Letters* 49.

30. Hawkins *Sketch* 26; ASPIA 1:647.

31. ASPIA 1:647.

32. Hawkins *Letters, Journals* 554, 559.
33. ASPIA 1:676.
34. Wright 59.
35. William Bartram, "Observations on the Creek and Cherokee Indians," *Transactions of the American Ethnological Society*, 3(1853):39.
36. Alexis de Tocqueville, *Democracy in America*, ed. Phillips Bradley (New York, 1945) 1:360-63.
37. ASPIA 1:607.
38. Pickering to Henry Knox, August 16, 1791, ASPIA 1:170.
39. Hawkins *Letters* 385.
40. Clarence Edwin Carter, ed., *The Territorial Papers of the United States*, Washington: Government Printing Office, 1937, 5:144.
41. ASPIA 1:678-9.
42. Hawkins *Letters, Journals* 577.
43. Hawkins *Letters, Journals* 508; Hawkins *Letters* 221, 239.
44. Hawkins *Letters* 293, 256, 250, 261.
45. Hawkins *Letters, Journals* 478.
46. Hawkins *Letters, Journals* 480.
47. Hawkins *Letters, Journals* 482, 485.
48. Hawkins *Letters, Journals* 541, 217.
49. Hawkins *Letters, Journals* 482-83.
50. Jefferson to the Senate, December 14, 1804, ASPIA 1:690-91. Emphasis in original.
51. Hawkins *Letters, Journals* 483-85.
52. Letter dated April 2, 1805, ASPIA 1:703.
53. Jefferson to the Senate, December 14, 1804, ASPIA 1:690-91.
54. ASPIA 1:684.
55. ASPIA 1:684. Hawkins *Letters, Journals* 192, 196, 243, 256, 284.
56. Hawkins *Letters, Journals* 490, 497.
57. Hawkins *Letters, Journals* 492.
58. Hawkins *Letters, Journals* 497.
59. ASPIA 1:690-1; Kappler 2:85-86. Hawkins *Letters, Journals* 505, 508.
60. Kappler 2:85-6; Reginald Horsman, *Expansion and American Indian Policy, 1783-1812* (Lansing, 1967) 138, 140; Peter J. Hamilton, "Early Roads of Alabama," *Transactions of the Alabama Historical Society*, 2.
61. "Hoboheithlee Micco to the President of the United States," May 15, 1811, "Letters Received, 1800-1823," Records of the Office of the Secretary of War Relating to Indian Affairs, Record Group 75, National Archives, Washington, D.C. Microfilm Publication 271; Wright 150.
62. Horsman 163-64.
63. Pound 210.

Chapter Eight:

1. B.J. Lossing, "War with the Creek Indians," *Harpers* 28(1864); J.F.H. Claiborne, *Life and Times of General Sam Dale* (New York, 1860) 45, 51-2. Dale's account is no doubt embellished but seems basically reliable. For a recent attempt to sort fact from myth, see John Sugden, *Tecumseh, A Life* (New York, 1998) chapter 19.

2. Claiborne 53-60. Tragically, while Tecumseh toured the south, General William Henry Harrison took advantage of his absence to attack Tecumseh's followers north of the Ohio in the celebrated Battle of Tippecanoe.

3. Thomas S. Woodward, *Reminiscences of the Creek or Muscogee Indians* (Montgomery, 1859).

4. Claiborne 53, 62.

5. ASPIA 1:839, 809, 813, 844.

6. ASPIA 1:839.

7. ASPIA 1:843.

8. Hawkins to Secretary of War William Eustis, December 31, 1810, in "Letters Received, 1800-1823," Secretary of War, Record Group 75, National Archives, Washington, D.C. (Microfilm Publication 271); Benjamin Hawkins, *Letters, Journals and Writings*, ed. C.L. Grant (Savannah, 1980) 590.

9. ASPIA 1:843, 841.

10. Claiborne 69-70; ASPIA 1:849, 846.

11. ASPIA 1:846. June 22, 1813.

12. ASPIA 1:847-48.

13. ASPIA 1:851.

14. Jackson to Willie Blount, July 13, 1813, ASPIA 1:850. Willie (or Wylie) Blount was a younger half-brother of William Blount.

15. Blount to General Thomas Flournoy, October 15, 1813, ASPIA 1:855-56.

16. ASPIA 1:853; Frank L. Owsley, Jr., *Struggle for the Gulf Borderlands: The Creek War and the Battle of New Orleans, 1812-1815* (Gainesville, 1981) 39; Hawkins, *Letters, Journals*, 665.

17. ASPIA 1:854.

18. ASPIA 1:861, 859, 849.

19. John Floyd, "Letters," *Georgia Historical Quarterly*, 33 (1949):235-36; Owsley 54.

20. Henry S. Halbert and Timothy H. Ball, *The Creek War of 1813 and 1814* (Chicago, 1895) 276; Owsley 83; Francis Paul Prucha, ed., *The Indian in American History* (New York, 1971) 71. Counterbalancing Jackson's rhetoric is the fact that he adopted a three-year-old Creek boy named Lincoyer whose parents had been slain by Jackson's troops. Lincoyer died at sixteen, so Jackson's ultimate intentions regarding him are unclear.

21. George D. Harmon, "Benjamin Hawkins and the Federal Factory System," *North Carolina Historical Review*, 9:147-48; ASPIA 1:860; J. Leitch Wright, Jr., *Creeks & Seminoles* (Lincoln, 1986) 177; For the text of the treaty, see Kappler 2:107-10. Only one hostile Creek signed.

22. Hawkins, *Letters, Journals* 762.

23. ASPIA 1:837.

24. Jackson tried to accept the land offered him without the condition of having to live on the land, but this proposal was rejected. See Florette Henri, *The Southern Indians and Benjamin Hawkins, 1796-1816* (Norman, 1986) 303-04.

25. Hawkins *Letters, Journals*, 698; ASPIA 1:860, 859; Owsley 90-91. Owsley's review of Spanish and British relations with the Creeks confirms that Big Warrior was justified in asserting that foreign instigation was not significant in the early stages of the Creek War:

> According to all available evidence, it is safe to conclude that the American suspicions were wrong and that the British government was not officially involved in any massive efforts to incite the Creeks before 1814. It is clear from the fact that it took the British eight months to respond to the Creek request for aid that the London government had had no advance plans to encourage an Indian war in the South. The Indians were sorely lacking in arms and other war supplies. Probably not more than one Indian in three had any firearm during the Creek War. Neither the Spanish nor the British had been able or willing to supply them. It was not until after Andrew Jackson had dealt the Creeks a major defeat at Horseshoe Bend that the British moved with their full force to reorganize, resupply, and regroup the Indians who had survived the Creek War. (Owsley 28-29)

26. William Sturtevant, "Creek into Seminole," in Eleanor Leacock and Nancy O. Lurie, eds., *North American Indians in Historical Perspective* (New York, 1971) 106; Hawkins *Letters, Journals*, 767.

27. Deepening the mystery is the fact that Hawkins' letters to the Secretary of War during these months were at some point removed from the War Department files. "That these letters were deliberately removed is certain," in the opinion of Frank L. Owsley, Jr.:

> They nearly all dealt with the Creek settlement and were probably all highly critical of Jackson....Unfortunately for the Jackson sympathizers who probably removed the letters, the register of letters received by the Secretary of War remained, and in most cases the register gives a brief summary of all letters received. Hawkins' specific criticisms are missing, but it is usually possible to see that the letter was not friendly. For example, on August 16, 1814, Hawkins wrote to the Secretary of War asking that Jackson be removed as a negotiator with the Creek Indians. Since this request was made after the signing of the treaty, it is probable that Hawkins hoped to repudiate its terms. (Owsley 90-91n).

28. Hawkins, *Letters, Journals* 742.

29. Hawkins, *Letters, Journals* 750.

30. Hawkins, *Letters, Journals* 754-57. Two speeches are here conflated.

31. Hawkins, *Letters, Journals*, 782.

32. Hawkins, *Letters, Journals* 765-66.

33. Hawkins, *Letters, Journals* 783.

34. Merritt B. Pound, *Benjamin Hawkins, Indian Agent* (Athens, 1951) 243-44. More skeptical assessments of the ultimate meaning of Hawkins' career have been offered recently by Gregory Evans Dowd, in his *A Spirited Resistance* (Baltimore, 1992); and by Joel W. Martin in *Sacred Revolt* (Boston, 1991).

35. Charles C. Jones, Jr., *The Dead Towns of Georgia* (Savannah, 1878) 243; Pound 237, 242.

36. ASPIA 2:762. Big Warrior died in 1824 or 1825.

37. James D. Horan, *The McKenney-Hall Portrait Gallery of American Indians* (New York, 1972) 142. For a detailed account of this period, see Michael D. Green, *The Politics of Indian Removal, Creek Government and Society in Crisis* (Lincoln, 1982).

38. John S. Bassett, ed., *Correspondence of Andrew Jackson* (Washington, 1955) 2:279-81.

39. 16 Stat. 566.

40. W.L.G. Smith, *The Life and Times of Lewis Cass* (New York, 1856) 256-261.

41. Annie Heloise Abel, *The History of Events Resulting in Indian Consolidation West of the Mississippi*, (Washington, 1908) 387.

42. Grant Foreman, *Indian Removal* (Norman, 1953)168-70, 187.

Chapter Nine:

1. Andrew Jackson to President James Monroe, March 4, 1817, in John S. Bassett, ed., *Correspondence of Andrew Jackson* (Washington, 1927) 3:277-82.

2. AA 4:5:988-89.

3. Jefferson to chiefs of the Ottawas, Chippewas, Potawatamis, Wyandots and Senecas of Sandusky, April 22, 1808, in Lipscomb & Bergh 16:429-30.

4. Massachusetts acquired fee title ownership of this Seneca-occupied region from New York State by the Hartford Compact in 1786, and sold this title to land speculators who then attempted to force the Senecas from their homelands. Cornplanter's 1790 appeal to President Washington included a plea that he protect the Senecas from these investors. Washington replied that the federal government could not help, since the Hartford Compact and the initial transactions based on it had taken place before 1789. ASPIA 1:142, 144.

5. Marshall in 1810 did not make separate mention of the two sorts of land subsumed under "vacant" but did take note of this in 1823, writing in *Johnson vs. McIntosh* that, "So far as respected the authority of the crown, no distinction was taken between vacant lands and lands occupied by the Indians."

6. Regarding Marshall's of colonial sources in this Opinion, see Lindsay G. Robertson, "John Marshall as Colonial Historian: Reconsidering the Origins of the Discovery Doctrine," *Journal of Law and Politics,* 13:4 (Fall, 1997).

7. Julian P. Boyd, ed., *The Papers of Thomas Jefferson* (Princeton 1961) 16:407.

8. *Proceedings of the Massachusetts Historical Society*, 2 Ser. 14(1901):337-38.

9. See Jackson's First Annual Message, December 8, 1829, and letter to the Senate, February 22, 1831, in *A Compilation of the Messages and Papers of the Presidents* 3:1005-22, 1099-104.

10. For Cherokee history in this period, see William G. McLoughlin, *Cherokee Renascence in the New Republic* (Princeton, 1986).

11. *Johnson vs. McIntosh* (1823).

12. This lack of agreement persists; see the three Opinions in the Supreme Court's five-to-four decision *Seminole Tribe of Florida vs. Florida*, March 27, 1996.

13. ASPIA 1:142.

14. *Cherokee Nation vs. Georgia* (1831).

15. *Worcester vs. Georgia* (1832).

16. Thomas Perkins Abernethy, *Western Lands and the American Revolution* (New York, 1959) 369.

17. Letter, Benjamin Hawkins to Thomas Jefferson, June 14, 1786, in Boyd 9:640-62.

18. Albert J. Beveridge, *The Life of John Marshall* (Boston, 1919) 4:551.

Chapter Ten:

1. Quoted in Joseph J. Ellis, *American Sphinx* (New York, 1997) 62.

2. Address to the Ottawas, Chippewas, Potawamaties, Wyandots and Senecas of Sandusky, April 22, 1808, in Lipscomb & Bergh 16:431-32.

3. May 4, 1808. Lipscomb & Bergh 16:434.

4. George Washington, *Writings*, (New York, 1997) 920, 894, 849.

5. Abstracts of Speeches made by Seneca chiefs at a treaty held in Albany for the purchase of lands on the Niagara River, New York State Archives, Legislative Assembly Papers 40:393-404.

6. W.L.G. Smith, *The Life and Times of Lewis Cass* (New York, 1856) 176.

7. *Carpenter vs. Shaw* (January 6, 1930).

8. Dissent by Justice Stevens, *County of Oneida vs. Oneida Indian Nation* (March 4, 1985).

9. Address to the Ottawas, Chippewas, Potawatamis, Wyandots and Shawnees, in Lipscomb & Bergh 16:472.

10. Annie H. Abel, "Proposals for an Indian State in the Union, 1778-1878," American Historical Association, *Report*, 1907, 1:89.

11. Regarding a Native American state within the Union, see Russel Barsh and James Henderson, *The Road, Indian Tribes and Political Liberty* (Berkeley, 1980) ch. 17.

12. "Archipelago" is used by Fergus M. Bordewich in *Killing the White Man's Indian* (New York, 1996) to describe modern-day tribal reservations.

13. The indigenous peoples of Alaska and Hawaii, the non-contiguous forty-ninth and fiftieth states, pose distinct issues which are not addressed here.

14. Regarding "Indian Country," see Charles F. Wilkinson, *American Indians, Time, and the Law* (New Haven, 1987); also Bordewich Chapter 3.

15. In 1980, Barsh and Henderson proposed that all tribes be simply declared to be "states" and therefore eligible for most if not all of the privileges guaranteed "states" by the Constitution. Tribes would collectively elect two members of the U.S. Senate and two members of the U.S. House of Representatives. This would achieve some of the purposes I envision through establishment of a unitary Native American state, but I believe Barsh and Henderson's proposal is less likely to gain acceptance than a single Native American state, which can be seen as an extension of the existing federal system rather than potentially at odds with it.

16. *New York Times*, July 7, 1993

17. Francis J. O'Toole and Thomas N. Tureen, "State Power and the Passamaquoddy Tribe: "A Gross National Hypocrisy?" *Maine Law Review* 23(1971):5-6. For the history of one group of "state" Native Americans, see Francis G. Hutchins, *Mashpee, the Story of Cape Cod's Indian Town* (West Franklin, 1979).

18. Robert A. Williams, Jr., *The American Indian in Western Legal Thought* (New York, 1990) 327.

19. Benjamin Hawkins, *Letters, Journals and Writings*, ed. C.L. Grant (Savannah, 1980) 187, 317.

Authors Cited in Notes

Text Index